976.4 S364a

Schoelwer, Susan Prendergast.

Alamo images

MAY 2001

FEB 27 1996			
JAN 18			
JAN 05 2004			
APR 14 2004			
JAN 02 2013	JUN 05 2006		

HIGHSMITH 45-220

D1805533

ALAMO IMAGES

The DeGolyer Library Publications Series

VOLUME THREE

Alamo Images
Changing Perceptions of a Texas Experience

By Susan Prendergast Schoelwer

with Tom W. Gläser

Foreword by Clifton H. Jones

Introduction by Paul Andrew Hutton

DeGolyer Library and Southern Methodist University Press

Dallas, Texas 1985

Copyright © 1985 by The DeGolyer Library
and Southern Methodist University Press, Dallas, Texas 75275

All rights reserved

Composed and printed by Princeton University Press, Princeton, New Jersey
Color printing by Meriden-Stinehour Press, Meriden, Connecticut

Designed by Laury A. Egan

Except as permitted under the Copyright Act of 1976, no part of this publication may be reproduced or distributed in any form or by any means or stored in a data base or retrieval system without prior written permission of the publisher.

The paper in this book meets the standards for permanence and durability established by the Committee on Production Guidelines for Book Longevity of the Council on Library Resources.

85 86 87 88 89   5 4 3 2 1

FRONTISPIECE: Title page illustration *Battle of the Alamo*, from Connecticut Senator John M. Niles's *History of South America and Mexico, with a Complete View of Texas*, 1838. Despite its title, this earliest known "view" of the Alamo fight bears very little resemblance to the actual event and depicts the Alamo itself as a battlemented turret strongly reminiscent of the romantic tales of Sir Walter Scott. The central figure, although unidentified, strikes the lunging pose traditionally assigned to Davy Crockett and may have provided the prototype for later imagery of Crockett's last stand. (DeGolyer Library)

Library of Congress Cataloguing-in-Publication Data

Schoelwer, Susan Prendergast.
  Alamo images.
  "An exhibition at the DeGolyer Library, Southern Methodist University, Dallas, Texas, November 16, 1985-March 14, 1986"—T.p. verso.
  Bibliography: p.   Includes index.
  1. Alamo (San Antonio, Tex.)—Siege, 1836—Exhibitions. I. Gläser, Tom W. II. DeGolyer Library. III. Title.
  F390.S36 1985   976.4'351   85-16210
  ISBN 0-87074-213-2

In Memory of Arnold Zohn

ALAMO IMAGES
CHANGING PERCEPTIONS OF A TEXAS EXPERIENCE

on exhibition at the DeGolyer Library
Fikes Hall of Special Collections
Southern Methodist University, Dallas, Texas
November 16, 1985 – March 14, 1986

This program is made possible in part by a grant from the Texas Committee for the Humanities, a state program of the National Endowment for the Humanities.

Matching funding given by Mr. and Mrs. Arnold Zohn, Sagaponack, New York.

Additional funding given by El Fenix Corporation, Dallas, Texas.

With special thanks from the project staff to Clifton H. Jones, Project Director, whose efforts made this exhibit possible.

LEFT: *Alamo*, by Eric von Schmidt, wax bas-relief, 1985. (Courtesy of the artist)

Contents

Foreword by Clifton H. Jones — viii

Introduction by Paul Andrew Hutton — 3

Chapter 1. Search for the Alamo
by Susan Prendergast Schoelwer — 18

Chapter 2. "Victory or Death" by Tom W. Gläser — 61

Chapter 3. Heroes Forgotten and Familiar
by Susan Prendergast Schoelwer — 104

Chapter 4. Memory and Mirage
by Susan Prendergast Schoelwer — 163

Notes — 174

Selected Bibliography — 190

Exhibition Checklist — 211

Index — 219

Color plates to follow page 162

Foreword

by Clifton H. Jones

THE ROLE of myth in American history is probably nowhere more effectively illustrated than in the battle of the Alamo. The encounter was violent and dramatic, its participants gallant. Most critically, there were no survivors, at least none among its white male defenders, leaving others free to reconstruct a history based more frequently upon conjecture and imagination than upon verifiable evidence.

The paucity of reliable primary sources documenting the battle, however, has not discouraged the writers of an extensive body of literature on the topic. While the numerous histories of the Alamo make fascinating and exciting reading, they may ultimately teach us more about those who write them—and about the culture that so eagerly absorbs such writings—than about the battle itself. Whatever its specific components, the battle itself was of questionable military significance. Once Santa Anna decided to assault the old mission, it fell quickly—if at unexpected cost to the Mexican army. Even the most commonly held premise—that the thirteen days Santa Anna delayed before attacking the Alamo provided essential time for Sam Houston to prepare an army—is difficult to prove. However gloriously, the Alamo's defenders lost their battle. Yet in the public mind, their defeat has paradoxically dwarfed Houston's overwhelming victory at San Jacinto, a stunning triumph which not only secured independence for Texas but also effectively opened the Southwest to North American expansion. Historically, San Jacinto is a much more significant battle, yet it has never captured the public's imagination like the battle of the Alamo.

The DeGolyer Library's first major exhibition and companion catalog, "Alamo Images: Changing Perceptions of a Texas Experience," attempt to explore the development of the Alamo myth itself and to suggest what that myth may reflect about the American character. This investigation has revealed much that is confusing and contradictory. The Alamo's defense certainly was heroic—strikingly reminiscent of the battle at Thermopylae—and has thus served well as a standard for subsequent American warriors, but this battle suggests a darker side to the American character as well. The Texas revolution deepened the split between North and South over the expansion of slavery into the

Southwest and West. To many of its contemporaries, such as abolitionist leader Benjamin Lundy, the Texas revolution suggested not a fight for freedom but the aggressive expansion of slavery. The link between the Alamo and slavery may or may not be historically tenuous—and in the popular legend it is nonexistent—but the broader question of racism in the development of the Alamo myth should not be casually dismissed. The exhibit explores this theme, specifically in respect to the myth's treatment of Tejanos, or Mexican Texans.

Although several Tejanos fought and died alongside the Alamo's Anglo-American defenders, popular depictions of the battle seldom include their participation. Actually, Tejanos were early participants in the Texas revolution. In 1832 the *ayuntamiento*, or town council, of San Antonio de Béxar had publicly issued a manifesto protesting Mexican governance of Texas and supporting Stephen Austin's struggle on behalf of the Anglo-American colonizers. Nonetheless, within a few years of the fall of the Alamo, Tejano contributions to both that battle and to the entire independence movement were being overlooked. At the beginning of the twentieth century, for example, San Antonio witnessed a struggle between two local preservationists, Adina De Zavala and Clara Driscoll, for control of the local Daughters of the Republic of Texas. This controversy—known somewhat facetiously as the "Second Battle of the Alamo"—also reflected a struggle between the Tejano and Anglo-American communities and their respective visions of the Alamo. While Driscoll's eventual victory may have been simply a reflection of San Antonio's particular social structure, the incident may also have reflected the rapid spread of Jim Crow and racism throughout late-nineteenth-century America.

Then again, racism and the years of open and intermittent warfare between Texas and Mexico after the Alamo's fall may have had little or no effect on the development of the Alamo myth. This exhibition and catalog endeavor to raise such questions not necessarily to supply answers about the battle itself, which may never be fully explained, but to explore what the myth says about ourselves. The aim of the project has been to raise questions, not to provide definitive answers, and to stimulate examination of various issues. The project is less concerned with such points as where and how David Crockett died that day than with why, in contradiction to the eyewitness testimony of several Mexican soldiers, he is commonly viewed as making a dramatic last stand surrounded by bayonets. Why are people today so concerned about his manner of death? Crockett—perhaps the quintessential American—died a hero whether he was bayoneted or shot by a firing squad, yet few questions will raise the ire of Texans so rapidly. Perhaps as the

French social philosopher Georges Sorel once wrote, the symbol soon becomes more important than the fact if that symbol fulfills a public need.

For whatever success this project achieves, credit must be given to several individuals. From a project proposal I originally developed, Susan Prendergast Schoelwer, former director of Special Collections at the Chicago Public Library, initiated work at the DeGolyer Library in November 1984. With the diligent and insightful assistance of Tom W. Gläser, a graduate student in American History at North Texas State University, Schoelwer has been responsible for the development of the entire project, which includes a public symposium as well as the exhibition and catalog. Taking the exhibit from the point of its original conception, she has conducted the necessary research, developed the theme and content, selected the materials, and designed the installation. She has also written the major portion of the exhibit's catalog, with Paul A. Hutton, Assistant Professor of History at the University of New Mexico and Editor of the *New Mexico Historical Quarterly*, writing the introduction, and with Gläser bringing his extensive military history background to the writing of the battle chapter.

Assistance to the project, particularly in the areas of bibliographic research, was given by all of the DeGolyer Library's staff, including Dr. James Phillips and Dawn Letson. Sally Gross and Deborah Carpenter in addition devoted considerable time to compiling the index. Special thanks is due to Betty English, a native Texan, without whose patient typing and persistent deciphering this manuscript would not have taken shape on schedule. Chuck Donaldson, Kay Bost, and other staff members provided additional administrative and clerical assistance. Acknowledgment must also be made of the support offered to the project by Robert W. Oram, Director, Central University Libraries; Dr. R. Hal Williams, Dean, Dedman College; and the administration of SMU.

In addition to general staff support, the DeGolyer Library also provided funding for supplies, equipment, and the publication of the catalog. However, without the generous support of the Texas Committee for the Humanities, a state program of the National Endowment for the Humanities, and matching funding given by Mr. and Mrs. Arnold Zohn of Sagaponack, New York, this endeavor could not have been initiated. It is to the memory of Mr. Zohn, a dynamic individual who died recently after a long and successful career in publishing, that this catalog is dedicated. Additional funds were given by El Fenix Corporation of Dallas.

Any project of such broad scope as this involves the assistance and cooperation of many individuals and institutions. In addition to the credit due to the project and library staff and to the financial supporters, thanks must also be given to others who lent their support. Outside of the DeGolyer Library, the heaviest use of research materials was at the Daughters of the Republic of Texas Library at the Alamo, San Antonio, Texas, whose staff, especially Sharon R. Crutchfield, Director, and Martha Utterback, Assistant Director, extended a warm welcome and exhibited patience beyond the call of duty in answering numerous requests. In San Antonio, the project was also aided by the staff of the University of Texas Institute of Texan Cultures, especially Tom Shelton and Al Lowman; by William Elton Green, Curator of the Witte Museum, who is presently preparing his own exhibition on the Alamo; and by Ron Bechtol, architect and author of an article on "Alamotifs," who generously loaned several of his personal photographs. In Austin, John Molleston guided us through the records of the General Land office.

As Alamo images are spread in numerous collections throughout the country, the DeGolyer Library is greatly indebted to those institutions, credited in the captions and checklist, whose staffs ferreted out and photographed the items indicated. In particular, George Miles, Curator of the Western Americana Collection at Yale University, devoted considerable attention to queries regarding three early Alamo drawings. Charles Colley, director of the Jenkins Garrett Library at the University of Texas at Arlington, was most gracious in allowing the project staff access to a newly acquired but not yet cataloged collection of Mexican documents and in agreeing to lend to the exhibit one significant pamphlet bearing on the Alamo. Peggy Riddle of the Dallas Historical Society was also extremely helpful in locating photographs and information on the Texas Hall of State murals.

The library is most grateful to artist Eric von Schmidt, who has graciously agreed to produce, especially for this exhibit, a new bas-relief, based on his epic painting of the Alamo battle which is to be unveiled in March 1986. Andy Reisberg, of Flying Horse Photography & Associates, Dallas, has produced most of the photographs for this catalog, and his artistry, dedication, and keen attention to detail have resulted in images of exceptional quality. Fred McElroy of the Meadows Museum, SMU, provided invaluable advice on lighting and designing the exhibition, while Max McKinney and Ed Richardson of the Physical Plant staff gave our ideas physical form.

Throughout its development, "Alamo Images" has benefited substantially from the support and suggestions of its primary advisor, Dr. Paul A. Hutton, and the advisory committee members: Dr. David J. Weber, History Department Chairman, Southern Methodist University; Dr. Arnoldo De León, Associate Professor of History, Angelo State

University; Dr. Ron C. Tyler, Assistant Director, Amon Carter Museum; A. C. Greene, Dallas author and historian; Dr. Frances Leonard, Director, Texas Humanities Resource Center, University of Texas at Arlington; and Trudy McMurrin, Director, SMU Press. As advisor to the project, Hutton, in particular, has far exceeded the requirements of his role, sharing unstintingly of his ideas, his enthusiasm, and his extensive collection of popular culture materials (without which this exhibition would have been far less lively). Hutton's own Alamo research, conducted over several years' time in preparation for his forthcoming book on the Alamo, has in turn been aided immeasurably by the assistance of Brian W. Dippie, Timothy J. Gravenstreter, Sergio Bonelli, Susan Wheeler, David Grossblatt, Jack Jackson, Don Graham, Carmen Perry, William Dean, and Charles Long. Finally, the exhibit staff wishes to most gratefully acknowledge their respective families, whose continuing encouragement and support has been essential to this undertaking.

In a very real sense, "Alamo Images" has been a group effort, and the DeGolyer Library extends its appreciation to all who participated. In organizing this project, the library hoped not only to suggest new insights on an important aspect of Texas history, but also to share the library's rich resources with a broader audience than ever before and to encourage increased use of its holdings—now nearly 100,000 titles—which comprise one of the more active Western History collections in the nation.

Former Director, DeGolyer Library
Director of the Library,
Saginaw Valley State College

July 1985

ALAMO IMAGES

INTRODUCTION

by Paul Andrew Hutton

ON MARCH 6, 1836, the 183-man garrison of the fortress Alamo, in San Antonio de Béxar, Texas, was overwhelmed and slaughtered by a vastly superior force of Mexican troops under General Antonio López de Santa Anna. Although in a military sense the battle was of little significance, it nevertheless became a symbolic rallying point for the Texan revolutionaries. It provided a battle cry that has become world famous—"Remember the Alamo!"

Similar battles, in which one side is annihilated, have of course long fascinated mankind. Peoples in many nations point pridefully to such events in their history. The story is always the same, although small details may differ. The heroes are always vastly outnumbered by a vicious enemy from a culturally inferior nation bent on the utter destruction of the heroic band's people. These men fight for their very way of life in a battle that is clearly hopeless. They know that they are doomed but go willingly to their deaths in order to bleed the enemy and buy time for their people. Oftentimes they are betrayed, sometimes by the failure of their countrymen to rescue them, and usually a lone survivor carries the tale of their sublime sacrifice to the world. They perish with a fierce élan that turns their defeat into a spiritual victory. The leader of the defeated band is often elevated to the status of a national hero, while the battle becomes a point of cultural pride, an example of patriotism and self-sacrifice. Such was the case with Saul at Mt. Gilboa, Leonidas at Thermopylae, Roland at Roncesvalles, Custer at the Little Big Horn, and Gordon at Khartoum. Such is clearly the case with the Alamo and its trinity of heroes: William Barret Travis, Jim Bowie, and Davy Crockett.

There have always been two Alamos—the Alamo of historical fact and the Alamo of our collective imagination. One was a mission and a fortress, and is now a shrine. The other has become a cultural and political symbol. But symbols have many uses and can be portrayed in many ways. Thus a name enshrined in historical memory has also been used to sell dog food and rental cars, banking services and real estate, history and propaganda. This book—and the exhibit from which it is derived—briefly explore the Alamo of history and myth.

The line between the Alamo of fact and the Alamo of popular fancy is often blurred. While there has been an amazingly large body of historical and popular literature generated on the battle, there has never been an adequate serious study of it by a professional academic historian. Thus competent popular historians such as Walter Lord, who has written the best book on the battle, have not had the usual body of solid secondary materials to draw upon when writing. The academic work usually cited as the best study of the battle and its heroes, Amelia Williams's doctoral dissertation, is of stunningly poor quality. Academic historians have thus deserted the field, leaving the battle to the popularizers and propagandists. Those who have written on the battle, for the most part, have simply repeated false stories told before in books, articles, and newspaper accounts. The written historical record is a sad one.

One of the reasons that academic historians have not written on the Alamo is because it is so popular a historical topic. So much has been produced on the battle and its heroes that many assume everything has already been covered. Others assume the subject to be too trivial to warrant their attention. As a result, the Alamo of our collective imagination has become dominant, assuming an importance in the national mind that is greater than that of the historical Alamo.

The development and nourishment of the Alamo in popular culture is a fascinating story. From popular histories, novels, poems, children's books, paintings, songs, television shows, and movies the Alamo that we know today has emerged. For the most part this body of material has treated the Alamo in a hagiographic manner, perpetuating false notions and developing powerful cultural symbols. The lives of heroes are a testament to the values and aspirations of those who admire them. If, by chance, their images change over time, these heroes may act as a barometer of fluctuating societal values. By looking at a symbolic event like the Alamo in terms of the way it has been portrayed in popular culture, we can learn much about the character of the people who create, nourish, and cherish the image. Thus, if we can understand what the Alamo means to Texans, we can learn much about their changing values, character, and self-image as a people.

Although the Alamo is an important national symbol, it is far more vital as a creation myth for Texas. Myth is used here in its folkloric form, not as a word meaning falsehood. Although a true myth may indeed bear little resemblance to historical fact, that is irrelevant to its folkloric function. A powerful mythic saga like the Alamo tale is embraced by a people and characterizes them, expressing shared beliefs and cultural symbols. As a creation myth for Texans, the Alamo story helps define them as a people, making them distinct from other Americans.

The tale embraces powerful themes of courage, sacrifice, betrayal, and redemption. Its trinity of heroes—Travis, Bowie, and Crockett—have since been deified beyond recognition as mere mortals. This was not necessarily a gradual development. Men at the time immediately saw the mythic potential of the battle. The *Telegraph and Texas Register* for March 24, 1836, proclaimed as much in an early account of the battle.

> Spirits of the mighty, though fallen! Honors and rest are with ye: the spark of immortality which animated your forms, shall brighten into a flame, and Texas, the whole world, shall hail ye like the demi-gods of old, as founders of new actions, and as patterns of imitation!

When Thomas Carlyle heard of Jim Bowie and his defiant last stand he was also swept up in the imagery of ancient heroic struggles fought anew. "By Hercules," Carlyle exclaimed. "The man was greater than Caesar or Cromwell—nay, nearly equal to Odin or Thor. The Texans ought to build him an altar!" The Texans, of course, did build Bowie an altar by turning the Alamo into a civil-religious shrine.

The Texans quickly recognized the parallels that existed between the Alamo and similar struggles in antiquity. Americans, of course, have long been burdened by an inferiority complex toward Europe and often point pridefully to national achievements that compare favorably to, or surpass, similar European events or cultural landmarks. The Texans were anxious to see elements of a unique regional identity coming out of their revolutionary struggle, but they could not help but compare it to an equally powerful symbolic battle from the past.

On March 26, 1836, the citizens of Nacogdoches, Texas, issued a resolution in praise of the defense of the Alamo that harkened back to ancient days.

> The tongue of every noble spirit of whom we speak is silent in death and we anticipate in a succinct and imperfect narrative the future Glory of their fame. They died martyrs to liberty; and on the altar of their sacrifice will be made many a vow that shall break the shackles of tyranny. Thermopylae is no longer without a parallel, and when time shall consecrate the dead of the Alamo, Travis and his companions will be named in rivalry with Leonidas and his Spartan band.

Thomas Jefferson Green, one of the leaders of the tragic Mier expedition, improved on that sentiment with a famous quote that was inscribed on the first Alamo monument in Austin: "Thermopylae had her messenger of defeat—the Alamo had none."

Thermopylae was, of course, a battle in Greece where a small band of Spartan warriors sacrificed themselves to momentarily stall the onslaught from the north of Xerxes' Persian hordes in 480 B.C. Although all but one were killed, the battle gave the other Greek city-states time to mobilize their forces and drive the Persians out of Greece, thus insuring the survival of western civilization and the birth of democracy. The Alamo had now matched that ancient struggle and gone it one better. No one, according to the myth, survived the battle of the Alamo. As with the struggle at Thermopylae, the early Texans viewed the battle at the Alamo as a contest of civilizations: freedom vs. tyranny; democracy vs. despotism; Protestantism vs. Catholicism; the New World culture of the United States vs. the Old World culture of Mexico; Anglo-Saxons vs. the mongrelized mixture of Indian and Spanish races; and ultimately, the forces of good over evil.

A creation myth does not pander to liberal sensibilities. The lines of good and evil are always razor sharp. The story is meant to give to a people a strong and unique self-image. It does not cater to the enemy in any way. Thus the myth of the Alamo is often stunningly racist. The myth is a nineteenth-century creation, and it reflects the racial sensibilities of that time. This racial mentality, however, lasted well into our own century and is still apparent today, although in more muted form.

The fact that Tejanos, Hispanic-Texans, had died fighting against the centralist government of Santa Anna at the Alamo was generally ignored in the historical and popular literature on the battle until the 1960s. Writers tended to share Colonel Travis's opinion of the Hispanic residents of Béxar.

> The citizens of this municipality are all our enemies, except those who have joined us heretofore. We have three Mexicans now in the fort; those who have not joined with us in this extremity, should be declared public enemies, and their property should aid in paying the expenses of the war.

Eight Tejanos died fighting with Travis in the Alamo, and another, Brigido Guerrero, may well have talked his way out of the Alamo during the battle by claiming to be a prisoner of the Texans. Three Tejanos were sent from the Alamo before the final assault as messengers. The leader of the Tejanos in the Alamo, Juan Seguín, was one of these messengers.

Seguín, scion of a wealthy and influential Hispanic family, had long been a friend of the Anglo settlers in Texas. His liberal sensibilities bridled at the centralist dictatorship of Santa Anna. His father, Erasmo, was a warm friend to Stephen F. Austin and Jim Bowie, and had been elected as a delegate to the convention that ultimately declared Texas independent. Juan Seguín's company of Tejano cavalry had proven invaluable as scouts in the early days of the war.

Seguín, who held the rank of captain in the Texas army, had scouted with Travis to insure that General Martín Perfecto de Cos's defeated army withdrew from Texas late in 1835, and they later rode into the Alamo together. On the night of February 25, accompanied by his aide Antonio Cruz y Arocha, Seguín made a daring ride through the encircling Mexicans to carry a message from Travis to Sam Houston. After delivering his message, Seguín raised a company of twenty-five Tejanos and hurried to Cíbolo to await the arrival of James Fannin's men from Goliad in order to march with them to the rescue of the Alamo. But the inept, timid Fannin never came, while Seguín waited impatiently and time ran out for the defenders of the Alamo. Texas has since raised monuments to the cowardly Fannin, who eventually surrendered his army and was executed by the Mexicans, while the bold patriot Seguín has been ignored, despite his heroic participation in the Battle of San Jacinto.

During the liberal revival of the 1960s, with interest in ethnic minorities, civil rights, and pluralism on the rise, Seguín was suddenly rediscovered. He became the standard Hispanic pictured in school texts and popular histories on Texas. He was featured in John Wayne's 1960 epic film, *The Alamo*, and in a 1982 public television biography. A fine pictorial biography in 1982 by the noted Texas graphic artist Jack Jackson, entitled *Los Tejanos*, presented Seguín as a heroic and tragic figure.

To the Hispanic left, however, Seguín was anything but an acceptable hero. Rudy Acuña, a well-known Chicano historian at California State University, Northridge, resigned from the advisory board of the PBS program on Seguín, protesting: "To make heroes of the Mexican people defending the Alamo is like making heroes of the Vichy government. . . . Seguín was interested in protecting his interests, not his nationality or the rights of the people. *Seguín* represents an accommodationist point of view that promotes the wrong kind of assimilation." David J. Weber, chairman of the history department at Southern Methodist University and the leading member of the PBS advisory board, noted that Acuña's problem with Seguín resulted from the fact that "[Acuña] sees Mexican-Americans as essentially lower-class people. His criticism is that Seguín was not himself a member of the lower class." Weber preferred to view Seguín as "a tragic figure in Mexican-American history caught between two cultures in collision."

Even after the brief liberal renaissance of the 1960s had passed, Seguín remained visible as a symbol of the Hispanics who fought for Texas independence. More conservative writers now pointed to Seguín in answer to charges that the revolution was nothing but an Anglo theft of Mexican land. The participation of Seguín and others, such as Lorenzo de Zavala, according to these writers, proved that the Texas revolution was a struggle for liberty against despotism, as traditionalists had long claimed.

One standard myth of the Alamo, in fact, portrayed the defenders as fighting and dying for their rights as citizens under the Mexican constitution of 1824. The flag of the Alamo pictured in books, paintings, and movies reinforced that view. It was a Mexican tricolor with the date 1824 replacing the Mexican eagle. There is no evidence to support such a flag ever flying over the Alamo. R. M. Potter seems to have made up the flag in 1860. Although Juan Seguín and his Tejanos may have been fighting for a more liberal Mexico, the Anglos in the Alamo were fighting for independence. They agreed with Travis, who wrote from the Alamo on March 3:

> Let the Convention go on and make a declaration of independence, and we will then understand, and the world will understand, what we are fighting for. If independence is not declared, I shall lay down my arms, and so will the men under my command. But under the flag of independence, we are ready to peril our lives a hundred times a day. . . .

Travis, who was viciously anti-Mexican, was not about to fight for his rights as a Mexican citizen under a modified Mexican banner, and neither were the men under his command. Almost all of them were recent emigrants to Texas, and it is unlikely that many of them knew anything about the Mexican constitution. The only flag captured at the Alamo was the blue banner of a band of Louisiana volunteers, the New Orleans Greys. Santa Anna sent it back to Mexico City as evidence that he was battling Anglo filibusters. His characterization of the Anglo defenders of the Alamo is probably closer to the truth than the Texan vision of them as a heroic band dedicated to the defense of liberty. After all, one of the major grievances that the Texans had with the Mexican constitution was that it banned slavery. The Texas revolution was generally regarded north of the Mason-Dixon line in 1836 as a conspiracy on the part of the Southern slavocracy to extend their power westward. The defenders of the Alamo certainly fought for freedom, but it was the freedom to economically prosper without Mexican economic or political interference.

Nevertheless, defenders of the Alamo myth are now quick to point to the Tejanos as proof that the battle was part of the eternal struggle for liberty and was not a racial conflict, a land grab, or an effort to expand slavery. Arizona Governor Bruce Babbitt dared to suggest in a 1979 speech in San Antonio that "the Alamo is a symbol of the problem in our relationship with Mexico ... a sacred symbol to Texans and an extension of the American ideal. But to Mexico, it's a symbol of territory lost, a nation plundered by overbearing gringo neighbors." He was loudly attacked by Texans who pointed to the Tejanos of the Alamo as proof that race had nothing to do with the battle.

"The Alamo stands as one of the most cherished examples in recorded history of mankind's eternal struggle for human rights," thundered an editor in the *Lubbock Avalance-Journal*. "It is not a racial symbol, nor even a nationalist symbol as Gov. Babbitt's ignorance would have him believe, but a beacon for all the world to see that man's struggle against repression is never in vain. Gov. Babbitt overlooks, if he ever knew, that many Mexicans living in what is now Texas joined in—and gave their lives for—the Revolution against a totalitarian regime personified by Santa Anna."

"The heroes of the Alamo don't need defending against a politician two states away," huffed then Texas Attorney General Mark White. "The Alamo was part of Texas' fight for liberty, which was backed by Mexicans and anglos alike and decided in 1836 at San Jacinto."

Texas House Speaker Billy Clayton chimed in as well, suggesting that Babbitt tend to his own state's relationship with Mexico and stop stirring up emotions in Texas. "Certainly Texas and Mexico have some problems, such as illegal aliens, but it's not going to help for a governor from some other state to come over here and try to fire up emotions," declared Clayton.

The Bryan, Texas, *Eagle* angrily pointed out that the Alamo was "a shrine representing, not war with Mexico, but a Texas struggle for liberty which was endorsed by most Mexicans as well." Juan Seguín and his handful of Tejanos, so long ignored by Texans, had by 1979 been magnified in numbers to represent "most Mexicans" in Texas.

Ruben Bonilla, national president of the League of Latin American Citizens, defended Babbitt's statement. "Texas suffers from an Alamo mentality," Bonilla declared. "As a result of that, Mexican-Americans have been denied access to political and social systems of this state and country." Bonilla said that Mexican-American leaders in Texas agreed with the Arizona governor's viewpoint. "We support Gov. Babbitt's statements. We have our pride as Texans in the Alamo, but we also recognize that the United States has a paternalistic attitude toward Mexico."

Bonilla, a Corpus Christi attorney, was surprised by the sudden interest in Tejano defenders of the Alamo as expressed by critics of Babbitt. "American and Texas history books have held up Hispanics for ridicule, embarrassment and humiliation," Bonilla said. "Contributions of Hispanics are lost in the back pages of history, like patriots such as Juan Seguín who fought valiantly for Texas' freedom."

The question of the Alamo as a symbol of racism, at least to some Americans, has yet to be settled. In 1980 and 1981 small groups of young people identifying themselves as Communists and protesting racism raised red flags over the Alamo. In 1982 and 1983 cloaked members of the Ku Klux Klan appeared before the Alamo on May 1 to defend the shrine from the radicals. Such defenders were, of course, hardly welcomed by the Daughters of the Republic of Texas, who control and operate the Alamo, or by city officials. When Charles Lee, grand dragon of the White Camelia Knights of the Ku Klux Klan, requested another parade permit in June 1983 for Klan members to rally at the Alamo to protest illegal aliens, it was the last straw for San Antonio Mayor Henry Cisneros and many other citizens of the Alamo City. The Klan was allowed to march, but it was kept away from the Alamo, and its route was strictly limited. Margot Moreno led a Hispanic group that rallied at the same time as the Klan march in counterprotest. Such incidents will undoubtedly continue, for the Alamo, like any powerful icon, is a handy rallying point for groups of various political persuasions seeking publicity.

If, for some, the "Alamo mentality" symbolizes racial repression, for most Texans and Americans the old mission remains symbolic of democracy triumphant through defeat. The most cherished moment of the Alamo myth perfectly captures that democratic spirit—Travis's line in the dust.

According to tradition, Travis called the weary garrison together during a lull in the Mexican bombardment the evening of March 3, 1836. James Butler Bonham had brought word that Fannin was not coming, and Travis now fully realized that the Alamo was doomed. He faced his men and shared with them the news of Fannin—news that was as sad as death. Although there was no hope of victory, he was determined to stay in the Alamo and sell his life as dearly as possible in order to buy more time for Texans in the north and east to organize an army. Drawing his saber, he drew a line in the pale dust before him and asked those who would stand with him and die for liberty to cross over.

It was a moment of sublime democratic choice as, one by one, every member of the garrison made his personal decision to die for freedom rather than to live under tyranny. Jim Bowie, too ill to lift himself from his cot, asked his friends to carry him across.

Finally, only one man remained on the other side of the line—a friend of Bowie's from France by the name of Louis "Moses" Rose. Later that night he climbed the wall and vanished into the darkness beyond.

Travis's drawing of the line became the most dramatic moment in the Alamo saga. The men of the Alamo voted with their physical beings—with their lives—for the cause of freedom, choosing death willingly and with Texan determination. The symbolic power of the line and the men's bold decision is overpowering. Painters, novelists, popular historians, and film makers have all embraced this as part of the Alamo story. (A painting of the episode hangs inside the Alamo today.) The story appears in various forms—sometimes the men are asked to cross the line if they wish to leave, and often all the men choose to stay.

In the 1955 film *The Last Command*, Travis speaks to his men in a driving rainstorm, and they all cross the line. In John Wayne's *The Alamo*, filmed five years later, Travis speaks to Jim Bowie's volunteers who have decided to depart and does not draw the line. After his speech, Bowie and his men all move over to join him and stay. In whatever form the story takes, the message is always the same—the defenders of the Alamo willingly chose to sacrifice themselves so that Texas might live. "But nobody forgets the line," wrote J. Frank Dobie in 1939. "It is drawn too deep and straight."

But did Travis really draw the line? For years historians found it a difficult tale to accept. It had not appeared until 1873, when William P. Zuber's article "An Escape from the Alamo" appeared in the *Texas Almanac*. According to Zuber, Louis Rose staggered up to his father's cabin in Grimes County a few days after the fall of the Alamo. They took in the exhausted man, and he related the story of the line to them, complete with a lavish version of Travis's speech to the men of the Alamo. Even though Zuber later admitted that he had made up much of the speech, the story of the line was quickly appropriated by poets, novelists, and historians. The most influential of the latter was Anna J. Hardwicke Pennybacker, whose *History of Texas for Schools* contained an even more embellished version of Zuber's story. First published in 1888, Pennybacker's history of Texas went through six editions and was historical gospel to generations of Texas schoolchildren.

Although the story never lost its fascination to poets and novelists, it did not fare as well with historians in the twentieth century. The revised edition of Pennybacker's history that appeared in 1908 dropped Zuber's story. Clarence Wharton's 1932 school text, which became the standard Texas history for years, ignored the story. Finally Amelia

Williams, for years considered the final authority on the Alamo, dismissed the story of the line as "the creation of a vivid imagination" in her 1931 doctoral dissertation.

But then, in 1939, a Texas history buff named R. B. Blake rummaged through court and land records in Nacogdoches County and discovered proof that Louis Rose had indeed lived and had been in the Alamo. Rose had testified in several cases concerning land claims for relatives of Alamo victims. Furthermore, Blake discovered that it was common knowledge among old-timers in Nacogdoches, Texas—where Rose operated a meat market—that the old Frenchman had been in the Alamo and had left the garrison. People often asked Rose why he had not stayed with the others in the Alamo, to which the reply invariably came, "By God, I wasn't ready to die."

Walter Lord, in *A Time to Stand*, concluded that although the story of the line was basically true, it had been garbled in Rose's original tale to Zuber or, more likely, greatly embellished by Zuber. Lord turned up an 1876 interview with Mrs. Susanna Dickinson, the only adult Anglo survivor, in which she stated that on the night before the final Mexican assault Travis had called the men together, explained that the situation was hopeless, and offered any who wished to depart the opportunity to do so. One man, she called him Ross, stepped out of the ranks and was gone before dawn.

So the shining legend is true, even though the actual line was never drawn across the dusty ground of the Alamo compound. But it happened on March 5 instead of March 3, which explains why the Alamo's final two couriers, John W. Smith and James Allen, never mentioned it. Even without the line, however, that sublime moment of democratic choice occurred in all its triumphant glory. Of course, the line will eternally live in the popular imagination whether it was drawn or not. And ultimately, that is more important than the historical record anyway. J. Frank Dobie understood this when he wrote: "It is a line that nor all the piety nor wit of research will ever blot out. It is a Grand Canyon cut into the bedrock of human emotions and heroical impulses."

Even though the story of the line is central to the symbolic power of the Alamo, it has never caused as much argument or bitter controversy as another part of the traditional tale of the Alamo—the death of Davy Crockett. This controversy would seem ridiculously unimportant if so many people did not get regularly exercised over it. After all, no matter the exact details of his death, Crockett still perished as the same martyr for freedom. Nevertheless, a grand debate continues to rage over whether he went down fighting like a tiger at bay or was overpowered and surrendered with several others only to be executed by direct order of Santa Anna.

Interestingly, the story of Crockett's surrender was quite common in the nineteenth century and seemed to upset no one. Contemporary newspaper accounts of the battle often stated that Crockett had surrendered only to be executed by the Mexicans. This was often used by the press in 1836 as further evidence of Santa Anna's barbarity. The story was retold repeatedly in early popular histories of the frontier. Even Theodore Roosevelt included it in his "Remember the Alamo" story in *Hero Tales from American History*, 1895. It was not considered to be a negative reflection on Crockett.

Edward S. Ellis, whose *The Life of Colonel David Crockett* was published in 1884 and went through numerous editions, recounted the surrender story in such a way as to cast Crockett in a heroic light.

> At last only six of the garrison were left alive. They were surrounded by General Castrillón and his soldiers. The officer shouted to them to surrender, promising that their lives should be spared. In the little group of Spartans were Davy Crockett and Travis, so exhausted they were scarcely able to stand. . . .
>
> There were a few brave and humane officers, and among them were General Castrillón and Burdillón. They spoke sympathizingly to Crockett and Travis, and with several other officers walked to where the scowling Santa Anna stood and asked that the surrender of the few survivors might be received.
>
> The reply was an order that all should be shot. Seeing his treachery, the enraged Crockett roused himself, and swinging his Bowie aloft, made a furious rush for the Mexican Nan Sahib. The intrepid Tennessean was riddled with bullets before he could pass half the intervening distance. Almost at the same moment, the other five were shot down.

This version of Crockett's death, often repeated in popular histories and children's books, is certainly fanciful. We know with some certainty, for instance, that Travis was killed on the north wall early in the final assault. Ellis copied his version from the spurious Crockett autobiography, *Col. Crockett's Exploits and Adventures in Texas*, 1836, which in turn used early newspaper accounts based on the eyewitness statement of a Mexican soldier. The point to be made here is not that the Ellis version is correct, but rather that it was accepted by most readers without argument. As late as the early 1950s juvenile histories and comic books were repeating this version of Crockett's death.

Then, in December 1954, the *Disneyland* television series on ABC aired the first episode of a three-part miniseries on Davy Crockett. By the time Fess Parker as Crockett went down swinging his rifle "Old Betsy" at the advancing Mexicans in the final episode, a craze of unprecedented proportions was sweeping the nation.

After seven incredible months of a merchandizing bonanza in which every conceivable kind of item carried the Davy Crockett label—coonskin caps, toy soldier sets, toy guns, bicycles, towels, pajamas, soaps, wallets, pillows, bedspreads, purses, and even ladies' underwear—the Crockett craze began a sharp decline. But the Disney version of Crockett had been indelibly fixed in the minds of a whole generation of young Americans. Ten million copies of "The Ballad of Davy Crockett" record were sold and every one of those buyers now knew for certain just how Davy had died—fighting to the bitter end with his rifle as a club. (Actually, the audience never sees Crockett die in the Disney show. There is a slow fade as he wades into the Mexicans—the last defender of the Alamo.)

Both the 1955 film *The Last Command* and the 1960 film *The Alamo* depict Crockett blowing up the powder magazine as the Mexicans rush upon him. This is a version of Crockett's death that is based upon nothing except a Hollywood scriptwriter's imagination. Robert Evans, in charge of the Alamo's powder, had attempted such an act near the end of the battle but had been shot before he could torch the magazine.

When Walter Lord published *A Time to Stand* in 1961 he trod a careful middle ground concerning Crockett's death. He included the story of the execution of the captured Texans but did not identify any of them. In an appendix he addressed the question of Crockett's death and noted that several reliable Mexican eyewitnesses agreed that the famous frontiersman was captured and then executed on order of Santa Anna.

Of the Mexican sources on the Alamo battle, none was more reliable than the diary of José Enrique de la Peña, an officer on Santa Anna's staff, first published in 1836. In 1975 a new translation of De la Peña's diary was published by Texas A & M University Press entitled *With Santa Anna in Texas*. Translated and edited by Carmen Perry, former director of the Daughters of the Republic of Texas Library at the Alamo, the 202-page book contained a single page relating the execution of Crockett. Said De la Peña:

> Some seven men had survived the general carnage and, under the protection of General Castrillón, they were brought before Santa Anna. Among them was one of great stature, well proportioned, with regular features, in whose face there was the imprint of adversity, but in whom one also noticed a degree of resignation and nobility that did him honor. He was the naturalist David Crockett, well

known in North America for his unusual adventures, who had undertaken to explore the country and who, finding himself in Béjar at the very moment of surprise, had taken refuge in the Alamo, fearing that his status as a foreigner might not be respected. Santa Anna answered Castrillón's intervention in Crockett's behalf with a gesture of indignation and, addressing himself to the sappers, the troops closest to him, ordered his execution. . . . Though tortured before they were killed, these unfortunates died without complaining and without humiliating themselves before their torturers.

Perry's book set off quite a controversy as journalists picked up on the Crockett death scene as a quick way to get a headline. "Students of American history and John Wayne fans take note. The legendary story of the Alamo may need revision," declared the Denver *Post*. "Has the King of the Wild Frontier been relieved of his coon-skin crown?" asked the *Jackson* [Tennessee] *Sun*. "Naturally, it will be hard for a generation that grew up singing 'Born on a mountain-top in Tennessee' to accept the mental image of a cowardly Crockett groveling in the Alamo corner," noted the *Jackson Sun* reporter, who had obviously not even bothered to read the one page in the book that she was writing the article about.

"Did Crockett die at the Alamo? Historian Carmen Perry says no," read the headline in the October 13, 1975, issue of *People* magazine. Above a picture of Carmen Perry the magazine ran a photo of John Wayne as Crockett. The press, absolutely ignorant of any historical works on the Alamo, consistently used movie versions of Crockett's death as a reference point for their readers. That was probably fully justified, since most people know nothing about the Alamo except what they have seen on television or in the movies.

People magazine quoted Mrs. Charles Hall, chair of the Alamo committee of the Daughters of the Republic of Texas, as condemning the book. "We don't believe Davy Crockett ever surrendered. We feel he went down fighting. And by 'we' I mean all Texans." Mrs. Hall later denied ever saying such a thing, and the DRT, in fact, rallied to support its former librarian. The Sons of the Republic of Texas even gave the book its prestigious Summerfield G. Roberts Award as the outstanding book of 1975. Another group that supported Perry was the Movimiento Estudiantil Chicanos de Aztlan of El Paso. "This seems to be another instance of the myths and legends which are contrary to facts of history . . . now being destroyed by scholarly work," commented Roberto Barcena.

Miss Perry was uncomfortable with all the publicity, and especially with the anonymous hate mail and late-night phone calls. Nevertheless, she staunchly defended De la Peña's account. "People don't believe his account because they don't want to believe it," she stoically noted. "We prefer to live by legend."

Partly in response to the controversy over the diary, Dan Kilgore, a certified public accountant in Corpus Christi who served as president of the Texas State Historical Association in 1977, delivered a speech on Crockett's death as his presidential address to the association. He expanded that speech into a carefully researched and intelligent little book published in 1978 entitled *How Did Davy Die?* Kilgore concluded that the mass of evidence supported the De la Peña account of Crockett's death. Kilgore, who admires Crockett but has a rather jaundiced view of the Crockett myth, noted dryly that "Crockett's heroism seemed to expand in direct proportion to the distance news about him had to travel" in the contemporary newspaper accounts.

The reaction to Perry's book was mild compared to the rantings directed at Kilgore. "Them's Fightin' Words. Davy's Legend Smudged," ran the headline in Kilgore's hometown newspaper, the *Corpus Christi Times*. "Any Texan worth his lizard skin cowboy boots and Willie Nelson albums knows better than to smear the legend of Davy Crockett."

Critics seemed to lump intellectuals and communists together in their defense of Crockett. A letter to Kilgore from Alabama labeled the author "a mealy-mouthed intellectual" who deserved to "have his mouth washed out with soap." Under pictures of Davy Crockett and John Wayne, a scandal-sheet tabloid called *World Weekly News* noted, "Some smarty-pants historians now claim Davy didn't die fighting at the Alamo—but instead surrendered when he ran out of ammo and was then executed." The paper noted that John Wayne must have been rolling in his grave over such lies, which were labeled "a commie plot to trash our heroes." A letter to Kilgore from Fort Myers, Florida, agreed. "We know the reason for this. This is one of the Communists' plans to degrade our heroes. . . . He's still king of the Wild Frontier."

This time the DRT was not in sympathy with the author. Peggy Dibrell, chair of the DRT Alamo Committee, disputed Kilgore's version of Crockett's death and then amazingly suggested that the version in John Wayne's movie was correct. "There were plans made before the battle to blow up the gunpowder stored in the main shrine if it was overrun," Dibrell was quoted as stating in the San Antonio *Express News* for March 6, 1985, "and Davy Crockett was attempting to do that when he was killed." Such a ridiculous statement is reflective of the absolute triumph of popular culture over historical fact. Among the very people entrusted with preserving the Alamo shrine, the

Alamo of our imagination has become more important than the Alamo of historical fact.

Dan Kilgore watched in amazement as the controversy swirled around him. He remained good-natured about it all but did note sarcastically: "I wouldn't have minded all this if they'd bought my books. Nobody even read the damn book."

With the approach of the sesquicentennial of the fall of the Alamo, which this exhibit seeks to commemorate, we can expect controversy to continue to surround the battle, as history clashes with myth. The proposal of Chicagoan Gary L. Foreman, now relocated to San Antonio, to redevelop the Alamo has already caused considerable controversy and should continue to do so. Efforts to retrieve the flag of the New Orleans Greys from Mexico continue to put the Alamo story before the public. Noted artist Eric von Schmidt has just completed a massive new painting of the battle which will be featured in *Smithsonian* magazine and will be on display at the Witte Museum in San Antonio. *American History Illustrated* is devoting its March 1986 issue to the Alamo. At least two film companies have announced Alamo productions. One will be based on Lon Tinkle's *Thirteen Days to Glory*. A new biography of Crockett by James Wakefield Burke and a novel on Texas by James Michener mark the beginning of what will undoubtedly be a massive wave of publications on the Alamo and its heroes to mark the sesquicentennial.

As Dan Kilgore and Carmen Perry discovered, the symbolic power of the Alamo nears the religious in many people's minds. Any attempt to tamper with the "Alamo of our imagination" will be resisted by staunch defenders of the true faith. To suggest that the battle was partly caused by racism or that Davy Crockett surrendered is to attack a symbol that people embrace as a part of their self-identification. Thus to attack the Alamo is to attack also the very identity of many Americans. During a period of rising patriotism, such as the 1980s, many people will be more defensive of their perceived history than ever before.

The purpose of this exhibit, at the DeGolyer Library and in travels throughout Texas, is to help explain both the Alamo of historical fact and the Alamo of our imagination. The historic documents, letters, photographs, books, and artifacts on display will explain the story of the battle and its heroes—including Juan Seguín and his Tejanos—the Alamo of history. At the same time, the iconography, paintings, movie memorabilia, novels, Alamo kitsch pieces, and popular culture artifacts will help trace the evolution of the Alamo myth—the Alamo of our collective imagination. We hope that the items, both historical and fanciful, will assist in explaining the difference between these two equally important Alamos.

Chapter 1

Search for the Alamo

by Susan Prendergast Schoelwer

A CENTURY and a half after its fall to Mexican forces on March 6, 1836, the Alamo chapel stands serenely in a park surrounded by the busy streets of downtown San Antonio. Gone are the mission walls that once enclosed it; silent are the thundering cannon that bombarded it; washed away are the blood and debris of battle. Despite many physical changes, the Alamo remains the preeminent Texas icon—the single most tangible and compelling link with the heroic events of the state's formation.

The evolution of the Alamo as both a symbol and a historic site, however, has been neither an accidental nor an inevitable process. The Alamo as it exists today is but one vision of its past—an enshrinement of one brief moment out of a long and complex history. Although this enshrinement began almost as soon as the Alamo's Mexican captors retreated in May 1836, the most decisive events occurred during the quarter century preceding World War I. During these years, preservationists struggled, first with the practical problems of acquiring the property and then with the far more difficult—ideological—issues of shaping a historic site.

This latter controversy—the "Second Battle of the Alamo"—determined the site's modern appearance, with its church-shrine dominating a tranquil memorial park and with few reminders of mortal combat. Although usually viewed as merely a petty organizational feud between the Alamo's caretakers, this controversy in fact reflected the sharply divergent historical perspectives of Anglo-American and Hispanic Texans. While the Hispanic Texans, or Tejanos, remembered the Alamo for its ancient, well-accustomed roles in the daily life of their community—first as mission and later as lodgings, hospital, military post, and other adaptive uses—the Anglo-Texans remembered it almost exclusively for its glorious role in the founding of a new order under the Republic of Texas. The latter vision—of the Alamo as a shrine—eventually triumphed, controlling the site's development to the present time.

The Alamo visitor today can only with difficulty form an accurate conception of the site's past appearance and of its many former uses. Where the Alamo park, plaza, and avenue, the Federal Building, and the commercial stores now encroach, once stood a

The Alamo, San Antonio, 1959 drawing by Edward Muegge (Buck) Schiwetz. (From *BUCK SCHIWETZ' TEXAS,* © 1960, courtesy University of Texas Press)

Bird's-eye view of the Alamo, about 1970, attributed to San Antonio photographer Harvey Belgin. As early as 1890, San Antonio historian William Corner had complained that "piecemeal, 'here a little, there a little,' the old mission has been improved off the face of the earth." Today, only a tiny portion of the original three-acre site remains, hemmed in by modern streets, public and commercial buildings, and the commemorative Alamo Plaza with its marble cenotaph designed in 1939 by Pompeo Coppini. (Courtesy Daughters of the Republic of Texas Library at the Alamo, San Antonio)

mission complex encompassing nearly three acres of ground and numerous structures—church, convent, granary, workrooms, storerooms, Indian houses, and outer walls. Of these, only two buildings have survived: the church and the convent or monastery, now known as the long barracks.

The Mission San Antonio de Valero, established in San Antonio in 1718, was but one of many Catholic missions organized as part of the official Spanish plan to Christianize native Americans and colonize northern New Spain. Franciscan monks began building on the present site, on the east side of the San Antonio River, about 1724 and

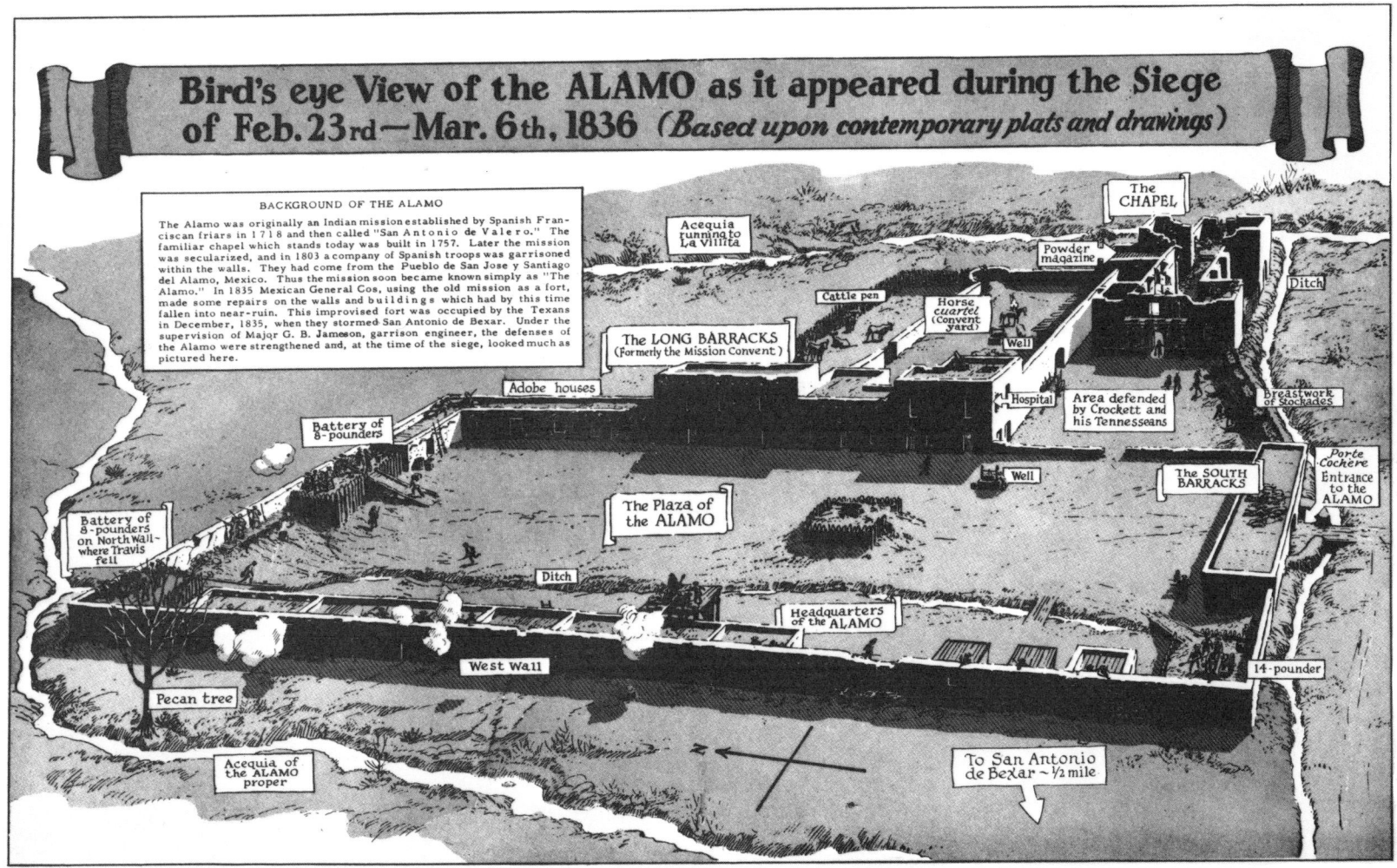

Conjectural bird's-eye view of the Alamo in 1836, drawn by Frederic Ray, ca. 1955. (From *The Story of the Alamo*, by Frederic Ray)

remained there until 1793, when the Spanish government legally dissolved the mission and distributed ownership of its lands and buildings.

After the departure of the Franciscans, the seventy-five-year-old mission entered a long period of rather haphazard use. In addition to its famous role in the Texas revolution, the site's subsequent functions have included quarters for both Spanish and Mexican frontier troops; housing for local Indians, Tejanos, and itinerant squatters; hospital; army supply depot; Masonic lodge; jail; commercial store and warehouse; public park; tourist attraction; movie set; and historic site. This multiple use has greatly complicated efforts to document or describe the Alamo at any given time. Another difficulty arises from semantic ambiguity in many descriptions of the site, with the title *Alamo* sometimes used to refer exclusively to the church building and sometimes to the entire mission complex.

Our knowledge of the eighteenth-century mission derives from the written descriptions of Spanish missionaries and government observers, from archaeological evidence, and from examination of the surviving structures.[1] Because much of this information has only recently become available, early Alamo historians and preservationists were forced to rely on oral tradition and outright speculation. Many of the resulting misconceptions have unfortunately become fixed in the popular image of the Alamo.

Regarding the church, for example, many nineteenth- and early twentieth-century observers assumed it had once been completed, then damaged by later military action. Contemporary reports indicate, however, that the mission church that now dominates Alamo imagery was never completed or actually used for religious services. Construction on it proceeded from the late 1750s, when Father Francisco Xavier Ortiz reported the collapse of an earlier stone church with tower and sacristy, until the decline of the mission during the late 1780s and early 1790s. The design for the new church was an ambitious one, clearly intended to be the architectural masterpiece of the mission. It followed a traditional cruciform plan, with a long nave crossed near its eastern end by a short, broad transept. The walls were sturdy—over three and one-half feet thick—and well built of limestone blocks, but only roughly finished.

Inside, the church was probably paved with flagstones and was intended to have a barrel-vaulted roof, supported by stone arches, and a dome or cupola over the crossing. The walls were evidently completed at least as high as the cornices, and several of the arches with their supporting pilasters were installed. Vestiges of these arches survived into the nineteenth century and are visible in Edward Everett's interior view of the Alamo (plate 3). There the project apparently stalled, however, as the mission's Indian population declined precipitously from a high of 328 in 1756 to a mere 44 in 1777. Surviving evidence suggests that the roof itself, the dome, and a second-story choir loft, designed for the west end, were never put in place.

Outside, the western facade of the church, which opened onto the mission plaza, was the chief architectural glory. The mission inventory of 1793 described this facade as "a showy and impressive piece of Tuscan architecture," with arched doors surrounded by elaborate floral carvings, twisting columns, and shell-topped niches for statuary. The central facade and front corners of the church were of carefully cut and fitted blocks, unlike the rough limestone used elsewhere. Although the facade was never finished, it is possible to project its intended design, based on similar Early Baroque style facades erected in Spain and its New World provinces.

Since the mission's ecclesiastical center was never finished, mission life must have revolved around the administrative center, the priests' residence or convent. Containing offices, kitchens, dining and guest rooms, the monastery was apparently the first permanent building constructed at the mission, replacing earlier adobe structures. By the close of the mission period, the convent included two two-story wings forming an L along the west and south edges of an inner courtyard, immediately north of the church.

The remainder of the mission complex, of less permanent construction than the two main buildings, is even more difficult to locate and describe. Workrooms, storerooms, and Indian residences were continually being repaired or replaced, and all apparently fluctuated considerably according to the size and vigor of the Indian population. During the mission's mid-century peak, the Indian pueblo included thirty finished adobe houses (most with open, stone-arched galleries) plus a number of brush huts, or *jacales*; by 1793, however, only twelve Indian houses were still habitable.

Theoretically, the Alamo was to have been the religious branch of the Spanish presidio-mission system established to reduce the savage frontier. A presidio, or strong defensive fort staffed by royal troops, would provide the needed military protection against both hostile natives and rebellious mission Indians. The presidio San Antonio de Béxar, however, was neither completed nor adequately garrisoned, compelling the Franciscans at San Antonio de Valero and other nearby missions to devise their own defenses against hostile Apaches and Comanches.[2] As a result, although religion dominated the Alamo's early years, the site also manifested clear military overtones. Protective walls, probably erected after the San Saba mission massacre of 1758, enclosed San Antonio de Valero's

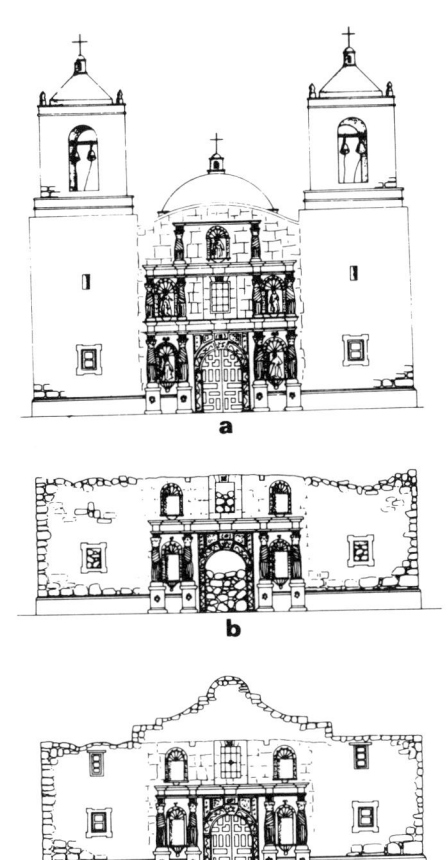

Drawing by Jack D. Eaton, comparing the Alamo facade today (c) with its supposed appearance in 1836 (b) and "suggested original elevation" (a) with a full three-level baroque retable facade, flanking bell towers, and a central dome. The presumed original design of the church has frequently been likened to that of nearby Mission Concepción. (From Jack D. Eaton, *Excavations at the Alamo Shrine*, 1980)

Conjectural view of Mission San Antonio de Valero, drawn ca. 1911 by San Antonio artist Rolla Taylor for early Alamo preservation leader Adina De Zavala. Granddaughter of Texas revolutionary leader Lorenzo de Zavala and one of the few prominent local Tejanos active in saving the Alamo, De Zavala based her conception of the site on careful research in historic documents then available, some of which she made public for the first time. Because she considered the convent the "main building," the usual relationship between convent and church is here reversed: the long, double-arcaded convent dominates the view, while the much less significant church fades into obscurity on the right. (DeGolyer Library)

The Fortified Building.
The Main Building of the Alamo where the heroes died, as it looked originally.
(Made from description in old manuscript, plans, pictures drawings, and descriptions of old settlers and pioneers.)

The Church in The Alamo.
Towers, Dome and Arched Roof fell in previous to or about 1762. Never restored or fully rebuilt.

main plaza in an irregular rectangle approximately 480 feet long (north-south) by 160 feet wide (east-west). The Indian houses lay within this enclosure, mainly along its western wall, but the church and convent buildings were outside and to the east of it. In 1793, the remaining walls (some had already crumbled) were about eight feet high and two feet thick, constructed of stone, mud, and adobe. The main gate, located in the south wall, had been fortified as early as 1762 with a turret and three cannons, and in 1793 a small one-pound cannon also stood on a rampart near the convent entrance.

After the complex ceased to be an active religious establishment in 1793, its military characteristics became even stronger. A company of Spanish cavalry, sent to protect the settlements around San Antonio, established its quarters in the old mission from at least 1801 until 1825. By the early nineteenth century, when Anglo-American visitors began to appear in Béxar occasionally, the site's essential orientation had changed to that of a military post. Zebulon M. Pike, who visited San Antonio in 1807, seemed unaware of its mission past, alluding to the Alamo simply as "the station of the troops" on the east side of the river.[3] Even its popular name, "the Alamo," apparently dates from this period, reflecting the Spanish cavalry company's origin at the Mexican town of "El Alamo," near Parra in Nueva Vizcaya. Since the Spanish word *álamo* means poplar or cottonwood, however, another tradition derives the name from a stand of trees that once grew near the mission.

Vista del fuerte de San Antonio de Valero commumemente llamado del Alamo tomada desde la azotea de la casa de Beramendi en la ciudad de Bexar por José Juan Sánchez Estrada

Drawing, probably a fair copy by Jean Louis Berlandier after an original attributed to José Juan Sánchez Navarro, ca. 1835–36. The Spanish title reads, "View of the Fort San Antonio de Valero, commonly called the Alamo, taken from the roof of the Veramendi house in the city of Bexar." The Sánchez view is the earliest known view of the site and the only one to depict the entire compound in elevation. Unlike more familiar church-oriented views, it focuses on the convent, center, a large tripartite building which rises on the right to a full two stories. Surrounding the compound is a high, crenelated wall, inside which can be seen the pitched roof of the old Indian lodgings, left, and the upper sections of the low barracks, right. Because the artist's position is evidently to the northwest of the compound (making its north wall visible), the convent building almost completely blocks the church from view—only a tiny corner can be glimpsed between the convent and low barracks.

Unfortunately, the authorship, date, and provenance of this important document are far less clear than its imagery. The drawing first became publicly known in 1913, when it appeared with a copy of Ygnacio de Labastida's map, 1836, in the *San Antonio Express* newspaper under the heading, "How the Alamo Really Looked." The Alamo view was there ascribed to Juan José Sánchez Estrada, a Mexican member of the first International Boundary Commission. Because both the drawing and the map were discovered in a sketchbook compiled by Jean Louis Berlandier, a French-born botanist who accompanied General Mier y Terán's expedition to explore the Texas boundary in 1828–29, however, later writers have attributed the Alamo view to another member of that expedition, artist José María Sánchez y Tapia.

Numerous arguments contradict this attribution, however. Mexican sources consistently assign the work to Captain José Juan Sánchez Navarro, a former classmate of Santa Anna's who, as Adjutant Inspector of Nuevo León and Tamaulipas, observed both the Texan siege of Béxar in 1835 and the Mexican siege of the Alamo in 1836. Sánchez Navarro's papers, as published in 1938 under the title *La Guerra de Tejas*, include two plans of the Alamo and a very slightly different version of this view, which appears to be signed "José Juan Sánchez, 1836." Since Berlandier's notebook, now at Yale University, apparently includes drawings by several artists, including some dated as late as the 1840s, it seems likely that Berlandier, who lived in Matamoros, must have had access to both Sánchez Navarro's sketch and Labastida's map, both of which he either copied himself or had copied by his assistant draftsman, Lino Sánchez y Tapia. The curious addition of "Estrada" to the artist's name may be an error by Berlandier, who could have confused the frontier army officer Sánchez Navarro with Sánchez Estrada (whom he may have met through boundary commission affairs), but Berlandier would hardly have been likely to forget his late expeditionary comrade José María Sánchez y Tapia. In addition, numerous martial details in the view itself suggest the war-torn months of 1835–36 rather than the more peaceful years of General Terán's expedition: a semicircular stockade guards the west gate, a partially completed trench encloses the southwest corner, both firing ports and artillery embrasures are visible in the west wall, and a two-star Mexican tri-color flies prominently over the long barracks. (Courtesy Western Americana Collection, Beinecke Library, Yale University)

Despite the very rudimentary nature of the Alamo's fortifications, its image as a military post proved irresistible to the various warring factions that battled across nineteenth-century Texas. From 1810 to 1865, the site changed hands at least sixteen times between Spanish, Mexican, Texan, Union, and Confederate forces.[4] In 1878 the departure of the U.S. Army, like the earlier withdrawal of the Franciscans, marked the end of an era for the Alamo. Its active military career was over, although it would be stormed yet once more—in jest if not without conflict—by ersatz Mexican troops in the 1969 filming of the movie *Viva Max!*

The physical appearance of the early-nineteenth-century Alamo remains as problematic as that of the eighteenth-century mission. In addition to the Spanish cavalry company, early-nineteenth-century tenants included patients in San Antonio's first hospital (which operated between 1806 and 1812) and the descendants of local Indians and Tejanos who had received land and housing at the mission's dissolution in 1793.[5] Although Spanish records indicate that considerable repairs were needed to convert the convent for use as a hospital, no detailed descriptions or visual records of the Alamo are available for the first quarter of the nineteenth century. The earliest known view of the Alamo, probably made in 1835–36 by Captain José Juan Sánchez Navarro, depicts a martial-looking compound with heavy blocklike structures surrounded by a high crenelated wall. Because Sánchez's drawing is the only view of the Alamo executed prior to its partial destruction during the Texas revolution, the site's appearance here differs markedly from later, more familiar images. The Sánchez view does, however, correspond closely to several contemporary descriptions. Jean Louis Berlandier, traveling with a Mexican exploring party led by General José Manuel Mier y Terán in 1828, observed of the Alamo, "An enormous battlement and some barracks are found there, as well as the ruins of a church which could pass for one of the loveliest monuments of the area, even if its architecture is overloaded with ornamentation like all the ecclesiastical buildings of the Spanish colonies." Several years later, George Kendall, a member of the Texan Santa Fe expedition, commented that the San Antonio missions "were all most substantially built; the walls are of great thickness; and in their form and arrangement they were frontier fortresses. They have generally, though not always, a church at the side of a square having one entrance. Seen from without, they present the form of a blank wall surrounding a square enclosure; within is a large granary, and the wall forms the back of a series of dwellings in which the missionaries and their converts lived."[6]

Even the earliest post-revolutionary visitors to the Alamo found the site vastly

Leonard Vosburgh's juvenile book illustration of "a big fort called the Alamo," an unusual example of the Sánchez view influencing popular Alamo imagery. Vosburgh has apparently not worked directly from the Sánchez drawing, however, but from an intermediate version painted ca. 1938 by Colonel Andrew Jackson Houston (last surviving son of Sam Houston) and published in Houston's own book *Texas Independence* as well as in Lenoir Hunt's *Bluebonnets and Blood*. Both Houston and Vosburgh reinsert the missing Alamo church by adding a decorative facade and bell tower to the largest block of the convent. (From the collection of Paul A. Hutton. Illustration by Leonard Vosburgh, reprinted by permission of G. P. Putnam's Sons from *DAVY CROCKETT*, A See and Read Biography by Anne Ford, illustrations © 1961 by Leonard Vosburgh)

altered, first by the construction of both Mexican and Texan fortifications, then by the inevitable battle damage, and finally by the intentional destruction of fortifications and artillery ordered after the battle of San Jacinto by Mexican commander General Vicente Filisola in order to remove the Alamo as an effective military threat to Mexico.[7] Dr. Joseph H. Barnard, who visited the Alamo just a few hours after the Mexicans left San Antonio on May 24, 1836, observed that a large fire burning inside the church had failed to injure its stone walls but that the remainder of the compound was "completely dismantled, all the single walls were leveled, the fossee [trench] filled up, and the pickets torn up and burnt." Barnard was but one of many pilgrims to the Alamo site, "sauntering about the Alamo and calling to mind the startling and interesting scenes that have at different times been acted in this little theater."[8]

Just as the roots of its martial role dated back to mission days, so the Alamo's development as a historic site can be traced back well into its military period. Anglo-American visitors of the early nineteenth century, perhaps coming face-to-face with a foreign culture for the first time, found the old Spanish missions fascinating and exotic, often without completely understanding what they were seeing. Already the buildings

The old church of San Antonio Valero — in the South East angle of the Alamo lay in ruins, appealing to the romantic taste for the picturesque, the brooding, the mysterious. Recalling the Alamo in 1845, one early settler reminisced many years later: "It was a veritable ruin, partly from the destruction caused by the battle, but mostly from its long abandonment as the abode of man. No doors or windows shut out the sunshine or storm; millions of bats inhabited the crevices in the walls and flat dirt roofs, and in the twilight the bats would pour forth in myriads. It was a meeting place for owls; weeds and grass grew from the walls. . . . We boys would run up the embankment to the outer wall and on to the roof of the convent building—it was a famous playground." This romantic vision of the Alamo persisted many years, even after the site had been turned to more prosaic uses. In 1897, William Brooker described the old chapel as a "frowning mass of stone," a "silent monument, grim, gloomy and peculiar, of all the horrors that were ever committed there."[9] Local Tejano legends of Alamo ghosts, religious statues that refused to be moved, underground passages inhabited by mysterious gift-givers, and the miraculous Margil vine only helped to increase the mysterious aura of the mission.[10]

Military men and British travelers seem to have been the most susceptible to the romantic possibilities of the site. Several of the known views of the Alamo between 1836 and 1846, when it lay in untended, picturesque ruins, were produced by British journalists or travelers like Thomas Falconer and William Bollaert, or by Anglo-American military officers, including Lieutenant Jacob Edmund Blake, Lieutenant Edward Everett (plate 3), and Captain Seth Eastman. Other views were the work of recent immigrants to San Antonio, like Mary Ann Adams Maverick, reputed to have been the city's first permanent female Anglo-American settler, or French-born artist Theodore Gentilz (p. 89). Despite differences in purpose, perspective, and artistic skill, these early views provide a remarkably consistent record of the Alamo's post-battle appearance.

Significantly, there are no known contemporary views of the Alamo ruins by Tejano artists. For the local residents, the old mission was neither a foreign exoticism nor a heroic monument; it was a familiar structure well integrated into the fabric of daily life. For many years after the revolution, Tejanos lived on the Alamo grounds and conducted business on its plaza. Local entrepreneurs guided tours through the ruins and carved souvenir pipes from Alamo stones, not unlike the pieces of the "true cross" offered for centuries at more formal religious shrines. For Anglo-American visitors, the revolutionary battle gave the Alamo a special status. Before then it had been considered simply one of the five old Spanish missions near San Antonio, but afterwards the Alamo became the most frequently visited mission, as well as a popular artistic and literary subject. Like

Earliest known post-battle view of the Alamo ruins, ca. 1838, drawn by Mary Ann Adams Maverick, wife of Declaration of Independence signer Samuel Maverick. According to her memoirs, Maverick visited the Alamo grounds in the fall of 1838, accompanied by Alamo survivor Juana Navarro and her husband Horace Alsbury. The sketch, inscribed "The old church of San Antonio Valero—in the South East angle of the Alamo," was sent by Maverick to her father-in-law in South Carolina and was apparently not published until 1952. (From Rena Maverick Green, *Samuel Maverick, Texan, 1803–1870*, 1952) ◄

Watercolor sketch, inscribed "Entrance to the Church, within the Alamo at Bexar, Texas—April 22, 1841," by Thomas Falconer, English-born draughtsman and scientific observer to the ill-fated Texan Santa Fe expedition. This strongly drawn view has not appeared in previous Alamo publications. (Courtesy Western Americana Collection, Beinecke Library, Yale University)

Pencil-on-paper sketch by Army Captain Seth Eastman, one of his views of the Alamo grounds executed during an 1848–49 tour of duty on the Texas frontier. Inscribed "Mexican house in San Antonio, Texas. Part of the Alamo—Nov. 22, 1848," this sketch was evidently drawn from inside the main plaza, in front of the long barracks, facing northwest toward one of the old Indian houses and a section of ruined arcade just inside the old west wall. Throughout the 1840s, the Alamo grounds provided quarters for a variety of permanent and transient residents—local Tejanos, impoverished European settlers, California-bound emigrants, and even Anglo-American families, like the Samuel Mavericks, who occupied an "old Mexican house" on the Alamo's western boundary while their new house was being readied. (From the *Seth Eastman Sketchbook*, 1848–49. Courtesy the McNay Art Museum, San Antonio, Texas, gift of the Pearl Brewing Company)

View of *The Alamo, San Antonio, Texas* by English traveler William Bollaert, probably made on September 20, 1843, when Bollaert's journal entry records "going to the Alamo to make sketches." At least three sketches from that expedition survive, none of which have appeared in previous Alamo publications. Of these, the most unusual and informative is this view from the southwest, showing, on the left, the one-story south wall of the low barracks, pierced by the main rectangular gateway into the compound. Above the low barracks can be seen the large two-story southern block of the long barracks, while to its right are the church and two small houses with low picket fences. Unfortunately, Bollaert had little skill in perspective, making it appear as though the low barracks, the church's west facade and south wall, and the neighboring houses are all on the same plane. (Courtesy Edward E. Ayer Collection, The Newberry Library, Chicago) ▶

William Bollaert, who in 1843 described the Alamo as a "sacred pile of ruin," many visitors considered a tour of the site an overtly spiritual experience. These English and American visitors focused primarily on the Alamo's revolutionary role; its long history as a mission became an ancient and disremembered prelude. The local Tejanos, in contrast, saw the 1836 battle as but one brief moment in a long and fondly remembered history; their tradition simply incorporated the Alamo defenders with other legends of the old mission. Bollaert's journal described meeting an old Mexican woman who recounted to him both the "horrors of the siege" and the beauties of the feast days.[11]

The arrival of the U.S. Army after the annexation of Texas in 1845 brought to a temporary halt both the romanticization and the decay of the Alamo. During the summer of 1846, preparations for the Mexican-American War brought some two thousand volunteers to San Antonio under Brigadier General John E. Wool. Wool's officers could not help noticing the "stately and melancholy ruins" of the Alamo and other nearby missions. Although the Alamo was then in an extremely ruinous state—with walls demolished, rubble strewn about, and squatters camping in the outbuildings—Captain George W. Hughes, head of Wool's Topographical Engineers, observed that, "if placed in a suitable state of repair, [it] would accommodate a regiment, and might at the same time be rendered a strong defensive work, well supplied with water."[12]

By the end of 1846, in fact, officers of the Quartermaster's Department had occupied the property, cleaning out and roofing several rooms for army stores and workshops. Captain Edwin B. Babbitt of the U.S. Army Quartermaster Corps is usually credited with having repaired and reroofed the Alamo buildings, but numerous army papers clearly indicate that this work had begun prior to Babbitt's arrival in 1849. According to a view and plan drawn by Lieutenant Edward Everett, by the end of 1848 the army had completed refurbishing the old mission convent for its offices and storerooms. The church itself remained unaltered, perhaps because, as Everett explained, "we respected it as a historical relic," but more likely because of continuing uncertainty over ownership.[13]

Beginning in 1849, the Alamo property became entangled in a three-way title controversy between the Roman Catholic Church, the United States Army, and the city of San Antonio. After extended litigation, the Texas Supreme Court in 1855 upheld the Catholic Church's title on the basis of "ancient possession," a presumed grant from the Spanish crown, and an act of the Congress of the Republic of Texas in 1841 confirming clerical ownership.[14]

Yet another claimant emerged in the person of Samuel A. Maverick, Alamo "sur-

The Alamo

vivor" and former mayor of San Antonio, who had complained of army preemption as early as 1847. In a letter to Captain S. M. Howe, Maverick argued that the Alamo was a religious establishment "only accidentally and recently used by the military." Maverick failed to dislodge the army, but he did purchase for forty dollars a large plot of land, held by Mariano Romano, bordering the northern and western sides of the mission and including sections of the outer wall and the Indian buildings. In erecting his new home on the northwest corner of the mission compound (now the corner of Houston and Alamo streets), Maverick partly obliterated the site for which he had ironically expressed to Howe a great affection. "I must add that I have a desire to reside in this particular spot. A foolish prejudice, no doubt as I was almost a solitary escape from the Alamo Massacre having been sent by those unfortunate men only four days before the Mexican advance appeared as their representative in the convention which declared independence."[15]

Despite the title controversy, the army apparently felt secure enough in its possession of the Alamo to begin repairs on the church sometime between 1850 and 1852. According to early San Antonio historian William Corner, the church was then "choked with debris, a conglomeration of stones, mortar and dirt forming on the inside a slanting heap [Cos's

RUINS OF THE ALAMO

Sketch of the *Ruins of the Alamo*, 1845, from a manuscript map of "the country in the vicinity of San Antonio de Bexar," executed by U.S. Army Lieutenant and Topographical Engineer Jacob Edmund Blake. The most extensive view of the Alamo ruins prior to repairs by the U.S. Army, Blake's drawing depicts the entire west facade of the convent, the church facade, and the connecting wall. Like Sánchez, Maverick, and Bollaert, Blake depicts the southern end of the convent as a two story block with arched entrances, flanked by a lower section of building to the north. Despite its significance and artistic quality, Blake's original drawing of the ruins has rarely been published and is known primarily through a less finely delineated but generally faithful copy included in Governor Oscar B. Colquitt's *Relating to the Alamo Property*, 1913. (Courtesy Cartographic and Architectural Branch, RG77:Q13-1, National Archives. Photographic enlargement by Flying Horse Photography and Assoc.)

Edward Everett's sketch of the Alamo, enclosed in a Quartermaster's Department report dated February 10, 1849. The sketch documents the extent of U.S. Army repairs at the end of 1848. To accommodate offices and storerooms, the army had raised the convent walls to a full two stories along its entire length, cutting new openings and partially filling others, adding exterior stairways, and replacing the old flat roof with a gabled one. The chapel ruins, in contrast, remain virtually unchanged from Everett's earlier sketch of 1846–47 (p. 46). (Courtesy Navy and Old Army Branch, Military Archives Division, National Archives)

THE ALAMO
1848

Rear elevation of the Alamo church, right, with new pitched roof and curvilinear gable, as seen by German-born artist Hermann Lungkwitz in 1852. The view is a detail from "San Antonio de Bexar," a hand-colored cityscape lithographed by L. Fredericks from Lungkwitz's original painting, which was completed in 1857, five years after his initial sketch, and sent to Rau & Sons of Dresden, Germany, for publication as an enticement to German emigrants. Also visible, to the left of the church, are several of the mission compound's old Indian houses, evidently still occupied. (From a reproduction published by Historic Urban Plans, 1975. Original in the collection of the Amon Carter Museum, Fort Worth)

artillery rampart] from the base of the rear wall to the top of the front." After removing this rubble, the church facade was "finished off in its present modest shape, the rest of the walls were raised to an equal height, a roof was added, and to assist in bearing up this roof, two stone pillars were built inside at points in the wings of the cross in line with the arch pillars. A second floor was added, and in the southwest tower, once a belfry, an office was made. Other offices were added on the ground floor."[16]

The most visible and lasting of these alterations was, of course, the capping of the church parapet by two local German contractors, John Fries and David Russi. Fries, described by local biographer Charles M. Barnes as a builder and contractor, and Russi, a builder and stonemason, evidently collaborated on numerous "prominent buildings" in the city, including the Greek Revival Market House and the First Presbyterian Church. Although their other buildings suggest that Fries and Russi possessed a certain familiarity

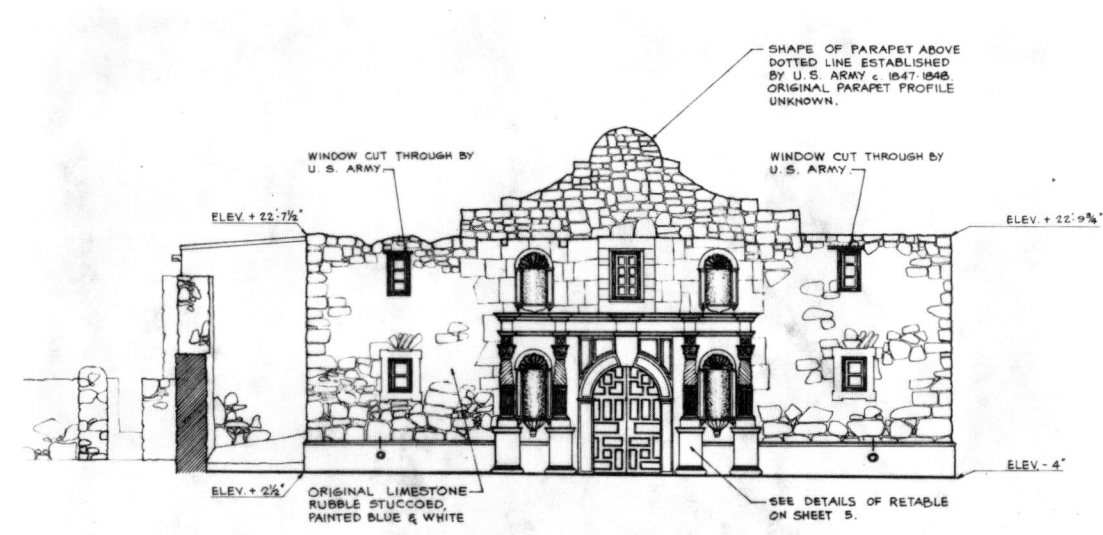

Architectural drawing, 1961, of the "West Elevation—Mission San Antonio de Valero (The Alamo)" by José Jiménez and James Emmrich for the Historic American Buildings Survey. In addition to clearly pointing out army alterations, HABS field notes describe the surface of the Alamo facade as "limestone rubble stuccoed, painted blue and white." Several early views confirm the existence of a stucco coating over the limestone blocks. Although this vision of the Alamo is at odds with more familiar images of its weathered limestone, the tradition of vivid surface decoration was well established in Mediterranean cultures, dating back to the ancient Greek temples whose pristine white marbles were also once brightly painted. (Courtesy Division of Prints and Photographs, Library of Congress)

Photograph variously dated to the 1850s and 1860s and attributed to several local photographers, including N. H. Rose and Ernst Raba. Where Alamo visitors of the 1840s had had to pick their way through fallen stones and overgrown weeds, visitors of the following decades found U.S. Army supply wagons busy loading and unloading commissary and ordnance supplies bound for posts on the Texas frontier. (Courtesy Catholic Archives, Austin) ▶

with formal architectural styles, the sources of the design for the Alamo gable remain a puzzle. This simple arched gable, no doubt intended to at least echo the original facade design, actually seems more reminiscent of urban Dutch architecture than of Spanish Baroque ecclesiastical buildings. Army artist Everett was among the few who seems to have found the new addition offensive, commenting in his memoirs, "I regret to see . . . that tasteless hands have evened off the rough walls, as they were left after the siege, surmounting them with a ridiculous scroll, giving the building the appearance of the headboard of a bedstead."[17]

The Alamo's preservation owes far more to the U.S. Army than has generally been acknowledged. The army's repairs protected the remaining buildings from further exposure to the elements, while the army's very presence halted deliberate pillaging of the site for souvenirs and building materials. (During the early 1840s, scavengers had carried off Alamo stone by the cartload.) The army's occupation of the Alamo also prevented renewed ecclesiastical use and eventually precipitated the Catholic Church's decision to sell the property. When the army had first occupied the site, Catholic Bishop John M. Odin requested a short tenancy, "as we think as soon as possible of using the whole as a seminary of learning." Three years later, Odin conceded occupancy of the property "so long as the U.S. Government may desire" in exchange for "its monthly rent."[18] Although

the Catholic Church retained legal title, it was never able to reoccupy its property. In 1865, diocesan officials politely requested that the army terminate its lease so that the Alamo could be used as a place of worship by the German Catholics of San Antonio. The army, having referred the request through its chain of command, refused to cooperate. "The Alamo building is now used for receiving Grains, and its vacation by the Government would be attended with great inconvenience and serious loss."[19] The proposal was dropped, the German Catholics built another parish church, and the Catholic hierarchy ceased to evince interest in its Alamo properties other than as a source of income. Without this change in ecclesiastical plans, the development of the Alamo as a secular shrine might never have occurred. The Catholic Church, which considered the years after the revolution the nadir of its history in Texas, would not have been likely to have encouraged a monument to Anglo-Texan heroes.[20] Finally, it is to the U.S. Army, not to Spanish missionaries, Texan pioneers, or even patriotic preservationists, that the Alamo owes its famous skyline. Despite the parapet's artistic and historic anachronism, it was quickly and irrevocably assimilated into the authentic fabric of both the Alamo site and symbol. That the army, which needed only a plain, utilitarian supply depot, instead erected a more expensive, decorative gable, suggests both the pervasiveness of mid-nineteenth-century romanticism and the nascent influence of the Alamo legend.

With the Catholic Church's abandonment of plans for reconsecrating the Alamo and with the army's departure in 1878, the way was opened for new uses of the site. In 1877, French-born San Antonio merchant Hugo Grenet purchased the old convent building and courtyard from the Catholic Church for twenty thousand dollars, remodeling them as a retail store. Over the convent building's old stone walls, facing the church and the Alamo plaza, Grenet erected two-story wooden arcades, embellished by crenelated cornices, octagonal turrets, and even false wooden guns. These additions were apparently designed to recall the building's original stone arcades, but the effect was generally reviled as an "atrocious lumber building" and a "hideous structure." One critic commented that fortunately "the elements were kind," sending "an unusual storm" that carried off both towers and guns, with "no general mourning for the loss." Grenet also operated a museum in one wing of the convent and obtained a lease on the Alamo church itself, which he employed as a warehouse, much as the army had done.[21]

After Grenet's death in 1882, another mercantile concern, Hugo & Schmeltzer, purchased the convent property. The chapel reverted to the Catholic Church and was sold to the State of Texas in 1883 for twenty thousand dollars. The city of San Antonio, which was then charged with maintaining the building as a historical museum, carried out minor renovations (notably removing the army's second-level wooden flooring) in an effort to return the structure "to its original condition, as far as could be done with safety."[22]

With the exception of the church and the badly disfigured convent building, little else remained of either the colonial mission or the revolutionary fortress. By 1861, historian Reuben M. Potter could find only faint traces of the outer walls. The old Indian quarters had fallen victim to civic progress in the 1850s, as a line of new residences and business buildings, beginning with Maverick's property on the north, obliterated the foundations of the west outer wall and the attached dwellings. Avenue D and Houston Street cut through the west and north sides of the old mission enclosure, the remains of which gradually evolved from a drab, dusty plaza into a sophisticated urban park. Along the south boundary of the grounds, the low barracks of revolutionary days served for many years as a jail but were torn down just after the Civil War; this site was purchased by the city in 1871 in order to complete the Alamo plaza. Behind the Alamo church, "a bunch of frame sheds" encroached on the old convent courtyard, providing quarters for "livery stable, blacksmith shops, etc." Finally, to the south of the church, not technically on Alamo property but highly visible to visitors, stood the public meat market and several busy saloons. The neighborhood had indeed been altered.[23]

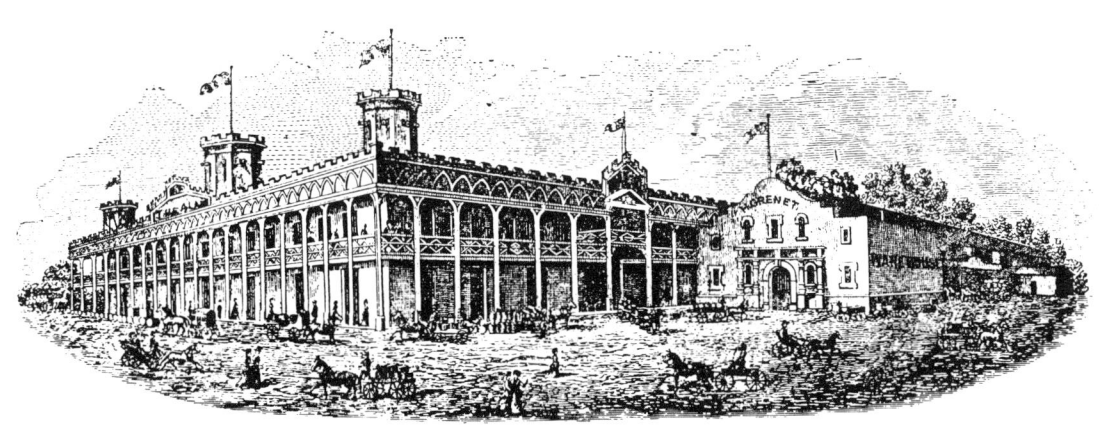

THE ALAMO AS REPAIRED BY GRENET.

Hugo Grenet's Alamo store, located in the converted convent building, seen here in an etching made between 1880 and 1882 and reprinted in Adina De Zavala's *History and Legends of the Alamo*, 1917. Grenet advertised "Groceries, Provisions, Dry Goods, Queensware, Glassware, Boots, Shoes, Whiskeys, Wines, Beer, Cigars, Tobacco, and Country Produce, second to none in the city." His architectural additions and commercial use of the property later became a major point of controversy in the struggle to preserve the Alamo. (DeGolyer Library)

Cabinet photograph of the Alamo from the south, ca. 1900, showing one of the Alamo plaza saloons. (Courtesy Daughters of the Republic of Texas Library at the Alamo, San Antonio)

As the Alamo site itself changed, so did the city around it. San Antonio had been gaining popularity as a health resort since the mid-nineteenth century but was accessible only via a long and uncomfortable stagecoach ride. With the arrival in 1877 of San Antonio's first railroad, the Galveston, Harrisburg and San Antonio, a new era began for the city. Tourism boomed, and the Alamo figured prominently in local promotions. Viewbooks and guides of San Antonio featured the site with front-page photographs carefully cropped to show only the chapel and not the adjoining mercantile establishments.

As a result, many travelers found their pilgrimage a disappointment. Harriet P. Spofford, visiting the Alamo the year before the army's evacuation, found it "a reproach to all San Antonio. Its wall is overthrown and removed, its dormitories are piled with military stores, its battle-scarred front has been revamped and repainted and market carts roll to and fro on the spot where flames ascended . . . over the funeral pyre of heroes."

Somewhat later, the authors of *On a Mexican Mustang Through Texas* found their tour impeded by cracker boxes, soap, and vegetables. "Do you see that angle in the wall, where those old cabbages and those boxes of Limberger cheese are piled? Right there at least forty Mexicans were killed." A local historian also alleged that "the Government hung fresh meat in the Alamo, and that stain stayed on the walls, which was later pointed out as results of the battle."[24]

As the Alamo site deteriorated, its popular image began to diverge from the physical reality. Historians, novelists, poets, and playwrights brought forth an increasing volume of Alamo literature, beginning with Reuben Potter's landmark article of 1860 (republished in 1878 in the *Magazine of American History*). In contrast to Potter's detailed description and measured plan of the Alamo, the poems, plays, and novels of this period provided little more than general impressions of the site, which served primarily as a backdrop and theatrical setting. In the early novels, such as Jeremiah Clemen's *Bernard Lile*, 1869, and Amelia Barr's *Remember the Alamo*, 1888, the Alamo passages seem almost incidental to the main plot, included perhaps as a means of attracting interest and encouraging sales.

The focus of artistic interpretation also shifted as photography came to provide the primary visual documentation for the Alamo's physical appearance. This change reflected both the availability of new technology and the site's diminished artistic potential. Cleansed of its romantic ruins, the army's modernized Alamo attracted fewer artists and amateur sketchers. The artistic productions that appeared after 1850 were less concerned with the site's contemporary appearance than with its role in the battle of 1836. Eventually Alamo imagery attained a significance and symbolic value independent of the physical site itself. This divergence began as early as 1838, when John M. Niles's *South America* published the first known "Alamo" battle scene, one fought before a turreted tower that bore absolutely no resemblance to the original (see frontispiece).

From its very beginnings, the popular image of the Alamo has centered exclusively on the church. Most of the early, on-site sketches of other areas of the compound remained unpublished and in private hands well into the twentieth century and so had little effect on popular perceptions of the Alamo. The first widely distributed views—such as Ikin's *Texas*, 1841; *London Illustrated News*, 1844; Hughes's *Memoir Descriptive*, 1850; *Gleason's Pictorial Drawing-Room Companion*, 1854—depicted only the facade of the ruined Alamo church, with the adjoining convent fading into obscurity at the left. By the 1870s, misconceptions of the Alamo increased as the army parapet now appeared in most views

Cover illustration from the well-known cartoon book *Texas History "Movies,"* 1928, by Jack Patton and John Rosenfield, Jr. Shown on the "movie screen" is a stock nineteenth-century view of the "Storming of the Alamo," which appeared in D.W.C. Baker's *Texas Scrap-Book*, 1875, and numerous other histories. Its imagery includes several prevalent misconceptions of the battle, notably the inclusion of the army gable and the placement of defenders firing out of an upper left window not installed until the 1850s. (DeGolyer Library. Reproduced courtesy of Pepper Jones Martinez, Inc., Publishers)

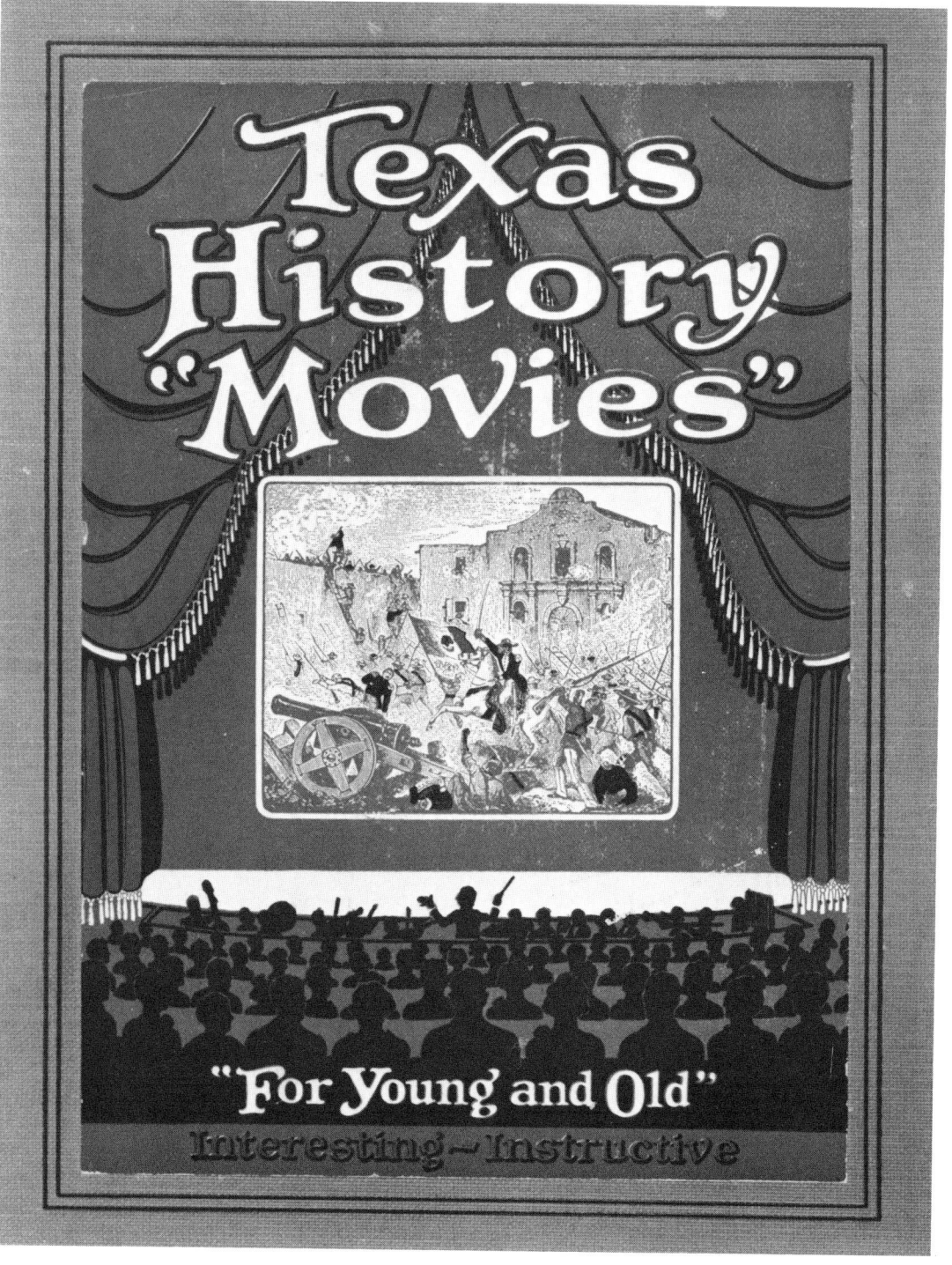

of the Alamo fighting. Although these early efforts contributed little to an accurate historical understanding of the physical Alamo, they did spread its fame and no doubt contributed both to the site's popularity as a tourist attraction and to the increasing concern for its preservation.

The Alamo church, having been delivered over to public ownership in 1883, was generally considered saved, but the old convent building presented a greater problem, both practically and theoretically. Practically, as long as the old convent remained private property, critics could only rail ineffectively at its commercialization. The theoretical issues involved in preserving the convent proved even thornier, for the various parties interested in saving it could not agree on how much of the convent was original, what its role had been, or how it should best be preserved.

Critics considered the Hugo & Schmeltzer convent building a modern fabrication that should be torn down completely. Henry Ryder-Taylor commented, in about 1905, that "the main idea is to remove the Hugo & Schmeltzer building, which crowds and obscures the Alamo, and to arrange the vacant grounds so that the Alamo can be well shown prominently, restore the convent building as it was originally and to be used as a museum."[25] Exactly how he expected to simultaneously remove and restore the same building remains unclear.

Other observers argued that, contrary to having been rebuilt, the convent had sustained surprisingly little battle damage and had required only minor alterations by its subsequent tenants—the U.S. Army, Grenet, and Hugo & Schmeltzer. Chief proponent for this view was Miss Adina De Zavala, founder of San Antonio's first chapter of the Daughters of the Republic of Texas and the granddaughter of the Mexican-born Texas patriot and first Vice-President of the Republic, Lorenzo de Zavala. She contended that the Hugo & Schmeltzer building was in fact the former convent, the main building of the old mission, and the last retreat of the Alamo defenders.[26]

As local leader of the DRT, De Zavala spearheaded early efforts to preserve the old convent. According to her own account, she met repeatedly with Gustav Schmeltzer during the 1890s and eventually obtained his promise of sale if she and the "De Zavala Daughters" could raise the necessary seventy-five thousand dollars. Unfortunately, De Zavala was not a wealthy woman, and fund-raising efforts stalled as the deadline approached. With an aggressive hotel firm eager to develop the property, Miss Clara Driscoll came to the rescue. A prominent and wealthy member of South Texas's Anglo-American elite, Driscoll advanced at no interest the funds necessary to buy the property and to pay

The Alamo (above), an anonymous title page illustration to Arthur Ikin's *Texas*, published in London in 1841, has been cited as the earliest published view of the Alamo. In fact, it was preceded by *The Ruins of the Alamo* (below), attributed to William Bissett and published in Philadelphia in 1840 as a frontispiece to Francis Moore, *Map and Description of Texas*. The latter image is extremely rare, since Moore's book evidently appeared in two editions in 1840—one with plates and one without. Bissett is reputed to have been a Scottish immigrant who worked on a surveying crew in San Antonio in 1839. Although his original drawing has not been located, several copies survive, including a 1912 watercolor by V. Chafsky, in the DRT Alamo Library, and an illustration in Frederick Chabot's 1931 book *The Alamo: Altar of Texas Liberty*. The latter is a copy by twelve-year-old Ida John, granddaughter of I. A. Clark, to whom the original was said to have been given by Bissett. A third copy, discovered in the papers of William Bollaert, seems to confirm Bissett's authorship of the unsigned Moore frontispiece and of other plates in the book signed by Bissett. Bollaert's view of the Alamo facade (facing) is inscribed "W. Bissett-del." and "WB copy," while elsewhere in his sketches the British journalist noted, "The Drawings in Moore's small volume [?] by Bissett—1841." (Ikin view, DeGolyer Library; Moore view, courtesy Barker Texas History Center, University of Texas at Austin; Bollaert, courtesy Edward E. Ayer Collection, The Newberry Library, Chicago)

THE ALAMO.

RUINS OF THE ALAMO

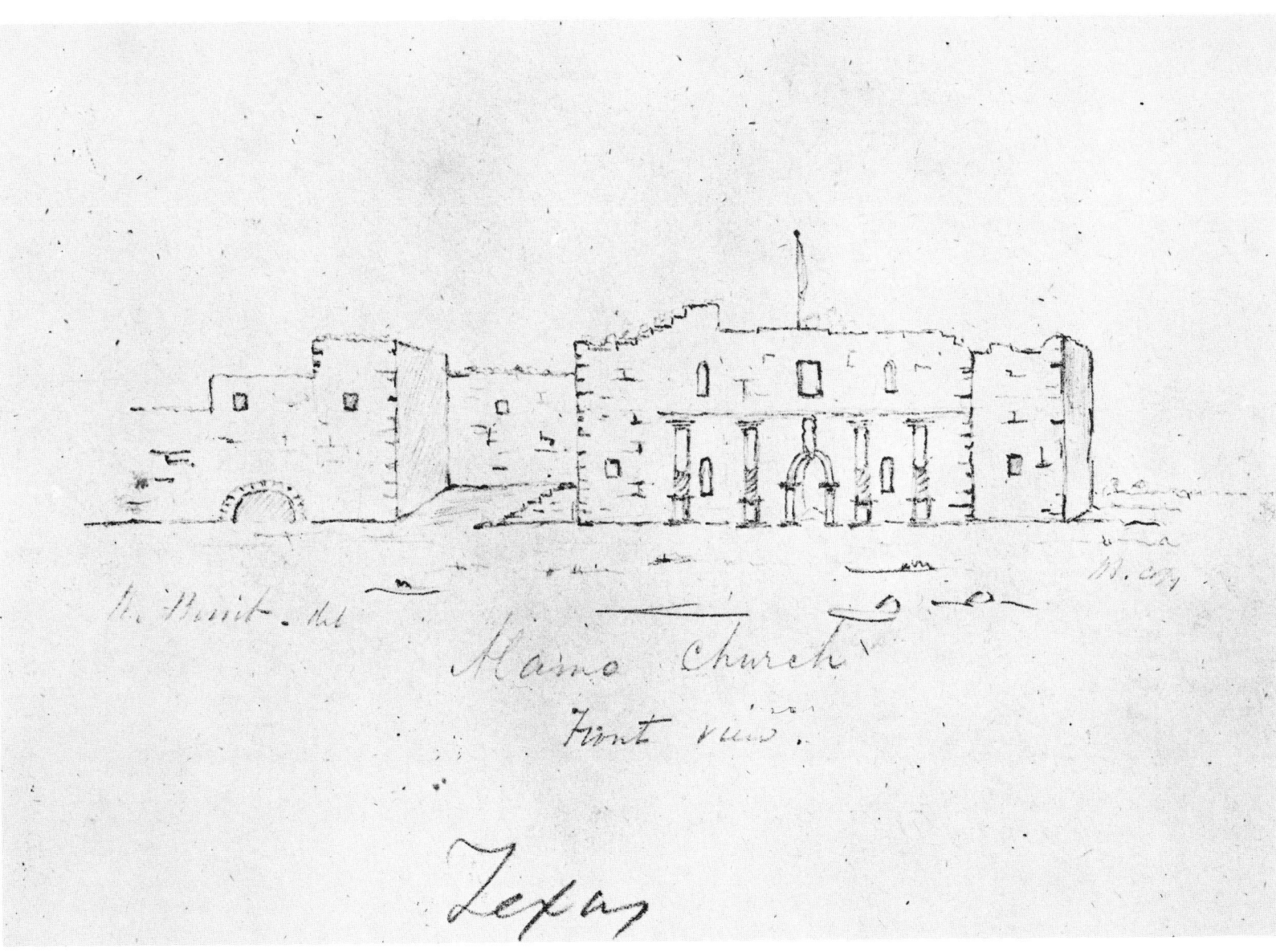

Ruins of the Church of the Alamo, San Antonio de Bexar, as lithographed by C. B. Graham after a view by U.S. Army artist Edward Everett. Later praised by his commanding officer as a "skillful and scientific draughtsman," Everett painted several of the San Antonio missions, and his views of the exterior and interior of the Alamo church became well-known and widely reproduced after appearing in the congressional publication, *Memoir Descriptive of the March of a Division of the United States Army Under the Command of Brigadier General John E. Wool, from San Antonio de Bexar in Texas to Saltillo, in Mexico,* by George W. Hughes, 1850. (Courtesy Amon Carter Museum, Fort Worth)

its taxes and insurance. Meanwhile, the DRT continued its private fund-raising efforts and renewed its appeal to the Texas State Legislature. In 1905 the Legislature appropriated sixty-five thousand dollars for the purchase of the Alamo property. The enabling legislation entrusted the Hugo & Schmeltzer building, "together with the Alamo church property already owned by the State, to the custody and care of the Daughters of the Republic of Texas, to be maintained by them in good order and repair, without charge to the State, ... provided that no changes or alterations shall be made in the Alamo Church proper as it now stands except such as are absolutely necessary for its preservation."[27]

Once in undisputed control of the hallowed shrine, the DRT ironically found itself severely divided. Supporters of Miss De Zavala argued bitterly with those of Miss Driscoll (now Mrs. Hal Sevier) over how best to preserve the site. De Zavala hoped to emphasize its mission background, restoring the main building (the convent) to its original arcaded appearance. The Driscoll faction, in contrast, focused primarily on the revolutionary battle and considered the church to be the main feature of the site, which could be better

Ruins of the Church of El Alamo, published in *Gleason's Pictorial Drawing-Room Companion* in 1854, clearly based on Everett's earlier facade view. In adapting the latter, Gleason's artist has cleaned up the site, removing rubble from the foreground and tufts of grass from atop the walls, embellishing the facade with a more decorative arched window above the door, and adding several groups of well-dressed Anglo-American tourists and a fancy carriage. Where Everett had seen a battle-scarred ruin, the American public saw a serene, stylish promenade ground. (Courtesy Daughters of the Republic of Texas Library at the Alamo, San Antonio)

Photograph of the Alamo chapel and convent building in 1912, with Grenet's wooden arcades partially removed. (Courtesy San Antonio Museum Association, San Antonio)

emphasized and appreciated if the convent were removed. The controversy escalated steadily for several years, becoming known as the "Second Battle of the Alamo" and culminating in a public meeting convened by Texas Governor Oscar B. Colquitt on December 28, 1911. Testimony provided on this occasion bears witness to both a dearth of reliable factual data and an excess of emotion. De Zavala's faction presented numerous historical accounts, letters, and plats documenting the location and role of the convent building. Driscoll's supporters countered that "the Alamo chapel is the real Alamo," while "the Hugo & Schmeltzer building is not historically sacred."

In support of this view, the DRT's Alamo custodian, Mrs. Sarah Eager, offered the opinions of "several priests whom she had interrogated" who had noted "that a monastery was never put in front of a church." Mrs. Susan Roach testified that "her mother had

Sheet music for "Remember the Alamo," by Jessie Beattie Thomas, 1908, featuring a vignette of Adina De Zavala, "The Heroine of the Alamo." (DeGolyer Library)

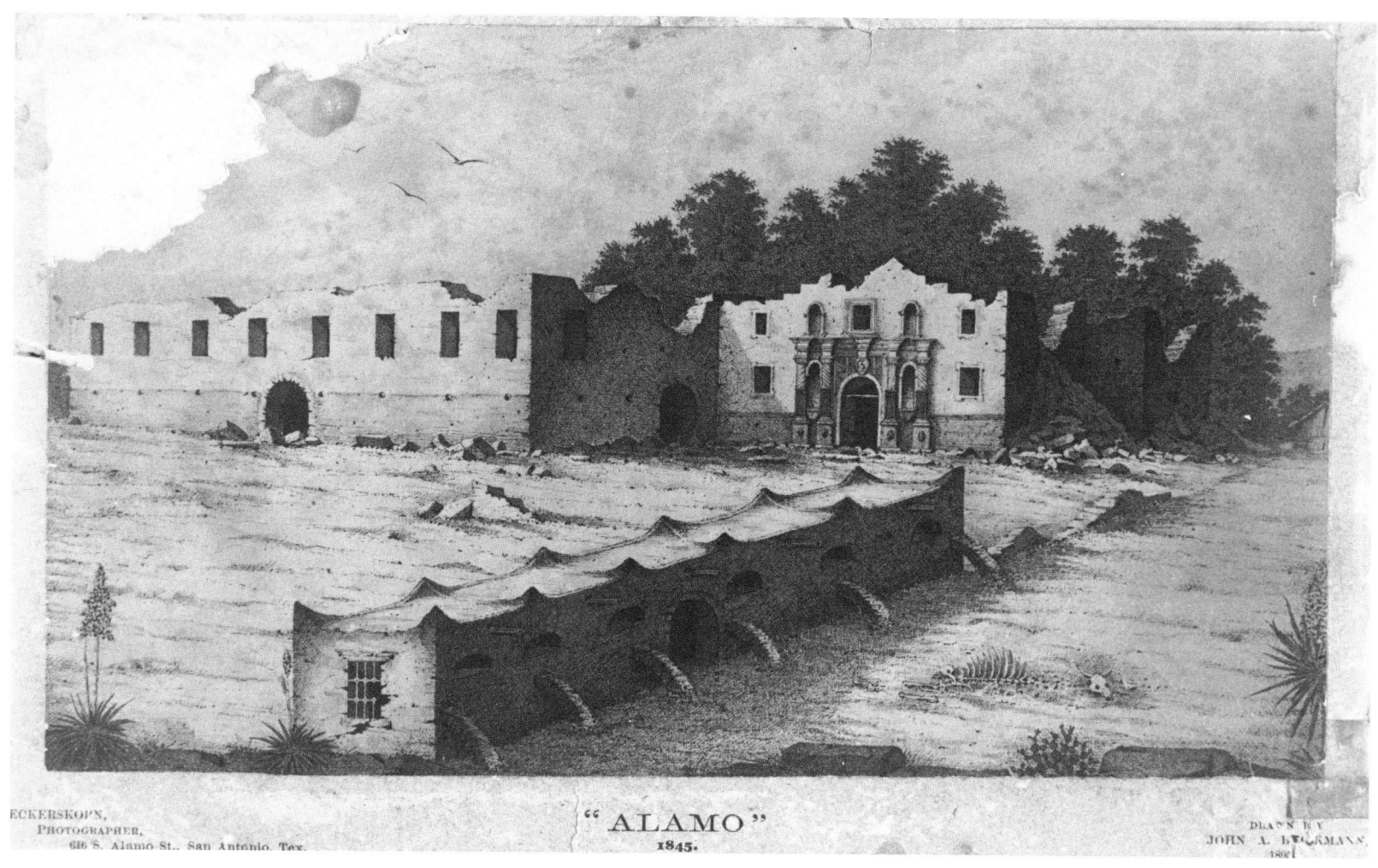

"ALAMO" 1845.

'Alamo' 1845, by John Antonio Beckmann. This view has been published very often as a documentary image of the ruins. However, it does not agree with authenticated on-site views by Maverick, Blake, Bollaert, and others. Since Beckmann was not born until 1847, his view must be considered conjectural, perhaps based on stories told by his father, John Conrad Beckmann, a German-born blacksmith who had worked for the army in renovating the Alamo. Beckmann correctly shows the chapel without the curved gable but mistakenly incorporates the two outer second-story windows added by the army. In addition, the convent block is joined directly to the corner of the church (omitting the connecting wall) and includes the row of second-story doorways added by Grenet for access to his arcade. This version of Beckmann's view, a souvenir photograph issued by San Antonio photographer J. Eckerskorn, is dated 1895. (Courtesy Daughters of the Republic of Texas Library at the Alamo, San Antonio)

lived within five blocks of the Alamo as early as 1827[?] and she never spoke of the walls as being two-story" nor "believed it was used as a convent." Mrs. Sevier herself offered what was evidently to many the most damning evidence against the old convent-store building. "I don't think the Alamo should be disgraced by this whiskey house, which obscures the most remarkable relic in the world."[28]

Governor Colquitt, who had vowed during the meeting "to put all the commercial vandals out of the Alamo," subsequently directed the removal of the Hugo & Schmeltzer building's frame superstructure, leaving the two-story masonry walls of the west and south facades. He then began restoration of the convent building, erecting a one-story stone arcade along the east courtyard wall, designed by University of Texas architecture professor F. E. Giesecke. The governor's efforts to resolve the controversy won little thanks from the DRT, however, which sought court injunction against this "usurpation of our authority." Funds ran out before Colquitt's restoration could be completed, and early in 1913, while the governor was out of the state, the lieutenant-governor authorized local officials to allow demolition of the upper-story walls.[29]

Photograph of the Alamo grounds, ca. 1912–13, showing surviving convent walls after the removal of modern commercial accretions. After bitter controversy, these two-story walls were reduced to one story about 1913 in order to better emphasize the Alamo church. (Courtesy Daughters of the Republic of Texas Library at the Alamo, San Antonio)

Post–World War I photograph by Eugene O. Goldbeck. The one-story remnants of the Alamo convent stood open to the elements from 1913 until the late 1960s. Reconstructed stone arches have here replaced the rectangular doorways, right, and a decorative gateway has been erected on the line of the old south wing adjacent to the church, but the army roof has not yet been superceded by the more shrine-like barrel vault in place today. The billboards and commercial establishments that litter this scene disappeared as the DRT gradually acquired land around the Alamo. (Courtesy Photography Collection, Harry Ransom Humanities Research Center, University of Texas at Austin)

Below the surface of petty organizational feuding, the DRT controversy reflected sharply divergent visions of the Alamo and its role in Texas history. The groundswell in favor of creating an Alamo shrine was predominantly an Anglo-American movement, with Adina De Zavala being the most notable, and eventually unsuccessful, exception. This preservation movement, significantly, did not gain any real momentum until well after 1860, as the Anglo-Americans ceased to be a minority population in San Antonio. On the eve of the Civil War, San Antonio's population consisted of three major ethnic groups: native Tejanos, Anglo-Americans, and foreign immigrants, mainly Germans.[30] In general, the Alamo could have been little more than a curiosity to most of the foreign immigrants, since its glory was not part of their own cultural heritage. Although the Alamo battle claimed several Tejano lives and destroyed extensive Tejano property, the site for them represented much more than a single battle (about which many no doubt harbored mixed feelings), but probably no more than any of the other missions. It seems significant that Tejano folklore of the Alamo focuses primarily on legends of the mission period; one notable exception is a tale of ghostly defenders whose flaming swords and sepulchral warnings frightened off Mexican soldiers ordered to demolish the walls in

1836.³¹ In legend, as in fact, the enshrinement of the Alamo had become an Anglo-American crusade.

The struggle to preserve the Alamo followed patterns observed in the historic preservation movement throughout the country. As late as the 1870s, some of America's most hallowed historic sites—the Old South Meeting House in Boston, Monticello, Washington's headquarters at Valley Forge—were still in private hands. Like the Alamo, many of the sites that survived did so through the efforts of private groups—the Sons or Daughters of the American Revolution, the Society of Colonial Dames, the Association for the Preservation of Virginia Antiquities, the Daughters of the Republic of Texas—whose

Tile mural at Alamo Stadium, San Antonio, a Works Progress Administration artwork by Ethel Harris and Henry Wedemeyer, 1940. The scene is a Mexican fiesta, featuring a cockfight and hat dance and set in front of the Alamo in 1860. (Photograph by Ron Bechtol, San Antonio, reprinted by permission)

View of the Alamo, *Harper's Weekly*, March 23, 1861, depicting the U.S. Army post's surrender to Confederate forces. The anonymous artist has replaced the church's baroque shell niches and twisted columns with classical Greek caryatids, perhaps following a similar illustration on an engraved stationery sheet issued ca. 1856 by San Antonio artist-printer Erhard Pentenreider and now preserved at the Amon Carter Museum. (Courtesy Daughters of the Republic of Texas Library at the Alamo, San Antonio)

motives were avowedly patriotic, if often narrowly chauvinistic. And, like the Alamo, many sites can point to the timely assistance of private citizens such as Clara Driscoll Sevier, whose financial intervention bridged the gap between good intentions and successful public funding. Many other preservation movements witnessed similarly painful schisms amongst their supporters.[32]

The Alamo preservation effort also fits neatly within the American Colonial Revival movement, which began as an eastern phenomenon but later spread across the country, encouraging the design of colonial style houses and public buildings, the collection of colonial artifacts, and the preservation of colonial structures associated with historically significant events. This movement received national impetus from the Centennial celebration of 1876 and the highly publicized World's Columbian Exposition of 1893, which included colonial exhibits from Texas and its western neighbors. Like the preservation of the Alamo and other historic sites, these exhibits were valued more for their potential

Movie set for John Wayne's *The Alamo*, designed by Alfred Ybarra and erected at Brackettville, Texas, ca. 1957–59. This full-scale adobe replica of the Alamo recalls John Beckmann's late-nineteenth-century conjectural view of the ruins: the second-story outer windows cut through by the U.S. Army are present, while the ruined skyline has been raised at the center to approximate the now-familiar arched gable. (United Artists, 1960)

as narrative history and ideological symbols than for their architectural authenticity. As narrative history, the sites and exhibits were seen to communicate—more personally, vividly, and directly than any schoolbook—the glorious story of the nation's origins. As ideological symbols, they fostered local pride, national unity, Americanization, and a sense of historical accomplishment.[33]

In Texas these nationalistic emotions were intensified by the presence of a long-standing non-Anglo culture. As events like the Spanish-American War and the continuing influx of Mexican immigrants aggravated local tensions, the Alamo also took on a heightened significance. Because the Alamo partook of both the Spanish Colonial past—as a mission—and the Anglo-American colonial past—as a fortress—its preservation and interpretation reflected the larger struggle for cultural dominance.

Like the crusade to preserve the Alamo site, the development of Alamo imagery has been an almost exclusively Anglo-American endeavor. In most other respects, however, the development of the Alamo as a symbolic image bears little relation to its evolution as a historic site. Thus, even as the actual mission site deteriorated during the late nineteenth century, its symbolic counterpart progressed. In time, the image came to influence the appearance of the actual, prompting the Alamo's custodians to lower the convent walls in order to emphasize the popular church facade. In the development of both the Alamo site and the Alamo image, symbolism, not accuracy, has been the overriding influence.

Thus it is not the authentic image of the ruined mission that dominates Alamo imagery; it is instead the intrusive, nineteenth-century curved gable that has come to summarize and symbolize the entire Alamo tradition. On book jackets, movie posters, toys, sweatshirts, telephone books, restaurants, motels, and shopping centers it appears, and in many cases the mere outline is sufficient to recall all that the Alamo stands for. This peculiar gable is so pervasive, and its symbolism so strong, that often those who should, and no doubt do, know better, find themselves compelled to humor popular perceptions. Thus John Wayne's extensively researched Alamo set, built at Brackettville, Texas, for his 1960 movie, depicted the Alamo church in ruins, but still with a slightly humped skyline.

Emotions stirred by the "Second Battle of the Alamo" lingered for many years. De Zavala's 1917 account of the Alamo, for example, did not once mention Driscoll's financial contribution, while the official history of the DRT in turn gave scant credit to De Zavala's initial preservation efforts, accusing her instead of "unauthorized and un-

Bird's-eye view of the Alamo grounds, 1937, showing the demolition of buildings to the east in preparation for the enlargement of the park. (Courtesy *The San Antonio Light Collection*, University of Texas Institute of Texan Cultures at San Antonio) ▶

Panoramic photograph of the Alamo Plaza, ca. 1935, by Eugene O. Goldbeck. (Courtesy Photography Collection, Harry Ransom Humanities Research Center, University of Texas at Austin)

warranted interference in the affairs of the Association," "continual arrogance" in the press, and "specious and sensational pleas for sympathy . . . in ensconcing herself in the Hugo & Schmeltzer building and refusing to leave the same." "Loyal" members of the association in 1907 obtained a court injunction forbidding De Zavala and her associates to claim any further association with the DRT, and the defunct De Zavala Chapter was replaced as custodians of the site by the Alamo Mission Chapter. Driscoll's forces triumphed, and their vision of the Alamo, with the church as the main building, has guided development of the site ever since.[34]

By 1919, the army's old pitched roof had been replaced by a more shrine-like barrel vault, supported by concrete arches and claimed by the caretakers to be as much "like the original roof of the Chapel in line as was possible to get." With the exception of this roof, however, the existing buildings received less attention during the 1920s and 1930s than did the acquisition of surrounding properties and the creation of a memorial park. Aided by enthusiasm for the Texas Centennial and by funding from Franklin Roosevelt's

New Deal programs, the DRT acquired the entire Alamo block; converted a former fire station into its chapter headquarters and library; cleared the grounds of other intrusive buildings; planted trees, shrubs, and flowers; erected arcaded stone walls and a new museum building, designed by Henry T. Phelps "in mission style to harmonize with the Alamo"; and excavated the old irrigation ditch, filling it with goldfish, water lilies, hyacinths, lotus, and reeds.[35] The resulting memorial park fulfilled Clara Driscoll's earliest visions of the site, expressed in a 1900 letter to the *San Antonio Express*: "Today the Alamo should stand out free and clear. All the unsightly obstructions that hide it away should be torn down and the space utilized for a park."[36]

The preoccupation with the church itself permanently altered the configuration and image of the Alamo. Rather than acquire the original mission plaza and walls lying to the west of the church and convent, the site was redefined according to modern street boundaries. Nor was any systematic effort made, during the many Centennial-period alterations of the site, to record, much less search for, archaeological evidence.[37]

Significantly, much of the actual labor required to carry out the Anglo-Texan vision of the Alamo shrine was provided by the Tejano community. In a 1981 column in the *San Antonio News*, Jesse Luna spoke proudly of her family's Alamo heritage. During the Depression, her father, José Luna, a stonemason and bricklayer, had worked on the WPA crews assigned to "restore the Alamo," and his work was regularly pointed out to his grandchildren. During an earlier restoration, Marguerite Routledge had suggested that "with slight imagination the noted fall can be realized again, as the crews of Mexican workmen scale the ladders and mount the aged walls with pick and crowbars. In the dazzling sunshine their varicolored clothing makes it appear as if a battle is at its height."[38]

Few significant changes have taken place on the Alamo site since the roofing of the long barracks for a museum at the time of the 1968 Hemisfair. A five-year master plan, prepared for the DRT in 1979 by San Antonio architects Ford, Powell and Carson, has been stalled, reportedly by lack of funds. Archaeological excavations, although often conducted as salvage operations racing just ahead of construction equipment, have nevertheless uncovered some significant finds. When the Hyatt Hotel corporation recently opened a new section of the Paseo del Rio, leading toward Alamo Plaza, excavations broke through a section of the old west wall and Indian lodgings. These foundation outlines were reproduced at street level, giving visitors for the first time in over a century a tangible sense of the extent of the original mission complex. The tablet installed in this area describes the site's use as a residence by the Losoya family, which not only was forced to move out of its home to facilitate military preparations in 1835, but also lost one son in the defense of the Alamo.[39] This emphasis on the role of local Tejanos in the Alamo's history marks an important new departure in interpreting the Alamo. Significantly, it was action taken by the city of San Antonio, led for the first time since 1842 by a Hispanic mayor, Henry Cisneros, and located on ground outside of the boundaries of the shrine itself.

After nearly 270 years, the Alamo site has not yet reached a point of static equilibrium, and even more sweeping changes in appearance and interpretation may lie ahead. A new site plan recently advanced by transplanted Chicagoan Gary Foreman has called for improved visitor interpretation and suggested such innovations as reconstruction of the long barracks' second story, the low barracks along the southern plaza boundary, and the timber and packed-earth stockades; placement of reproduction artillery; and use of costumed guides.[40] If enacted, such proposals could vastly alter both the physical fabric of the Alamo site and the popular perceptions of its meaning.

Chapter 2

"Victory or Death"

by Tom W. Gläser

COMPARISON of the defense of the Alamo to the ancient Greek stand at Thermopylae began within weeks after the Texas battle, reflecting the new republic's need to identify its experience as both unique and universal. The Alamo was seen to be distinctly virtuous and distinctly Texan, yet at the same time to embody and clearly express such basic truths about the nature of man that all of humanity could instantly perceive its worth. History repeatedly offers examples of the valiant few nobly sacrificing themselves for the benefit of the many: the Biblical Samson, the Spartans at Thermopylae, the "embattled farmers" at Lexington and Concord, and the Texan defenders of the Alamo all fit this heroic mold. Even the siege and assault fell comfortably within the established parameters of early-nineteenth-century warfare.

The military prelude to the Alamo opened on October 9, 1835, when the Mexican army of General Martín Perfecto de Cos arrived at San Antonio de Béxar. In sending these troops to Texas, the Mexican government conformed to established European patterns of civil unrest and governmental response. Since the mere presence of troops was probably expected to subdue the fractious Texans, Cos assumed a passive attitude. He contented himself with preparing defensive fortifications at Béxar and the nearby Mission San Antonio de Valero and with dispatching desultory cavalry patrols into the surrounding countryside.[1]

Cos's troops were a mixed lot, encompassing the professional Battalion of Morelos, less-disciplined soldiers from the frontier presidios, convicts pressed into military service, and elements of the Texas-Coahuila Civil Militia. The latter groups had not been thoroughly trained as soldiers, and continuing news of Mexican defeats in skirmishes such as Gonzales greatly weakened their morale.

The army's lassitude extended to the physical preparations for defense. Cos had ordered barricades erected in the streets of Béxar, in the tradition of Parisian street fighting. He then had some parts of the Alamo's walls torn down and earthen ramps and embankments constructed for artillery emplacements inside the old convent complex.[2] This was as much as he was able to do before the Texans took advantage of the freedom

The wrapper of Hiram McLane's 1886 play, *The Capture of the Alamo*, tidily sums up the late-nineteenth-century view of the Alamo, combining a standard illustration of the assault with the two most often used phrases regarding the battle. (DeGolyer Library)

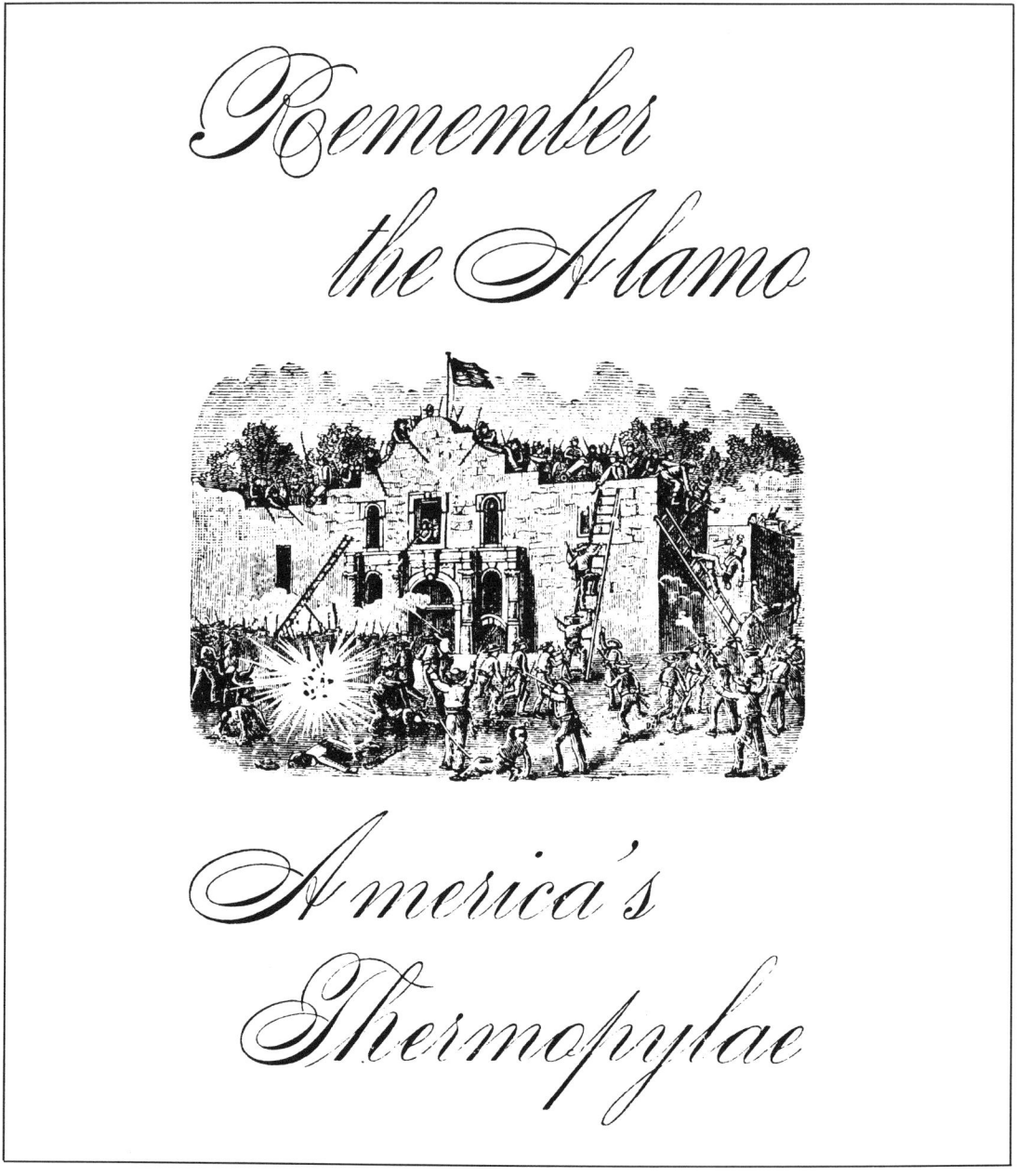

of movement that Cos had given them. With the Battle of Concepción on October 28, the full, formal siege of Béxar by the Texans began.

The siege, however, was hardly more vigorous than the defense. In classic military tradition, Cos remained stolidly behind his works, while the Texans tried to lure him out with cavalry demonstrations. Although the fortifications were not up to European military standards and the attackers dug no siege trenches, the problems faced by both armies were the same as have faced beleaguerer and beleaguered since time immemorial. Cos began to run low on food for both his men and his animals, an important consideration in the open reaches of South Texas. Moreover, Mexican soldiers began deserting in increasing numbers to avoid the now inevitable fight. As is usual in battle, more losses were caused by morale than by mortality.

The Texans also suffered morale problems, but for a different reason—ennui. The Texans became restive and bored with the enforced inactivity required to conduct a siege, wanting instead the intense involvement of pitched battle. Camp brawls erupted, resulting in a murder and the first Texan execution. Not just the ranks were affected; like the Homeric Achilles retiring to his tents in a fit of pique, Colonel James Bowie threatened twice to resign, and Lieutenant Colonel William Barret Travis not only tried to resign but also actually left the Texan siege lines briefly in November.[3] While this sort of action was not that of a Byronic Romantic hero—to which Travis has been frequently compared—it certainly was that of a classic Greek.

This situation was not entirely the fault of the Texan commanders but was simply one of many problems confronting a volunteer militia force. The troops not only chafed against the inaction of siege operations and drifted in and out of camp at will but also were very selective in what orders they obeyed. General Stephen F. Austin ordered an assault on Béxar for 3 A.M. on November 23 but canceled it at 1 A.M. when he was informed that the troops opposed the plan. A similar response blocked Austin's successor, General Edward Burleson, and his assault of December 4. It was not until Benjamin Milam exerted the sort of charismatic leadership necessary to influence such men—with his cry of "Boys, who will come with old Ben Milam into San Antonio?"—that the Texans finally launched their assault on the morning of December 5.

Advancing slowly into Béxar, the Texans first tasted urban warfare and the rigors of house-to-house combat. Protected by barricades and strong adobe walls, the Mexicans opposed the advance at every point, firing from the rooftops down onto the Texans. From Acequia Street to Soledad Street to Presidio Street to Zambrano Row, the Mexicans

Presidial trooper, painted ca. 1828, by Lino Sánchez y Tapia. This watercolor is one of the earliest representations of the soldiers of the new Mexican Republic. The uniform is dark blue with red facings. Stationed on the frontiers to protect settlements from the Indians, these soldiers often did not agree with the policies of far-off Mexico City. (Courtesy the Thomas Gilcrease Institute of American History and Art, Tulsa, Oklahoma)

1971 watercolor by Joseph Hefter. The uniforms illustrated are that of a trooper of the Coahuila-Texas Civil Militia, 1835, left, and of an officer of the Texas Dragoons, 1836, right. The militiaman wears a dark blue uniform with red facings, while the dragoon wears a green uniform with gold facings. (From Hefter, *The Army of the Republic of Texas.* Reproduced courtesy Old Army Press)

defended doggedly while the Texans were forced into murderous street fighting. Milam himself was killed on the morning of December 7 trying to cross Soledad Street. The streets ablaze with gunfire, the Texans took up axes and crowbars to smash through walls in order to move from house to house. The Navarro house, the De le Garza house, the Veramendi house, the "priest's house" were all hotly contested and tortuously taken as the Texans advanced inexorably toward Cos's defenses at the Alamo and at the main plaza. Yet here again morale played the decisive role: as a rumor of Cos's death spread like wildfire through Mexican ranks, entire units quit the line. At 2 A.M. on December 11 Cos capitulated his entire army, and at 11 A.M. the following day he led 1,105 men under parole toward Laredo. After forty-four days of siege and battle, the Texans held Béxar.

The cost of the victory was high, though, and not just in lives lost in combat. From Troy and Carthage to Berlin and Stalingrad, the fate of a city turned into a battlefield has been harsh. As the armies ate, private supplies and livestock were pillaged. As the soldiers sought advantages in attack and defense, homes and other private property were sacrificed, and the victorious Texans had no means of paying their troops, much less making reparations. Moreover, many Anglo-Texans believed that the portion of the predominantly Tejano population of San Antonio that hadn't fought should contribute to the cause with their goods.

With Béxar in Texan hands, the volunteer soldiers of the Texas army behaved exactly as volunteers have long been wont to do. Like the Minutemen of the American Revolution and the state militias of the War of 1812, many Texans abandoned the army after the fighting to return to their lands and their families. Others left with Dr. James Grant and Colonel Frank Johnson on December 30 to carry the war into Mexico itself. The ill-conceived Matamoros expedition stripped San Antonio of almost everything militarily useful, leaving the commander, Colonel James C. Neill, with no food, no clothing, and 104 soldiers, later decreased to 80 when the paymaster did not arrive in January 1836. As this force was plainly not enough to hold all of San Antonio, Neill ordered his troops to concentrate at the old mission of the Alamo, a fortification that Cos had not been able to hold with over ten times that many men.

The precariousness of this position was not lost on the Texan commander-in-chief, General Sam Houston. On January 17 he dispatched Jim Bowie with orders to remove the artillery from San Antonio to Goliad and Cópano, to evacuate San Antonio if necessary, and to blow up the Alamo since Houston considered it indefensible. Houston's plan was never carried out, however, as Neill protested that there were not enough draught animals to move all of the artillery, and Bowie, who arrived on January 19, avowed that they would "rather die in these ditches than give them up to the enemy."[4]

Many writers have suggested that the Alamo cast some sort of elusive "spell" on its defenders, but this attributed mystique reflects a later romanticism that probably did not exist in 1836.[5] Unlike Houston, many Texans did view the Alamo as a defensible position, if for no other reason than that others before them had so considered it. The Texans forgot, however, that previous defenders of the Alamo had been defeated. Moreover, most of the Texans had no intentions of dying but expected to carve new lives and futures in the new republic. To this end, they regularly requested and expectantly waited for reinforcements that would never arrive.

Yet there were also other, less mystical reasons that the Texans were loathe to abandon the position. In 1836 San Antonio de Béxar was the political capital and the largest city of the Department of Béxar. Many Anglo-Texans saw the Alamo as the key to holding all of Texas. With it, they struck a powerful blow at Mexican pride and morale; without it, they left the enemy in a position to gather strength and counterattack. San Antonio also represented a military outpost on the western frontier of Texas. Such a vanguard, many Anglo-Texans hoped, would keep the theater of war as far removed from the Anglo-American colonies in East Texas as possible, centering the fighting in the area of the Tejanos, whom many considered both inconvenient and expendable. Without Béxar, thundered the *Telegraph and Texas Register* in December 1835, "the theater of war may be in the heart of our country; and, instead of our troops being fed at the expense of the enemy, the whole burden of supplying our own forces, and those of the enemy, will fall upon our citizens." Finally, Béxar psychologically represented a victory not only over the Mexican army itself but also over all that army stood for—the Catholic Church, the Latin culture, despotic government. The ancestral wellsprings of protestantism were deeply ingrained in the Anglo-Texans, and their hatred of Catholicism and "popery" would emerge again later with the "Know-Nothings," the "Crusader Zeal" of the Mexican-American War, the Ku Klux Klan, and similar xenophobic groups.[6]

For the Tejanos, however, San Antonio was home, not a battlefield of convenience. Their motivation for opposing the centralist government of President Antonio López de Santa Anna, Cos's brother-in-law, was political, not racial, and specifically protested Santa Anna's abrogation of the Republican Constitution of 1824. Their actions thus reflected San Antonio's long-standing tradition of political unrest whenever local rights were threatened.

Whatever reasons motivated each defender, whether Anglo-Texan or Tejano, the

Illustration from Jack Jackson's 1979 comic book *Recuerden El Alamo*. Anglo-Texan commander Travis and Tejano leader Juan N. Seguín obviously have different visions of the Alamo. Travis views the Alamo as a castle out of an Arthurian romance, where to live or die gloriously is all-important. Seguín simply sees an old, abandoned building that has stood in his hometown longer than anybody can remember. (DeGolyer Library. Reproduced courtesy of Jack Jackson)

decision was made to remain, fortify, and hold the Alamo, even though most informed observers agreed with Alamo engineer Green B. Jameson, who wrote to Sam Houston on January 18 that the Alamo "was never built by a military people for a fortress." Jameson remarked to Governor Henry Smith nearly a month later that "the Mexicans have shown imbecility and want of skill in this fortress as they have done in all things else." While soliciting a permanent appointment to the Texas corps of engineers, Jameson sent to both Smith and Houston a "neat plat of the fortress exhibiting its true condition" and enumerated both the changes that he had already made and those that he intended to make. It was, however, in the midst of a Texas winter, and "the men I have will not labour and I cannot ask it of them until they are better clad and fed."[7]

With limited resources and manpower, Jameson set about his task. A picket barrier was erected between the chapel and the convent wall, trenches were dug to divert water and to increase the difficulty in scaling the walls, and more emplacements and lunettes were made to accommodate the captured Mexican artillery pieces that the Alamo garrison had been able to restore to service. Much work was yet to be done, though, when the Mexican Army, now led by Santa Anna himself, returned on February 23, forcing the Texans to defend the mission complex with their preparations incomplete.[8]

One major problem that delayed Jameson's efforts and weakened both morale and discipline was a crisis in the command of the Alamo garrison. The strong characters of Bowie and of Travis, who had returned on January 30, were further augmented by the arrival on February 8 of David Crockett, Colonel of Tennessee militia. Neill apparently felt overshadowed, and he departed February 11 on "family business." Though Crockett called himself a "high private" and evidently did not press for command over more than his small band of men, his reputation exerted a strong influence on all the men of the Alamo. When Travis assumed command of the Alamo as the ranking "regular service" officer, Bowie demanded that his rank as full colonel of volunteers be recognized over Travis's lieutenant colonelcy. This was an intriguing distinction because both "regular" and "volunteer" ranks were conferred by a "government" that as yet had no recognized legal status, no draft, no issued uniform except that of Mexican origin, no regulations, no staff, no supplies, no pay for soldiers in either status, almost no chain of command due to political machinations, and precious little leadership. Nor was there a constitution or official flag for which to fight and die.

Even if both Travis and Bowie had been commissioned officers in an established army, their strong personalities and differing life-styles and political beliefs inevitably would have conflicted. Bowie—the widower of Ursula de Veramendi, daughter of Juan Martín de Veramendi, the former vice-governor of Coahuila and Texas—was well-known and accepted by the Tejano community in San Antonio. Travis, in contrast, mistrusted and disliked almost everything Mexican and had scant use for the local Tejanos. Travis's supercilious attitude apparently alienated much of the garrison, and he lost to Bowie an election held among the volunteers to choose their commander after Neill's departure. On February 14, a letter signed by both Bowie and Travis announced that "Col. J. Bowie has the command of the volunteers of the garrison, and Col. W. B. Travis of the regulars and volunteer cavalry. All general orders and correspondence will henceforth be signed by both until Col. Neill's return." Despite this truce, conflicts continued as Bowie's reportedly drunk and disorderly behavior offended Travis almost to the point of resig-

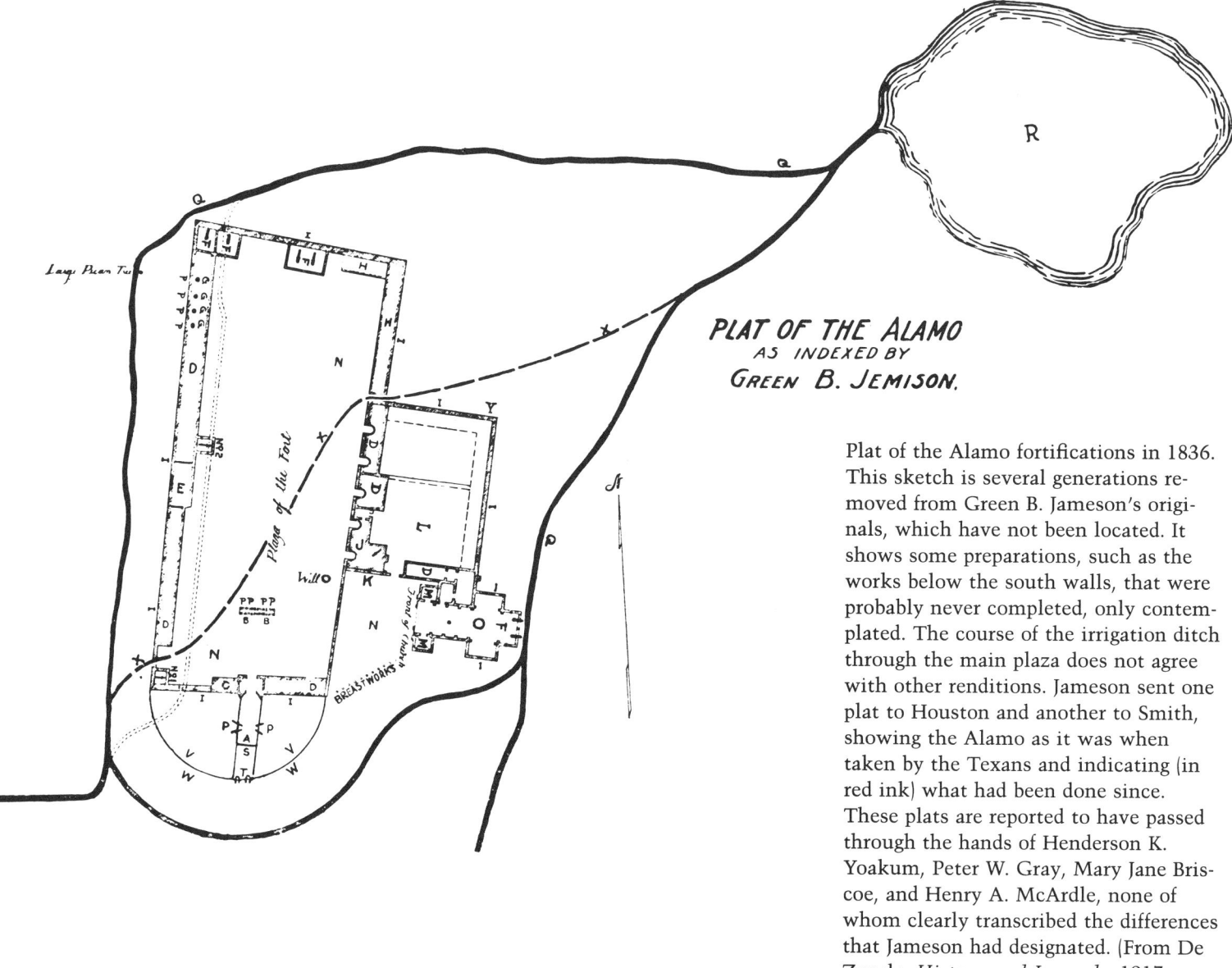

Plat of the Alamo fortifications in 1836. This sketch is several generations removed from Green B. Jameson's originals, which have not been located. It shows some preparations, such as the works below the south walls, that were probably never completed, only contemplated. The course of the irrigation ditch through the main plaza does not agree with other renditions. Jameson sent one plat to Houston and another to Smith, showing the Alamo as it was when taken by the Texans and indicating (in red ink) what had been done since. These plats are reported to have passed through the hands of Henderson K. Yoakum, Peter W. Gray, Mary Jane Briscoe, and Henry A. McArdle, none of whom clearly transcribed the differences that Jameson had designated. (From De Zavala, *History and Legends*, 1917. DeGolyer Library)

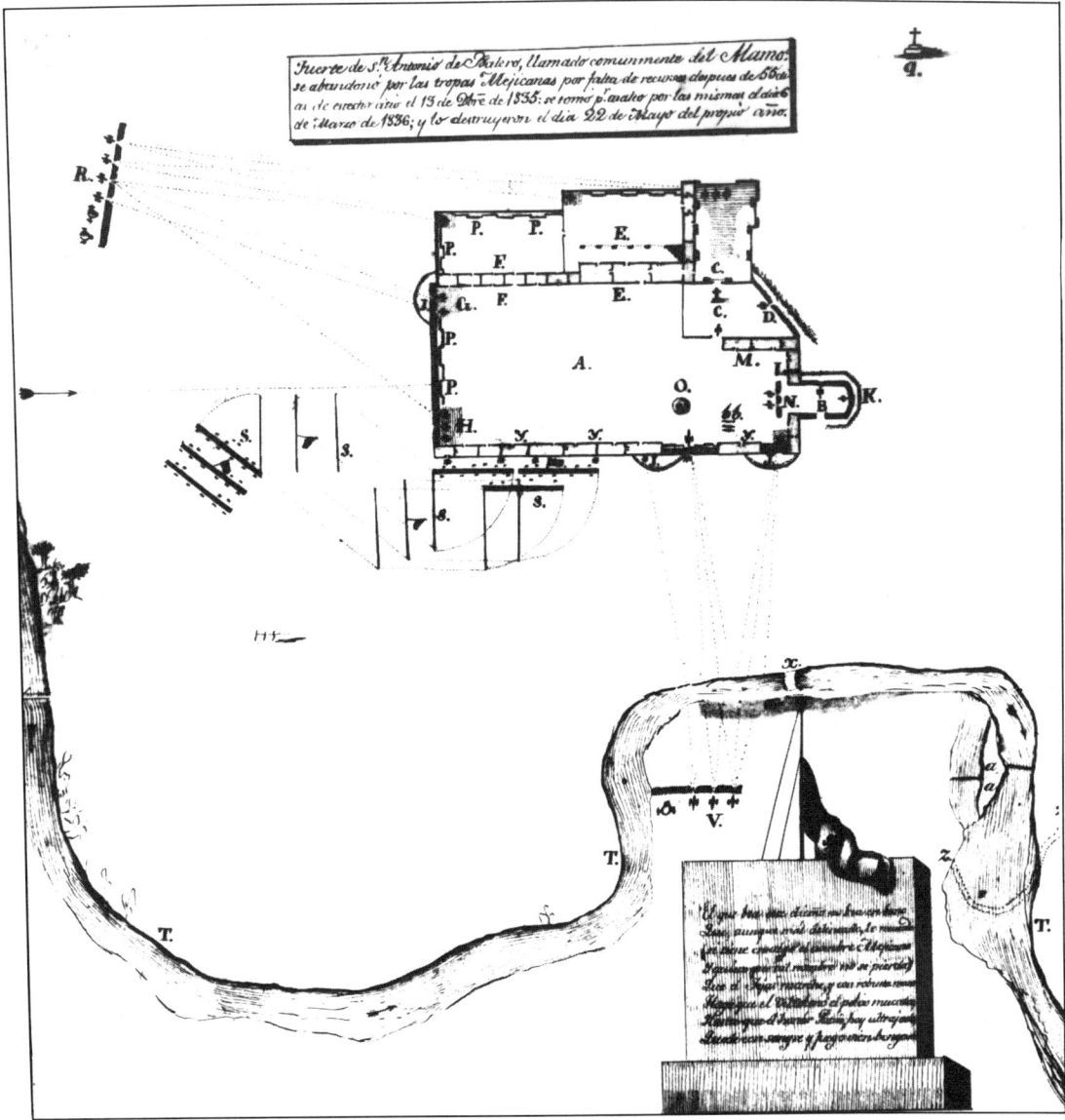

Map of the Alamo, 1836, by José Juan Sánchez Navarro. As Adjutant Inspector of the Departments of Nuevo León and Tamaulipas, Sánchez Navarro was present for both Cos's defeat and for that of the Texans. His map, made after the battle of San Jacinto, differs greatly from later Texan plats in both shape and arrangement of buildings as well as in completed outworks. The artist identified the columns maneuvering at "S" as Cos's troops, "G" as the site of Travis's death, "L" as that of Bowie's death, and "Q" as the location of the funeral pyre. An aspiring poet, as well as professional soldier and amateur cartographer, Sánchez Navarro also included on his map a memorial tablet inscribed in Spanish.

> Let him who sees this crude device
> Remember every patriot must
> (If name of Mexican suffice
> To proudly bear its fame in trust)
> Return to Texas, seal the price
> Of vile rebellion low in dust,
> Until our honor, now outraged,
> In blood and fire shall be assuaged.

(Courtesy Barker Texas History Center, The University of Texas at Austin)

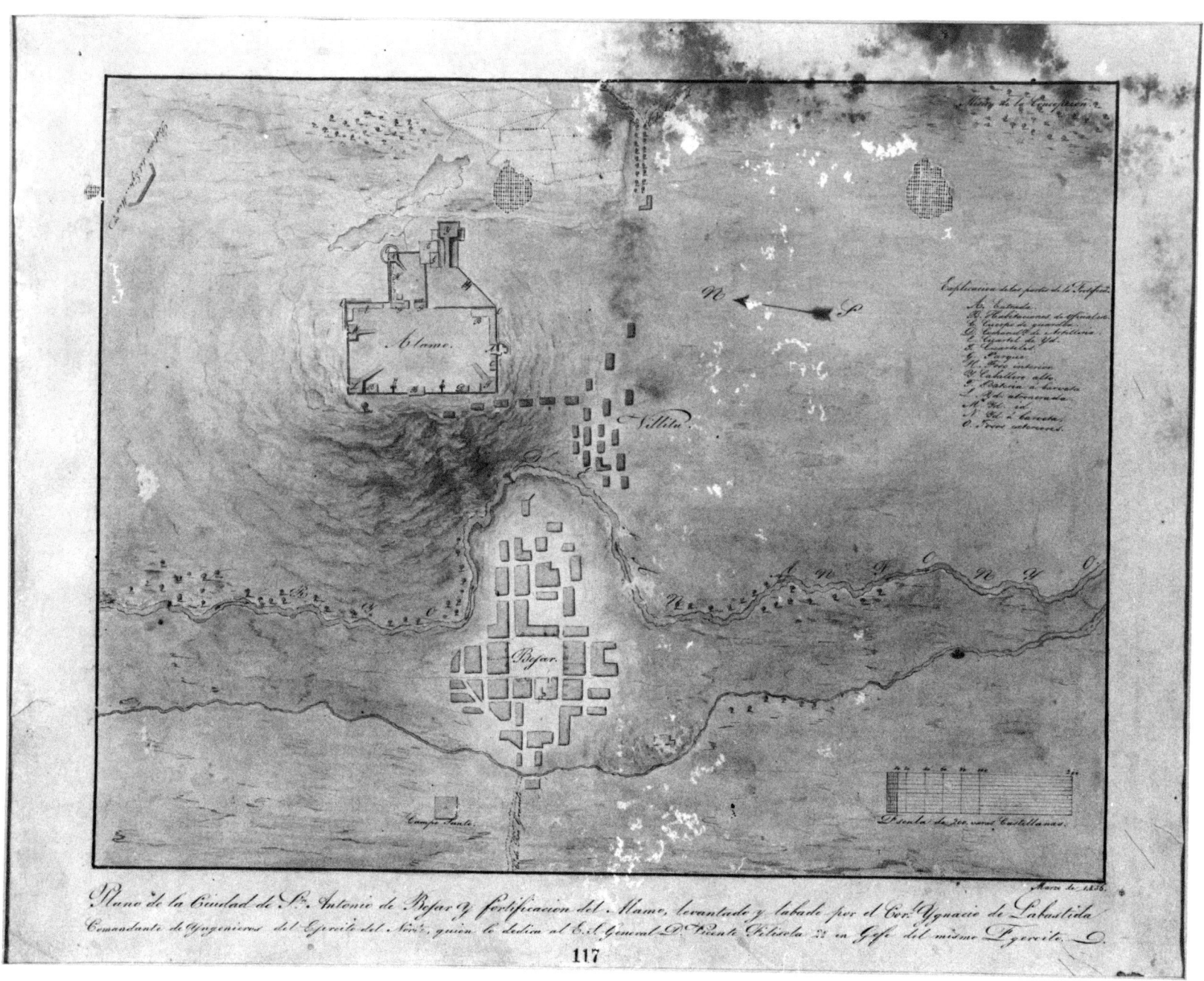

nation and possibly hastened Bowie's physical collapse and removal from active duty.⁹

While the Texans—both soldiers and politicians—wasted valuable time squabbling, military preparations proceeded to the south. Santa Anna, "the Napoleon of the West," was busy gathering and training troops to crush the rebellious Texans in the same manner as he had seen General Joaquín de Arredondo crush them in 1813 when Santa Anna was but a twenty-one-year-old lieutenant. Embarking early in life upon a military career under the Spanish empire, Santa Anna had supported and fought for the republican Plan de Iguala during the Mexican Revolution of 1821 only to break with its leader, Augustín de Iturbide, shortly before Iturbide's abdication as emperor. Santa Anna alternately rebelled and retired his way into power by shifting his position expediently as situations changed. First elected President of Mexico in 1833, he was to be the leader of Mexico four more times, was exiled five times, retired repeatedly, and fought more battles than George Washington and Napoleon combined before he died of old age, unwept and unhonored, on June 21, 1876. His reports, memoirs, defenses, and autobiography contradict each other repeatedly, and even the year of his birth is questionable. The only truly consistent image that can be formed of Santa Anna—one of the most mercurial figures in the history of the Americas—is that of survivor, first and foremost.¹⁰

Like Arredondo in 1813 and subsequent leaders of the Mexican Republic, Santa Anna viewed the Texan unrest of 1835–36 as the result of agitation by Anglo-American filibusters. To oppose these interlopers, he began mobilizing an army in December at Saltillo in northern Mexico. Although the data available is contradictory and indefinite, his total forces apparently numbered between six and eight thousand men. To this force were added Cos's men, now numbering about eight hundred after desertions and attrition on the return from Béxar, and another fifteen hundred men under General Joaquín Ramírez y Sesma. The inclusion of Cos's troops in the invasion force was, of course, a violation of their parole—which Santa Anna ignored as treasonous and, therefore, invalid. Santa Anna viewed the conflict in Texas not as a war between nations but as treason, just as George III had viewed the American Revolution. To Santa Anna, the Texan rebels were not internal freedom fighters but outside agitators, to be regarded and treated as pirates. The word of a Mexican soldier to a traitor, then, was in no way a binding pact between two men of honor, and could not be tolerated as an impediment to the swift restoration of law and order.¹¹

While Santa Anna's army was hardly the body of men that such a dynamic officer would hope to lead, it was the best that a country worn out by continual revolt and

Map prepared in March 1836 by Colonel Ygnacio de Labastida, Commander of Engineers, for Santa Anna's use during the siege. The Alamo proper, sketched from observation and reports of its interior, may have been augmented after the battle. This map, with its graphic scale and compass rose, shows clearly the hand of an experienced cartographer, while its politically self-serving dedication to Filisola also reveals its creator as a career soldier. (Courtesy Barker Texas History Center, The University of Texas at Austin) ◄

Portrait of Antonio López de Santa Anna, as published several years after his death, in the 1883 edition of Homer Thrall's *Pictorial History of Texas*. This often-reproduced etching by Richardson, New York, was evidently taken from a painting made late in Santa Anna's life and does not reflect how dashing and handsome he was reported to have been in his younger days. If this image seems unflattering, earlier images made by his enemies, both domestic and foreign, often reduced him to a grotesque caricature, reflecting his current political status. (DeGolyer Library)

SANTA ANNA.

Edward James Olmos as Santa Anna in the made-for-television movie *Seguín*, a revisionist film intended to correct many Anglo-American perceptions of the Tejanos. To clearly delineate good from bad, Olmos portrayed Santa Anna at his worst—as mean, vicious, and snarling as his harshest critics would have had him. (PBS, 1982)

Mexican soldiers in John Wayne's 1960 *The Alamo*. The army was correctly depicted as a regular army, but this version incorporated numerous inaccurate details. The costumers, told that the Mexican soldiers were uniformed, stylized the typical white cotton peasant garb that was an unofficial uniform into formalized issue, complete with shako, epaulettes, and one of the scarcest commodities in the army, shoes. The property master, told to procure single-shot muskets with bayonets, issued these extras Remington rolling-block rifles, first adopted by the United States in 1870. (United Artists, 1960) ▶

economic collapse could raise. Like Cos's army, Santa Anna's forces included professional troops, presidial soldiers, militia, impressed convicts, and even a battalion of Mayan Indians from Yucatán. Not only did these Indians not speak Spanish, they had never before left the tropics. During the ensuing winter march to San Antonio, however, those that survived became intimately acquainted with snow and cold.

Such, then, were the soldiers of Santa Anna. They have been popularly portrayed as the flower of Mexican soldiery and as a murdering barbaric horde. There are probably elements of truth in both of the contending interpretations, for so much depends on point of view. If only the convict battalions are considered, the Mexican force may indeed have seemed a ravening, demoralized rabble, as capable as any other undisciplined army of committing outrages and ignominies. These particular soldiers would have had little cause for pride in their appearance or unit, concentrating instead on their very survival. If, on the other hand, an observer encountered an elite unit, such as the *Zapadores*, his perception could be radically different. Many of these officers were men of scruples and honor, and their soldiers behaved accordingly. Historically, only those soldiers who have transcended the threshold of self-concern enjoy the luxury of observing—or even of knowing—the established rules of warfare, written or unwritten.

Another weakness of the Mexican forces was clearly discernible at the headquarters of the army. Graft and corruption were a way of life among some of the senior Mexican officers; Generals Adrian Woll and Vicente Filisola, Santa Anna's second-in-command, were little more than soldiers of fortune from France and Italy, respectively. General Antonio Gaona accumulated all of the supplies that he could, and then sold them back to the government for a tidy profit. General Manuel Fernández Castrillón took advantage of the forty-eight percent annual interest charged to the government by money lenders Rubio and Errazu to lend some of his own money to the firm at the same rate.[12]

Even a well-trained, well-supplied, and unified force, however, would have suffered grievously from the long winter march to San Antonio, across 365 miles of desolate, uninhabited Southwest Texas. As they wended their way north, through extremes of choking dust and drifting snow, men and animals died of thirst or starvation from reduced rations. Others contracted a fever known as *telele* from bad water, or got diarrhea and dysentery, history's two greatest killers of soldiers, from chewing mesquite nuts and other berries. Still others fell to rashes, itches, and simple exhaustion. The only doctor in the entire column was Santa Anna's personal physician, and there was not a single chaplain to administer the last rites.

Howard L. Hastings's cover and frontispiece illustration for J. Walker McSpadden's *Texas, a Romantic Story for Young People*, 1927. This is indeed a romanticized image for Anglo-American children, with almost all pretence to accuracy abandoned. More important than history was the message that the Texans fought against the shako-wearing soldiers and sombrero-wearing peasants of a foreign empire and an "inferior race." (DeGolyer Library)

Moving slowly beside the long column of soldiers were baggage wagons, artillery, and, the accompaniment of almost every army, camp followers or *soldaderas*. Although the large *soldaderas* train further strained limited Mexican logistics, the followers also provided certain benefits. The puritanical Americans had officially disdained camp followers as early as the French and Indian War, but their more experienced English allies suffered far fewer casualties, largely because of them. Not only did camp followers care for the wounded after the battle, they also improved morale and encouraged camp sanitation by their insistence on clean soldiers. To this day, many armies bring wives, children, and livestock with them to war as tangible proof of what is worth fighting and dying for. If the soldier dies, he dies secure in the knowledge that the extended family of the *soldaderas* will care for his survivors.

The movements of such a large and inchoate force, about six thousand strong, were bound to be noticed, even if Santa Anna had tried to keep them secret. Mexican newspapers printed reports of training and troop movements, and Tejano border spies carried a stream of information back into Texas. Nevertheless, a surprise Mexican attack on San Antonio was foiled February 21 only by a rain-swollen river; as some Bexareños reported to Santa Anna, the staunch Texan defenders were busy celebrating at a fandango.[13]

Texan unreadiness reflected many factors. As Jameson had complained, the men were unpaid, unmotivated, underfed, and not properly clothed to labor in inclement weather. Funds, materials, labor, and skilled craftsmen were in short supply. Still, the approach of thousands of enemy soldiers should have caused even the most sluggardly of defenders to either prepare or flee. The Alamo garrison did neither. While many Tejano families left San Antonio, some on the flimsy pretense of going farming, the Alamo defenders feuded amongst themselves. Compounding the Anglo-Texans' lack of decisive leadership were their prevailing perceptions of Tejanos as inveterate liars, as traitors who wished to betray the Texans to Santa Anna, or as fools who scared at shadows and reported imaginary armies. As a result, military intelligence gathered by local residents went largely ignored by the amateur Texas soldiery.

The Texans were indeed amateurs at soldiering, and not only in their unpaid status. Although there were many with militia experience, those with a regular service background were scarce and were frequently ignored. The American public held a long-cherished aversion to professional armies, distrusting the caliber of their men and fearing their abuse of power. More important, standing armies had to be paid by tax dollars, whether or not there was a war in progress. In contrast, militias were cheap to organize and operate, and they provided a means to repay political favors with honorary commissions (thus the disproportionate number of colonels and lieutenant colonels to privates in the Texas revolution). To all of this was added a widespread belief in American marksmanship and innate military superiority. The Minutemen of '76 were continually hailed as the cause of that American victory, although it was rarely recalled that these same Minutemen had never decisively defeated a British field force in open battle or siege.

Such myths were fostered by such men as David Crockett, who vociferously disdained trained regular soldiers, apparently preferring the drunken brawls that passed in those days for militia muster. Since Crockett's own prowess with a rifle was even then legendary, those accompanying him were assumed to have similar abilities with flint, powder, and ball. But Crockett was a professional frontiersman who had lived by his skills as scout and hunter. Lawyers, such as Travis or James Butler Bonham, doctors, shopkeepers, farmers, and other ordinary settlers would hardly have had the same time to hone such skills. Moreover, the Scottish, Welsh, Irish, and English members of the Alamo garrison, all recent immigrants, could not have had much of a background in marksmanship due to the British laws and the settled and populated nature of their home islands.

In contrast to their earlier lassitude, the Texans became industrious indeed on the morning of February 23, when Dr. John Sutherland and John W. Smith rode pell-mell into San Antonio accompanied by a sentry's frenzied ringing of the bell atop San Fernando Church, alerting all to the arrival of Santa Anna's army. Food and supplies were hurriedly gathered, as were friends and families.

Santa Anna did not, however, rush in to crush the disorganized Texans as many critics have argued that he should have done. As a devout follower of Napoleon, Santa Anna heeded the great general's maxims, particularly regarding the needs for overwhelming odds and artillery superiority when assaulting a fortified enemy position. On his arrival at Béxar, Santa Anna lacked both. Besides, El Presidente had intended simply to use San Antonio, with its presumably friendly Tejano population, as a base of operations.[14] He may have been surprised to find the Alamo still defended, and his troops were in no condition to make an assault after their arduous forced march across the desert. Every minute of movement had taken him farther away from his source of supplies and funds, and San Antonio, the only substantial Texas settlement that could have been classified as potentially loyal, offered little else, for any possible supplies had already been confiscated. His troops were also dispirited by being so far from home, fighting men of a different race, religion, language, and nationality in Mexico's first truly foreign war waged, nonetheless, on its own soil.

Santa Anna did have trained and veteran engineers, but they had not previously plied their trade in a siege, and the vast bulk of the Mexican army had not been trained in the specialized skills required for a siege. Yet time was on the side of the besieger, for he had but to wait for reinforcements and supplies and to simultaneously deny the same to the defenders by a blockade. With the water in the Alamo probably fouled, personal hygiene and sanitation became mounting concerns, and each day witnessed the dwindling of irreplaceable supplies of food, powder, shot, and medicine.[15] Since historically most forts have fallen not to assault and barrage but to the inexorable constrictions of want, famine, and pestilence, the key question becomes not why Santa Anna delayed his attack but rather why he attacked at all. The expeditions of Grant and Johnson and the forces at Goliad were defeated by separate detachments, so the troops engaged in the siege were not vital to the continuation of the rest of the campaign; they instead could have served as the pivot point for General José Urrea in his sweep of East Texas.

Again, much of the answer must lie within the personal makeup of Santa Anna. Events ensuing immediately upon the arrival of the Mexican army in Béxar were quite confused. According to Travis, Santa Anna's demand for the surrender of the Alamo was answered by a cannon shot toward town that only by happenstance caused no damage. At some time during the confusion, reports arrived of a Mexican bugle sounding the call to parley, followed by the dispatch of a Mexican messenger under a flag of truce with Santa Anna's demands, the dispatch of Green Jameson by Bowie to inquire after terms, the dispatch of Albert Martin by Travis on the same mission, and the Mexican raising of a red flag over the same San Fernando church where the sentry had earlier sounded the alarm. This flag was interpreted to mean that no quarter would be asked and none given, the same interpretation that the Texans had given Cos's black flag. This was curious in light of the fact that Santa Anna had not told the Alamo defenders that prisoners would be executed. Quite the contrary, he had announced in his answer to Bowie that surrender was the only chance the Texans had to survive. It was the Texans who fired the first shot, resolving to "never surrender or retreat."[16]

All of the above activity sent several unspoken messages to Santa Anna. The dispatch of two separate messengers testified eloquently to dissension in the Alamo command, dissension that would only be aggravated by the boredom of an enforced siege. The defenders, moreover, had fired on him, on the flag of Mexico, and possibly on a flag of truce, and to Santa Anna this made all the difference. This was confirmation writ large that he did not face an army of honorable soldiers but rather a den of traitors, a nest of thieves, murderers, agitators, and malcontents. Their crime was *lese république*, and, for Santa Anna, "*La République, c'est moi.*" Such a stain on the escutcheon of his honor, and incidently on Mexico's, could only be expunged with the blood of the profaners. Men such as these had no honor—it had been clearly demonstrated—and were therefore not entitled to the respect of the laws of land warfare, to those niceties extended an honorable foe in order to ease somewhat the horrors of war. And yet even within this framework, there existed a long military tradition of no quarter asked, and none given, so the fate of the Alamo defenders was within established practice.

While Santa Anna could suspend the laws of warfare, even the "Napoleon of the West" could not ignore the principles governing the conduct of sieges—the rules and procedures that a commander must follow if he expects victory. These dictates Santa Anna obeyed as best he could, beginning his physical and psychological probing of the Alamo's defenses while the Texans also strengthened their position as best they could. Trenches had already been dug outside of the mission walls proper as an outer line of defense, but the Texans soon noticed that the Mexicans were able to advance fairly close under cover of some of the *jacales*, or wooden houses, near the Alamo. To prevent this and to gain firewood, these dwellings were either torn down or burned to clear the fields of fire, leaving many Tejanos homeless.

Nor was this the only breach in the Mexican siege, for even though reinforcements straggled in daily, Santa Anna did not have enough men for an impenetrable cordon around the Alamo. Some local citizens reportedly brought meals to the defenders. Texan messengers came and went with relative impunity, the defenders sallied forth more than once to raid Mexican lines, and on the first of March, thirty-two men from Gonzales rode through the Mexican lines and brought the Alamo its only reinforcements. In addition, messengers rode in and out of the Alamo as late in the siege as March 5.[17]

Santa Anna had not been idle, however. Many of those who passed in and out of the Alamo also spread rumors of the defenders' status and morale. The Mexican cannonade, although relatively ineffective against the mission walls, had a much more important psychological effect. Every round fired reminded the Texans of their position and their inability to respond because of low ammunition stores. Later, at San Jacinto, Houston would borrow Santa Anna's other psychological ploy—a band. While Houston's band played "Will You Come to the Bower I Have Shaded for You?" Santa Anna, at the Alamo, simply ordered his band to serenade the troops. The Texans responded to the Mexican serenading with a cacophonous combination of Crockett's fiddle and John McGregor's skirling bagpipes. The bulk of Santa Anna's actions, though, focused on physically tightening the encirclement of the Alamo and on finding the weaknesses in its defenses. This involved particularly the location and advancement of artillery batteries, for Santa Anna, like Napoleon, knew that "artillery is the final argument of kings."[18]

The guns of both sides played a pivotal role in the siege, for the Texans in the Alamo possessed the largest artillery park in that part of the world at that time. Although reports as to exactly how many guns the Alamo had vary to extremes, it is generally agreed that the Texans had between eighteen and twenty-one guns firing during the siege. Their inability to move them and their loathing to abandon them indubitably influenced the Texans' decision to hold the Alamo. Big guns have always held a special fascination for the soldier. Since artillery first ended the invincibility of walled fortresses, the artillery corps has attracted the better elements of society to its service. The man who aimed and fired artillery utilized a combination of art and science, generally living a cleaner, more civilized life than the infantryman or cavalryman, who had to physically attack the enemy in close proximity. Yet even this is not enough to explain the devotion of gunners who have historically fought with trail-spike and ramrod against bayonet-armed infantry rather than abandon their guns.

While the Texans' reputed plan to blow up the powder magazine at the end of the battle indicates a plentiful stockpile, many of the guns were in short supply of cannonballs. Moreover, the various calibers, including several four-, eight-, and twelve-pounders plus a single eighteen-pounder, all smoothbore, presented a formidable task in procurement. Where balls were not available, jagged pieces of broken rock and metal were rammed over the powder, creating in effect a giant shotgun. While such a charge had a very limited range, its effect on massed infantry was devastating.[19]

As a final difficulty, a muzzle-loading cannon of that day required at least a five-man crew in order to fire, including a rammer, a loader, a thumbstall, a gunner (who could double as gun commander), and a powder monkey. If the Texans had indeed had all eighteen guns firing, it would have required ninety men, almost half of their total strength, and would have left the extensive walls of the mission dangerously bare of the much-vaunted riflemen. More likely, many of the guns remained silent.

When Santa Anna arrived in San Antonio he was out-gunned approximately five to one by the Alamo. By the time of the final assault, he had received enough guns to reduce the odds to two to one, still far short of the overwhelming superiority considered necessary for the successful storming of a fortress. He also lacked the heavy caliber artillery needed to reduce the outer walls. This probably influenced his decision to assault in the dark, when the night would hamper the Alamo batteries as much as his own.

Santa Anna also shared many of the Texans' logistics problems. Both sides used identical Mexican artillery pieces, and both quartermasters had to supply the guns with a bewildering array of different caliber ammunition. Also, there were no military supplies to seize in San Antonio, as both Travis and Santa Anna must have found to their profound disgust. The advantage to the Mexican army, apart from its freedom of movement, lay in its trained gunners, who could be expected to remain calmer under counterbattery fire and to operate their guns more efficiently and therefore faster, making up somewhat in volume and in accuracy of fire for what they lacked in number.

It was in small arms that the Texans had the unquestioned advantage during the siege. In addition to the captured Mexican muskets, the defenders were armed with hunting knives, shotguns, pistols, and most significant, hunting rifles. The Mexicans were not fully aware of the accurate range of a hunting rifle—about three times that of their *escopetas*—and at first ventured too close to the walls. Experience quickly taught them to keep a more respectful distance. While there may have been some of the new percussion cap rifles in the Alamo, most were probably of the same flintlock ignition system as the muskets. The difference lay inside the barrel. These rifles—called Kentucky, Pennsylvania, squirrel, or long rifles, depending on the owner's preference—were designed for hunting. The barrels were rifled to give spin to the ball for increased accuracy in order to kill dangerous game quickly, cleanly, and economically with only one shot. The rifles were loaded through the muzzle, just like the muskets, but since the rifles used a ball larger than the bore of the barrel, a greased patch of cloth had to be wrapped around the ball and then hammered down the barrel for the tight fit that insured maximum accuracy. This made loading a slow process, not particularly important in hunting, but crucial in battle.

The *escopetas* of the Mexican army, in contrast, were Third Model "Brown Bess" muskets, purchased as surplus from the British East India Company and virtually unchanged since their use by the British in the American Revolution and the Napoleonic Wars. These guns fired a lead ball over one-half inch in diameter with marginal accuracy

Lobby card from the 1955 movie *The Last Command*, illustrating some of the problems and questions of the Alamo's weaponry. The gun is shown on a field carriage, which was much more probable than the small-wheeled naval or garrison carriages in the John Wayne movie (see p. 55). Once the gunner has fired it, though, there seems to be no one to reload it. Instead, the other defenders are shown with their hunting rifles, which were slower to load than the cannon and far less effective. (From the collection of Paul A. Hutton) ◄

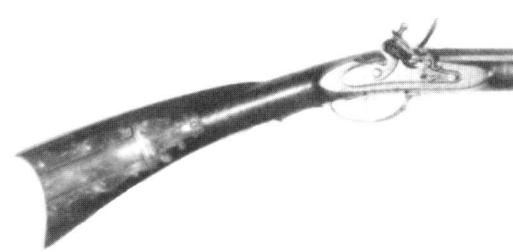

Flintlock rifle, a fairly typical early-nineteenth-century hunting rifle. This one is on display in the Alamo shrine as the only individual weapon presently verified as having been at the battle of March 6, 1836. The hinged metal lid in the stock covers the cavity where the greased patches were kept. The graceful full-length stock is decorated with several disassembly keys of German silver and with ferrules to hold the wooden ramrod. Rudimentary sights are mounted atop the octagonal barrel, and the hammer is shown in the fired position, with the frizzen flipped up. Additional accoutrements necessary to load the rifle included a ball-starter, powder horn with gunpowder, priming horn with priming powder, and lead balls. (Courtesy The Alamo—Daughters of the Republic of Texas. Photograph by Frank Haecker)

out to seventy yards. Their main use as infantry weapons was on the firing line, when volley fire was used to make up in volume for what it lacked in precision. In contrast to the rifles of the Texans, the barrels of these muskets were smoothbore and used a ball smaller than the bore. As a result, a trained unit could load and fire up to three rounds per minute.

The main theoretical use of musketry, however, was not to inflict casualties. Up until the American Civil War, gunfire rarely decided a battle. Rather, it was used to break the enemy's morale; the battle was won or lost by press of bayonet. The bayonet was essentially a knife fitted to the muzzle of a musket for close combat, basically converting the musket into a spear. It was a Spanish invention, initially intended to supplement pikemen in warding off cavalry attacks, and Santa Anna had specifically ordered that his troops be instructed in its care and use. The Texan hunting rifles, in contrast, were usually stocked out to the muzzle and often had heavy octagonal barrels with no provision for mounting bayonets. As a result, the final hand-to-hand combat forced the Texans to fight with knives against the longer bayoneted muskets. It also reduced the Texans to using their finely crafted rifles as clubs—as Crockett is so often depicted as doing (plates 5, 9)—for at close quarters, rifle fire was no match for the massed *escopetas*.

Throughout the siege the Mexicans prepared their works both defensively and offensively. Santa Anna saw no advantage to massing his artillery, where its effects would not be increased as greatly as the risks from a massed counterbattery fire. Instead, he distributed his artillery around the Alamo as anchor points upon which to build his lines. This also gave a variety of angles for fire into the fort, so that the defenders in turn could not afford to mass their guns against any one position. The Mexican guns necessarily covered the routes into and out of the Alamo and were situated so that other batteries could fire in support of any position that might be threatened or attacked. The engineers obviously played a part in siting the batteries, enabling the attackers to advance closer to the Alamo in relative safety during the siege. In addition, the batteries were aimed

Brown Bess musket. First adopted in the early 1700s, the Brown Bess remained the British empire's service arm for well over a century. Supplies of the Third Model, purchased by the British East India Company for its semi-autonomous army, were later sold as obsolete surplus to Mexico with the lock markings changed as illustrated. Outmoded as it was by technological advances, the Brown Bess was still a rugged, serviceable arm capable of mounting another weapon—whose design and use have not changed significantly to this day—the bayonet. Many of these muskets, captured during the revolution, subsequently formed a large part of the arsenal of the Republic of Texas. (Courtesy Old Army Press)

not so much at futile perpendicular pounding of the mission's masonry, but at sweeping the ground before the walls and landing rounds inside the compound proper.[20]

The problems of the Mexican situation were compounded by other factors beyond their control. The weather was typically Texan—cold and blustery. Shelter was scarce, and the men suffered from the cold. Food was fairly plentiful, but disease took its toll. Indeed, until the First World War more soldiers died of diseases than of combat action, and the Texan campaign of Santa Anna was no exception. The same situation, if not worse, raged inside the Alamo. A significant number of those in the Alamo must have been incapable of active duty due either to illnesses or to wounds suffered in the siege of San Antonio. The cooking was done communally, the water supply was fouled, contagious patients were impossible to isolate, and sanitary conditions were primitive.[21]

The final decision to launch the assault was made solely by Santa Anna, unencumbered by the consensus process used by the Texans. Councils of war are, with few exceptions, conservative events that usually vote for no action. When Santa Anna's generals balked, however, he simply disbanded the council and told them to await his orders. The timing of the assault, thirteen days after the start of the siege, has been criticized as being both too late and too early: why wait so long, or why not wait longer to starve the Texans out? To the first question, the answer usually given is artillery—Santa Anna was waiting for General Gaona to arrive with more men and, more important, more artillery. In addition, it was rumored that a Tejano female left the Alamo on the night of March 4 to inform Santa Anna of the fort's defenses and weakened morale. These surely would have been excellent reasons to await the Texans' inevitable collapse.

But Santa Anna did not wait. The Texan garrison from Goliad, numbering several hundred men under the command of Colonel James Walker Fannin, was thought to be on the move. If Fannin attempted to relieve the Alamo, the Mexican army could be pinned between the artillery-strong anvil of the fortress and the hammer of Fannin's troops maneuvering behind their lines. The concept of an annular position, both defending and attacking, was untenable. The only alternative was to seize the Alamo and its artillery, eliminate that threat, and turn the guns against Fannin when he arrived. Santa Anna again followed Napoleon: "Strike the fragments of the enemy with the masses of your own."

From late in the night of March 4 until 2 P.M. on March 5, Santa Anna devised and then dictated his plan to his secretary, Ramón Martínez Caro. It was a complex concept of operations, perhaps needlessly so, but it fully suited Santa Anna's taste for the grandiose

Fall of the Alamo, epic battle painting in oil by Jean Louis Theodore Gentilz, destroyed in a fire in 1906. Arriving in San Antonio in 1843, French-born artist Gentilz produced numerous sketches of the Alamo prior to its renovation as a U.S. Army depot. He also compiled copious notes on the battle—interviewing witnesses; measuring the ruins; describing the uniforms, flags, and weapons; listing the officers and survivors—and executed numerous individual figure sketches, perspective studies, and scale drawings. The final painting was evidently not completed until ca. 1885, prior to its publication in McLane's 1886 play *Capture of the Alamo*. A second copyright, dated four years after the artist's death in 1906, was held by C. H. Mueller, a San Antonio paint manufacturer who had owned and displayed the original prior to its destruction by a fire in his store. Pictorially, the scene is rather wooden, with tiny soldiers almost like lead toys, and somewhat disoriented in time. Although Morales has not yet breached the southern pallisade, the columns from the north have already entered, swept the plaza, and turned the guns on the long barracks. Possibly more informative are Gentilz's extensive sketches and notes, in the collection of the Alamo Library. (Courtesy Daughters of the Republic of Texas Library at the Alamo, San Antonio)

and spectacular. At 4 A.M. on March 6, four columns would assault the Alamo; Cos with about 350 men from the northwest, Colonel Francisco Duque with another 350 men from the northeast, Colonel José María Romero with 300 men from the east, and Colonel Juan Morales with 100 men against the southern pallisade. Approximately 1,100 men would actually assault the Alamo, all of them chosen from the veteran regulars. Santa Anna would personally control the 400 reserves, composed of the *Zapadores* and the infantry battalion's grenadiers, their best troops, to the north. As cavalry would be singularly useless in such an assault on high walls, Sesma would deploy his 300 horsemen to cut off any attempted escape to the east.[22]

The largest problem on the battlefield, then and now, is the span of command and control. In ideal conditions, signals could be sent from the commander to his subordinates by hand signals, flags, heliographs, bugle calls, or just plain shouts. None of these would be possible with Santa Anna's plan, for quiet stealth under the cover of darkness would be needed to position troops in order to take the Alamo defenders by surprise and so reduce casualties. Therefore, each column had to have few enough men for their leaders to control in the dark and yet enough to accomplish their mission. The division was necessary to insure that the defenders could not simply mass all of their defenses at one point, and also to separate the commands to avoid confusion.

One problem usually attendant on such an assault was that at some time during the advance the troops would mask their own artillery, preventing them from firing lest they hit their own soldiers. To avoid this, and to avoid betraying his intentions, Santa Anna elected to eschew an artillery preparation of the Alamo prior to the assault. Attacking an entrenched enemy across open ground without artillery support was risky business, as witnessed by Confederate General George Pickett's later unsuccessful charge at Gettysburg, but it was a calculated risk. If all went according to plan, the battle would be over very quickly.

If the plan did go awry, it would not be for Santa Anna's lack of preparation. The attack was to start while the defenders would be in deepest sleep in the pre-dawn, and the cold, cloudy sky would hide most of the waning full moon. Furthermore, in the dark the soldiers could see neither how small their columns were nor the fates of the other columns or their companions around them. The dark also dehumanized the enemy, obscuring individual faces so that one had only to shoot at muzzle flashes and slash at movements.

Now the troops prepared, moving to assembly sites, turning in early for sleep. All was quiet by ten o'clock on the night of March 5. Then, at midnight, the chosen troops were roused and made ready to move. At 1 A.M., the soldiers began their long, cold, silent trudge around the Alamo to their assault positions, leaving campfires, belongings, and *soldaderas* behind while Santa Anna nervously drank hot coffee and snapped at everyone. By 4 A.M. the men were positioned roughly two hundred yards from the Alamo, an insignificant distance except when under fire.

The Mexicans were instructed to lie down, and without coats and blankets the cold of the ground crept in. Breath fogged in the air, fingers numbed on the cold steel of the muskets as they waited to advance, and still the order did not come. Why Santa Anna delayed the assault for about an hour is unclear. He himself later said he had been waiting for the Texans to respond to his latest demand for surrender. More likely, he had been watching the light conditions, which may have been too dark for movement or too bright for concealment. Every step his men took toward the walls without being observed was a savings of several lives, yet he could not afford to wait too long, for dawn approached and with it the Texans would be rising.

Suddenly, the issue was resolved for him. Santa Anna, always either a hero or a villain to his men, heard the cry "Viva Santa Anna!" arise spontaneously from the ranks at around five o'clock. Accepting the stroke of fate, he signaled his bugler, José María Gonzáles, to sound the attack, which was picked up and repeated by the buglers in all of the columns. Only later in the battle would the Mexican bands play the "Degüello." Known as the "Assassin's" call, the "Degüello" was used by most armies and navies of that time in attacking an enemy who had refused an honorable surrender: no quarter asked, and none given. It was not simply a warning to the defenders that they would be killed, it also served notice that the attackers would not surrender, even if defeated, but would die to a man. The Mexicans accepted this equal footing not knowing the outcome, but knowing how wars were customarily fought. It was kill or be killed or both, and death, given the Mexican lack of medical facilities, was preferable to being wounded.[23]

Committed, just as the Texans, to victory or death, the columns surged toward the mission. This was no formal, measured advance to the tattoo of drums; this was a screaming, frenzied dash of hundreds of bunched-up soldiers, trying to maintain ranks while crossing the open space quickly and staying alive in the face of fire from the Alamo. Not all of the Texans had been sleeping, and the rest rose quickly to the defense. By the broken light of the moon, and the twinkle of flashpan and musket, linstock and muzzle, the battle was fought.

Contrasting versions of the Mexican assault. Patton and Rosenfield's *Texas History "Movies,"* 1935 edition, (above) depicts the Mexican troops as cowardly buffoons whipped on by a demonic Santa Anna. (Right) John Severin's 1952 comic "Alamo!" portrays the attackers' viewpoint, rushing from all directions into gunfire and death. "The Texians cut us down, like wheat! . . . Now we were angry!" The curious analogy of pouring in "like sheep" comes directly from the testimony of Travis's slave, Joe. Patton and Rosenfield's work, which originally appeared as a comic strip in the *Dallas Morning News* in 1926, became a long-standing favorite of Texas schoolchildren through a condensed version issued by Magnolia (now Mobil) Oil Company. Despite, or perhaps because of, its popularity, the book has recently come under heavy criticism for its racially derogative stereotypes, particularly of blacks and Hispanics. (Patton and Rosenfield image, from the abridged Magnolia Petroleum Company ed., DeGolyer Library, reproduced courtesy the Texas State Historical Association. Severin image from *Two-Fisted Tales*, no. 28, July-August 1952, © 1985, William M. Gaines)

Yet even in this fitful illumination, Santa Anna could see that things were not going according to plan. The Texan rifles and cannons in the church had halted Romero's men to the east, and a storm of grapeshot from the Alamo's artillery raked the columns from the northeast and northwest. Colonel Duque fell and was run over by his troops advancing through the dark. The Mexicans halted, fell back, and reformed, again charged the mission, and once again were repulsed. Santa Anna had after all overlooked a salient feature. He had prevented the riflemen from massing in one point for the defense, but by spreading his attack, he gave targets to more of the Alamo's cannons than if he had sent only a single column.

WE RUSHED FROM THE **NORTH** INTO THE MOUTH OF A BATTERY OF CANNON!

WE RUSHED FROM THE **SOUTH** RIGHT UP TO THE WALLS WITH OUR LADDERS!

WE RUSHED FROM THE **EAST** INTO A STORM OF FIRE FROM THE CHAPEL!

WE RUSHED FROM THE **WEST** INTO DEATH FROM THE LONG BARRACKS!

¡AY QUÉ ESTABA TERRIBLE! THE TEXIANS *CUT US DOWN, LIKE WHEAT!* ONCE THEY REPULSED US!... 150 AGAINST 4,000 AND THEY REPULSED US! NOW WE WERE ANGRY! ONCE MORE WE CHARGED, AND THIS TIME WE *POURED THROUGH THE NORTH WALL LIKE SHEEP!*

Lajos Markos's oil painting *Siege of the Alamo*, part of the permanent collection of the State Capitol of Texas and one of the few epic-scale Alamo battle paintings attempted in recent years. Like its predecessors by Gentilz, McArdle, and Onderdonk, it contains many curious contradictions. First, considering the placement of the chapel with Markos's ersatz humped gable, the view appears to be from the west wall where no columns are reported to have attacked. The sword-wielding gentleman on the wall is obviously intended to be Travis, but he was probably among the first to die during the initial assault on the north wall. The Mexicans appear to have not yet entered the Alamo compound, yet a huge conflagration blazes to the Texans' rear, set against a dawn that none of them lived to see. Despite cold spring weather, a large number of both Texans and Mexicans seem to have bared their chests in true macho passion. (Courtesy of Mr. Lajos Markos and the Texas State Capitol) ▶

This consolidation of columns occurred by chance. After the second repulse, Romero's column moved to the north, and Cos's drifted to its left, both converging with Duque's column, which Castrillón now commanded. Incredibly, the soldiers plunged into the firestorm a third time, finally reaching the north wall, only to discover that most of their ladders had been lost or destroyed. Now Santa Anna committed his reserves, who rushed in cheering to the strains of the "Degüello" to help the troops milling at the base of the walls.

It was obvious to the soldiers that to stay in the open was to die and that their only hope lay inside the walls. They began climbing up the stone walls of the mission and over the rough fortifications thrown up by the defenders. Some wriggled through embrasures, and little by little, there were more Mexicans inside than the defenders could repulse. As in the fall of the great castles, when the Alamo's northern wall was breached and the enemy rushed in unchecked, the end was inevitable.

At this time, Morales gained the south wall. He had been mauled by Crockett's Tennesseans firing over the pallisades and had been forced to shift to the west, out of their line of fire. Some of Morales' men turned the eighteen-pounder into the compound and began firing on the Texans, while the rest engaged with bayonets the defenders in front of the chapel in fierce hand-to-hand fighting. The melee was now general, and Mexican soldiers were killing and wounding each other in the confusion. The fighting proceeded room-by-room in the long barracks, darker still than the courtyard, reeking of sulphur and saltpetre from the gunpowder. Movement was restricted in these cramped quarters, and the fighting was particularly vicious as opponents grappled in the blackness. The guns still manned by Jameson and Almeron Dickinson on the chapel now came under intense counterbattery fire from the Texans' own captured guns, and the crews fell at their posts, cut down by the same ammunition that their colleagues had just before been using against the Mexicans.

The Texan defense was broken. According to Mexican accounts, some defenders tried to flee outside the fort but were run to the ground and killed with lance and sword.[24] Lieutenant José María Torres saw the flag of the New Orleans Greys flying over the Alamo and gave his life in raising in its stead the Mexican tricolor and eagle. Other flags began appearing around the Alamo, though. Handkerchiefs and even white socks were reportedly used to signal for quarter, but Travis and Santa Anna had both pledged the lives of their soldiers, and Travis had lost. The sick and wounded were killed where they lay, either as helpless victims or while trying to defend themselves. In the frenzied gloom

of the final fighting in the church, even some children were killed, but most were spared. Between fifteen and twenty-five occupants of the Alamo, all noncombatants, survived the battle, and in addition some five or six defenders surrendered to Castrillón, who promised them quarter. Santa Anna, however, standing amid the steaming blood and sweat in the compound, repeated his order that no prisoners be taken. Castrillón and others turned away in disgust at such pointless slaughter after such a battle, but Santa Anna was determined the Texans know that if they chose to oppose him, the only alternative to surrender was death. Whether still inflamed by bloodlust or simply eager to toady to Santa Anna, other Mexicans carried out the order.[25]

As the sun finally rose over the carnage, the morning's toll became apparent. Some six hundred Mexicans had been killed or wounded, just ten percent of the total army but over one-third of the assaulting force. Decimation, or reduction by ten percent, was usually the maximum amount of loss that a unit would accept before its morale broke. With three times that amount lost, against high walls and murderous fire, the Mexicans attacked three times and emerged victorious, while the Alamo defenders inflicted only slightly more than three-to-one losses on the Mexicans. In terms of numbers, it was not in any way the Pyrrhic victory that Lieutenant-Colonel José de la Peña thought it was, particularly in light of concerns over Fannin's movements. The battle ended at dawn, giving Santa Anna the entire day to prepare to fight Fannin, should he arrive. More important, the vast majority of Santa Anna's forces were fresh and rested to meet any contingency with morale boosted by the victory.

The only Alamo defender apparently accorded the dignity of a Christian burial was Gregorio Esparza, a local Tejano whose brother fought in the Mexican Army. For the others, Santa Anna ordered cremation. He evidently intended to leave no memorial to the fallen, to scatter their unshriven ashes ignominiously in the wind so that their crime would be evident even unto Judgment Day. This was probably Santa Anna's single most provocative action of the entire campaign, for to the Texans it represented sacrilege and dishonor.

This is a peculiarly Christian concept, for many other religions and civilizations have considered funeral pyres an honor to their dead, committing their remains to all of nature in such rites as the Roman *rogus* and the Viking burial-at-sea in flaming longboats. Most likely, though, both Santa Anna and the Texans perceived the fire in its Christian role as a purgative, the dispeller of evil from witches and heretics. As the promised resurrection was then widely expected to be a bodily one, if the body were not complete,

The Alamo, by H. Charles McBarron, from *Americana: Portraits of the Growing Nation*, a portfolio of prints issued by American Oil Company in 1963. McBarron has chosen to depict the most oft-repeated scene, the fight before the chapel with Morales' men, and despite the slight glimmer of sunrise on the horizon, he does suggest the darkness in which the battle was fought. The accompanying caption identifies both Bowie and Crockett among the fighters and implies that the entire battle was fought here. In contrast to his vivid portrayal of the final melee, McBarron's chapel appears distorted, a looming edifice much larger than its actual modest size. (From the collection of Paul A. Hutton. Reproduced courtesy Amoco Corporation) ◄

there could be no resurrection. Cremation had vanished from Western Europe by 500 A.D. and was not reintroduced until 1866 and not legalized in the United States until 1876. Thus Santa Anna's act was specifically intended to gall the Texans. Even in this, Santa Anna's plan backfired, for the windblown ashes mixed inextricably with the dust of the smouldering Alamo to create a monument and an undying memory.

In Mexican eyes, the view of the Alamo battle has been no more consistent than that of Santa Anna. Militarily, the battle was overshadowed by the Mexican-American War and "Los Niños," the heroic martyrs of Churubusco. Politically, the Texas revolution

Illustration from a 1904 World's Fair souvenir book, W. W. Dexter's *Texas: Imperial State of America*. This version of the battle is another of many variations of the *Storming of the Alamo*, published in Baker's *Texas Scrap-Book*, 1875. Its intriguing anachronisms include numerous gunners firing out of windows that did not exist (as on the south side of the chapel) and what appears to be a white flag flying atop the army gable. The scene does, however, convey a sense of the action and the obscurement of battle smoke. (DeGolyer Library) ◄

Illustration of *The Mexican Assault on the Alamo*, by Armand Welcker for Buffalo Bill Cody's *Story of the Wild West and Camp-Fire Chats*, 1888. In the style of the 1880s, nearly every combatant, Texan and Mexican, appears with beard or mustache. San Antonio looms as a major city to the south of the compound, where only small *jacales* stood, and the Texans fire not only from the army windows but also from the statue niches. (DeGolyer Library)

José Cisneros's evocative drawing *Alamo Funeral Pyre*, in *San Antonio Legacy*, by Donald E. Everett, 1979. (DeGolyer Library. Reproduced courtesy José Cisneros and Trinity University Press)

Santa Anna and the cast of Mexicans surveying the wreckage in a scene from the John Wayne movie *The Alamo*. In the background, the chapel smoulders from the explosion of the powder magazine. What Major Robert Evans had been unable to accomplish in 1836, John Wayne, as Crockett, did in 1960. The resulting blast destroyed much of the Brackettville set; had it actually occurred in 1836, it would have killed the women, children, and sick and wounded soldiers inside the chapel. (United Artists, 1960) ◄

has been viewed as the first dismemberment of Mexico, a symbol of United States expansionism at its southern neighbor's expense. In 1835, Secretary of War and Marine José María Tornel y Mendivil announced the creation of a Legion of Honor for the veterans of the Texas campaign. On April 27, 1836, Tornel stated that the legion would have as its date of establishment March 6, 1836, in honor of the victory at the Alamo. Within a month, however, upon receiving the news of San Jacinto, Torrel reneged, explaining that the captured president's promises were no longer valid. Mexico would as soon *olvidarse del Alamo*, forget the Alamo.[26]

The American image of the Alamo has been no less confused and shifting. A variety of factors account for this, including illiteracy, prejudice, partisan politics, and careless research. The only men of letters to survive the battle were Mexican soldiers and officers, and their work was suspect by even those few Anglo-Texans who had the opportunity or bothered to read them. Moreover, as most of these Mexican accounts were written after San Jacinto, they tend to be more partisan than objective, either exculpating the writer's own actions or blaming others for the final defeat and withdrawal. The non-Mexican sources from the Alamo have included interviews with survivors, memoirs of those associated with the Alamo, and often pure conjecture and speculation. Most of the interviews with survivors came much later, as did the memoirs, and the remembrances so evoked could not help but be colored by events after the Alamo and by the fading of memory. Some stories have gained currency simply by their long existence—the major doctoral dissertation on the Alamo cites a novel as a source of information.

Yet none of this explains the widespread and persistent fascination with a small military action of such ambiguous documentation. Much of the attraction probably comes from the curious appeal throughout history of the "Grand Military Folly." The monumental failures persist in the public imagination as often as the triumphs. The stunning Revolutionary War victory of the Battle of Cowpens, South Carolina, is unknown to a public that considers Bunker Hill a triumph. America remembers the burning of Washington, D.C., by the British much better than it remembers the battles of the Chippawa or Lundy's Lane. Lee and "Pickett's Charge" come to mind when Gettysburg is mentioned, not the stubborn Union defense. The brilliance of Crazy Horse, the determination of Major Reno and Captain Benteen, the steady progress of Generals Terry and Crook pale in the mind when compared to "Custer's Last Stand" at the Little Big Horn.

The "Grand Folly" alone is not enough to explain the Alamo's mystique, however, for similar Texan debacles at Goliad and Mier have not achieved the same stature. The only event in American history to have the same allure, the same aura as the Alamo, is the Custer Massacre at the "Greasy Grass," and for basically the same reason. The "truth" will never be known. There are no documents to be discovered in an obscure repository, no artifacts to be unearthed, that will ever give a definitive form to events. Markers dot the hill where the bodies of Custer's men were found, but what happened before then, after his column galloped off toward the Indian camp, is as unknown and ultimately unknowable as the locations of the deaths of the Alamo heroes. This vacuum has opened the way for myriads of interpretations, each contending with the other for recognition. Within these impenetrable secrets lies the Alamo's continuing fascination. Of such stuff are legends made; no era has been exempt from the enduring appeal of the retold tale.

Chapter 3

Heroes Forgotten and Familiar

by Susan Prendergast Schoelwer

THE TALE of the Alamo has long revolved around the deeds of Jim Bowie, Davy Crockett, and William Barret Travis. The other defenders—some 183 Anglo-Texan and Tejano men, plus several women and children and at least two negro slaves—remain shadowy in both fact and fiction.

The best known of these defenders is James Butler Bonham, popularly remembered as a dashing cavalier who chose certain death in the Alamo rather than desert his commander and supposed boyhood friend, Travis. For over fifty years, descriptions of the battle did little more than repeat Travis's own terse notation of the event: "Col. Bonham (a courier from Gonzales) got in this morning at 11 o'clock, without molestation." In 1889, however, Texas novelist John Henry Brown published a much more detailed description, placing Bonham on a cream-colored horse, with a white handkerchief in his hat as a signal to Travis, dismissing all warnings of danger and dashing through the Alamo gates amidst a shower of Mexican bullets. An even more romantic version appeared in the *Dallas Morning News*, March 8, 1931. "A great round Southern moon rose over the plains. Riding down from Goliad came Bonham . . . cold and alone . . . riding with a dream, a promise riding with death . . . to go down immortally in history for the freedom of Texas."[1]

Despite its obvious contradiction with the only documented contemporary report of the event, the image of Bonham's midnight dash remains a compelling element of the Alamo tradition. From a literary standpoint, it represents one flash of dramatic action amidst the tedium of enforced inaction. It also provides several opportunities for linking the Texas revolutionary experience to earlier historical and literary traditions—the medieval knight in shining armor, Regulus returning to ancient Carthage, and even Paul Revere's ride in the American Revolution.

Bonham's solitary ride has long overshadowed the only other occasion on which Mexican lines were crossed by incoming traffic—the arrival of thirty-two men from Gonzales on the night of March 1. Although widely hailed as "The Immortal Thirty-Two," the courageous action of the Alamo's only reinforcers has received surprisingly

Section of wall mural by Howard Cook, San Antonio Post Office, ca. 1935–37, featuring Travis (with sword), Crockett (with long rifle and coonskin cap), and Bowie (with pistol, in right background). (Courtesy Daughters of the Republic of Texas Library at the Alamo, San Antonio. Photograph by Robert Benavides)

little attention. John Wayne's *Alamo* epic, for example, completely lost its Gonzales sequence after critics declared the film too long.

The historical record on these men remains painfully silent, offering little more than brief, tantalizing glimpses of individual valor—Isaac Millsaps's blind wife parting from her husband, William P. King substituting for his father, young Galba Fuqua struggling to speak through shattered jaws. Much of the information available derives from John W. Smith, who had guided the Gonzales unit into the fort but survived by being sent

Harry Anthony DeYoung's 1939 painting of James Butler Bonham. DeYoung incorporated all of the important legendary elements of the gallant courier's daring ride—waving handkerchief, bullet-ridden steed, buckskin-clad defenders throwing wide the gates. Because no contemporary portraits of Bonham are known to exist, most purported likenesses of him are in fact based on portraits of his nephew, also named James, who was said by the family to greatly resemble the Alamo hero. (Courtesy The Alamo—Daughters of the Republic of Texas)

The men of Gonzales preparing to reinforce the Alamo in a scene from *Heroes of the Alamo* (Sunset, 1975) ▶

out again on courier duty. Smith later related his experiences to fellow Alamo veteran Dr. John Sutherland, who in turn described the gathering of volunteers, their route to Béxar, the near escape from a Mexican trap, and the single file passage through enemy lines into the Alamo, amidst mistaken Texan fire that injured one volunteer. Fictional treatments are equally sparse, primarily John Culp's novel *The Men of Gonzales*, 1960, and Ramsey Yelvington's moving poetic drama *A Cloud of Witnesses*, 1959, which takes up the unusual viewpoint of the "weeping widows"—those left behind to watch "men dying willingly for ideals they could not easily share."[2]

That "The Immortal Thirty-Two" should be so inconspicuous in the Alamo tradition seems curious indeed. Their ranks included two men, Albert Martin and John Smith, who had left the fort earlier on courier duty and, like Bonham, voluntarily chose to return. Since word of Fannin's refusal to leave Goliad had not yet arrived, the men of Gonzales probably expected to join a stream of reinforcements and, unlike Bonham, may not have been fully aware of the odds facing them. Yet they all shared Bonham's resolve to forsake personal safety by entering the besieged fort.

The men already inside the Alamo are hardly better known. Of the nearly two hundred defenders present at the beginning of the siege, at least ten and possibly more were Spanish-speaking residents of Béxar, recruited by local Tejano leader Juan Nepomuceno Seguín. The remainder of the men were largely newcomers to Texas—only a handful had been there longer than five years. Some had families and established farms or businesses to protect, but many others had come to Texas specifically to fight and, not incidentally, to share in the spoils of victory. It seems quite clear from the letters of defenders like Daniel Cloud, Micajah Autry, and even Travis himself that patriotism mixed easily with adventuring, that land and liberty were powerful dual lures. As the battle approached, Travis wrote hurriedly to his son's guardian, "If the country should be saved, I may make him a splendid fortune; but if the country should be lost and I should perish, he will have nothing but the proud recollection that he is the son of a man who died for his country."[3]

With the exception of literate men like Cloud and Autry, whose letters prior to the siege provide some insight into their experiences and expectations, the Alamo garrison remains a faceless lot, frequently identifiable only in the most general terms: name, origin, possibly age or occupation. The compilation of an accurate roster of Alamo defenders has long been one of the most vexing problems facing Alamo historians. No official muster roll survived the Mexican assault, and the numerous reconstructed lists found in early newspaper accounts, letters, histories, and on the various Alamo monuments have been subject to continuing review and correction. The generally accepted count of defenders killed stands currently at 183, of which some 20 to 30 were probably ill or wounded. To this number must be added perhaps 15 to 20 noncombatants (women, children, servants) and another 10 to 15 able-bodied men sent out as couriers during the siege. Thus, the maximum population of the besieged garrison almost certainly exceeded 200, even though most of the messengers had gone out before the Gonzales contingent arrived.[4]

Considering the dearth of reliable biographical information, it is hardly surprising that some of the most well-known and intriguing Alamo defenders are entirely imaginary. Davy Crockett's loyal companions, Thimblerig (played by Hans Conreid in the 1955 *Davy Crockett* movie and by Denver Pyle in the 1960 John Wayne film) and the Bee Hunter or Beekeeper (subject of a full-length 1966 novel by Christopher Bryant), were both legendary characters spawned by the inventive yarns of *Col. Crockett's Exploits and Adventures in Texas*, 1836. Children's authors and comic book writers have been especially adept at inventing Alamo characters: Margaret Cousins' memorable Billy Campbell, *The Boy in the Alamo*, 1958; Marvel Comics' "Two-Gun Kid," keeping vigil for his slaughtered friend Jim Bowie; *Eerie* magazine's "Rook," going back in a time machine to save his great-great-grandfather; "Little Orvy," stepping from a snowball fight into the Alamo battle; and the French comic book western hero Manos Kelly, Alamo survivor.[5]

Manos Kelly has to be an imaginary character, for as every loyal Texan well knows, "Thermopylae had its messenger of defeat—the Alamo had none." The Alamo had no survivors, at least none in the strictest possible nineteenth-century sense of the term: no adult white males, present at the onset of the battle in the pre-dawn hours of March 6, 1836, remained alive at day's end. There were, however, several survivors of the siege, members of the garrison who had passed out through enemy lines (mainly as couriers) prior to the final attack: Launcelot Smithers, Benjamin Highsmith, Juan Seguín, Antonio Cruz y Arocha, Alexandro de la Garza, James Allen, a Johnson, and possibly four or five others. Dr. Sutherland and San Antonio carpenter John Smith, while not technically part of the garrison, also carried messages out of the fort and through enemy lines.[6]

These men hold a curious place in Alamo lore. Although several lived many years after the battle and became quite prominent in local affairs—both Smith and Seguín served as mayors of San Antonio, while Allen was mayor of Indianola—they left re-

1950 painting by John Francis Lewis. "I go the whole Hog in the cause of Texas," wrote Micajah Autry to his wife in January 1836. A Tennessee lawyer hoping to start anew, Autry joined up with Crockett's band on the way to the Alamo and, like all the Tennesseans, was reputed to have been a great marksman. Here, Autry is about to take aim (unsuccessfully) at Santa Anna himself. (Courtesy The Alamo—Daughters of the Republic of Texas)

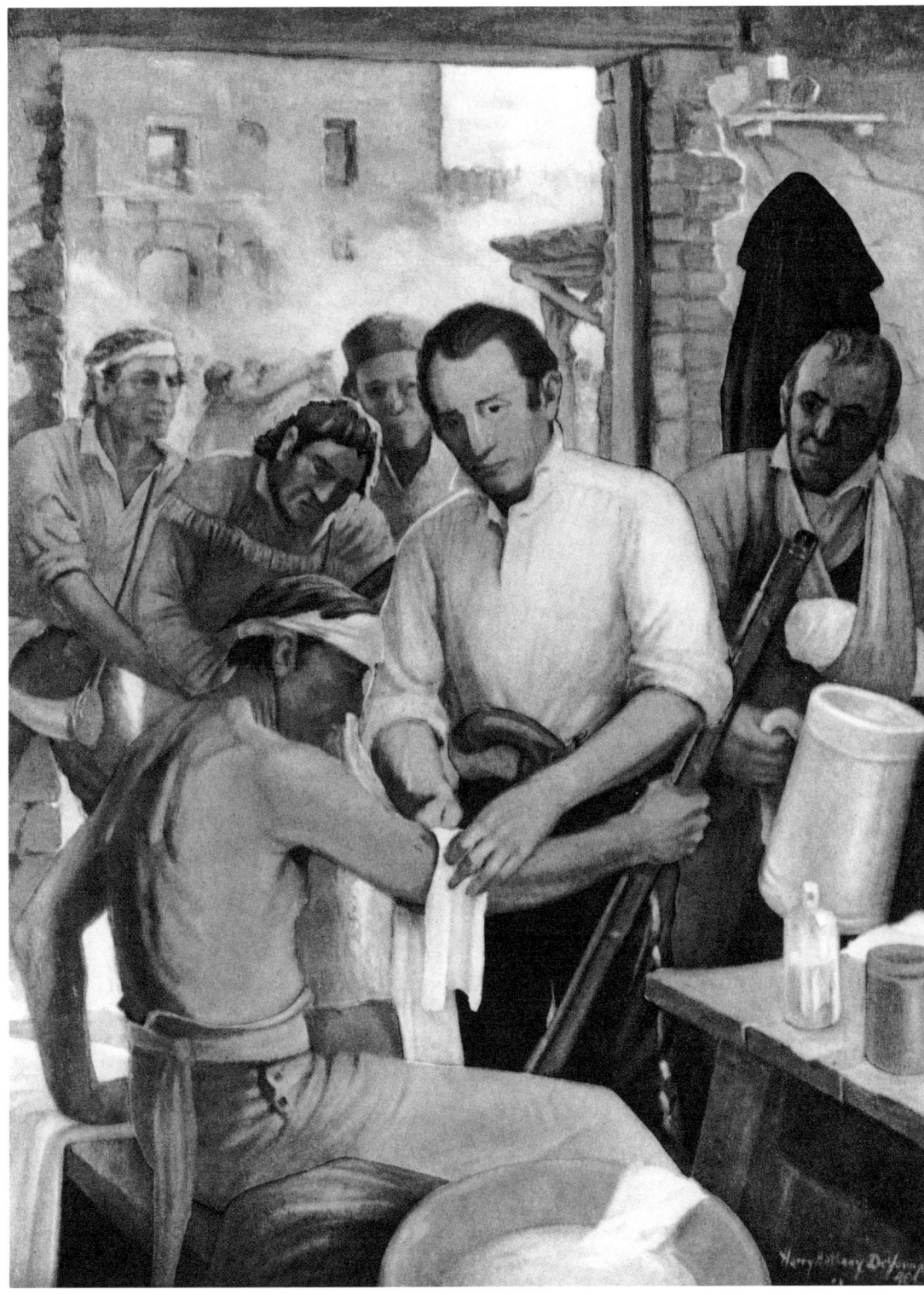

Alamo surgeon Dr. Amos Pollard treating the garrison's wounded. Painting by Harry Anthony DeYoung for the Fiesta San Jacinto, 1940. Pollard's portrait is one of several (including those of Bonham and Autry) painted by various artists as program illustrations for the annual Fiesta San Jacinto. Now hanging in the Alamo chapel, the Fiesta series includes some of the only known "portraits" (all conjectural) of the men of the Alamo—Jacob Darst, Tapley Holland, Robert Evans, Green B. Jameson, and others. (Courtesy The Alamo—Daughters of the Republic of Texas)

markably little record of their experiences inside the besieged fort. Unlike the heroic messenger of ancient Marathon, who had the good grace to expire after speaking his piece, these men survived to lead ordinary lives. Their memoirs, when they exist, tend to play upon their relationships to the "Great Ones" rather than on their own accomplishments, to focus on their perilous passages through the lines while revealing little of conditions inside the doomed fort.[7]

That these men should be so reticent suggests a certain embarrassment toward not having shared in their colleagues' glorious deaths. Potter took great pains to point out that Seguín's departure was not of his own choosing, while Williams elaborated the tale further, relating how Travis called for couriers but got no response, "so lots were cast" and the "die fell upon Seguín." Other writers have been equally careful to avoid even the slightest suggestion of disloyalty, emphasizing that the couriers were "unable" to return in time for the final battle.[8]

In addition to the couriers, actual combat survivors who turned up elsewhere shortly after the battle are mentioned in early references: Henry Warnell, escaping to Port Lavaca only to die there of his Alamo wounds; two unnamed refugees, one wounded, bringing Nacogdoches a report of the "general massacre" a full week before the official news arrived. Another defender, Mexican-born Brigido Guerrero, apparently survived by claiming to have been a Texas prisoner held in the Alamo against his will.[9]

The most well-known male survivor, Travis's Negro slave Joe, was evidently spared by the Mexicans as a conscious signal of their opposition to slavery, which had been legally prohibited throughout the Republic. Joe was dispatched with Susanna Dickinson to notify Sam Houston of Santa Anna's victory, and he subsequently testified before the Texas cabinet. Being black, Joe had little opportunity to share in the glory of his comrades; in 1837 he was the object of a manhunt when he fled Texas for the Travis family home in Alabama. Many writers have downplayed Joe's role, portraying him as a cringing noncombatant, but recent black historians have used the same bare facts to recreate a plausible image of Joe as a full-fledged member of the garrison. At least two other blacks figure in the Alamo legend. Less fortunate and less well-known than Joe, a second slave named John perished in the battle after being left in the Alamo when his owner, San Antonio merchant Francis De Sauque, rode out on courier duty. Jim Bowie is also widely reported to have had a slave, variously called Ben, Sam, or Ham, but this character is apparently a confusion with Mexican officer Juan Almonte's black cook, Ben, who was sent as an escort with Mrs. Dickinson to Gonzales.[10]

The Defender of the Alamo, dressed in buckskins and armed with a long rifle, in an oil painting by Dallas-born western artist Joe Ruiz Grandee. (From the collection of Mr. and Mrs. Jack L. Erickson)

The most controversial Alamo survivor is certainly Louis "Moses" Rose, the only defender who refused to cross Travis's famous "Death Line." Instead, he climbed over the Alamo walls, slipped through enemy lines, and vanished into the night. Several weeks later, he appeared in East Texas, where he recounted his experiences to the Abraham Zubers. By the time their son, William P. Zuber, eventually retold the family story, the Alamo legend had been firmly established by historians like Henderson Yoakum and Reuben Potter. Many Texans refused to accept the possibility of any deserters.[11] The real obstacle to incorporating the Rose story into the Alamo legend, however, has never been its dubious historical provenance or the lack of confirmation by other eyewitnesses, but rather its juxtaposition of selfless patriotism with self-interested pragmatism.[12] Escape clearly runs counter to the Alamo tradition. When Senator John F. Kennedy visited the Alamo, he is said to have asked to leave through the back door in order to avoid the throngs gathered in front. "Senator," he was told, "there is no back door. That's why there were so many heroes." Many versions of the Alamo legend feature Travis's line in the dust but ignore Rose's dissent. In John Wayne's *Alamo* no one flinches: "To the last man, they chose to stay."[13]

Symbolically, Rose is the "arch-coward of Texas history," a cowering, yellow sneak who disgraces himself by whining, un-Texanlike: "I can't. I don't want to die." Only a few accounts attempt to excuse his actions. In Robert Penn Warren's *Remember the Alamo*, 1958, Rose is not really a soldier but a businessman, accidentally trapped inside the fortress. Universal's 1953 film *Man from the Alamo* features an unwilling deserter chosen by lot to return home and look after his comrades' soon-to-be fatherless families.[14]

The most famous family left fatherless by the Mexicans was that of artillery captain Almeron Dickinson, whose wife Susanna and infant daughter Angelina were apparently the only Anglo-American females then in San Antonio. Having accompanied Dickinson from their home in Gonzales in the months before the siege, they withdrew with him into the Alamo for safety. Remaining with the garrison throughout the siege and final assault, Susanna Dickinson became the only adult Anglo-Texan to witness the entire encounter and survive. She evidently aided in caring for the garrison's sick and wounded but took no active part in the fighting, being secluded in one of the small rooms of the church during the final assault. Her very presence inside the Alamo, however, has been sufficient to guarantee her recognition as a preeminent Texas heroine. Until Yelvington's inclusion of the widows of Gonzales in *A Cloud of Witnesses*, Susanna Dickinson rep-

Scene from John Wayne's *The Alamo*. Travis's servant Joe—described by many nineteenth-century sources as a "slave boy" despite his adult age—in John Wayne's movie becomes indeed a young boy, "Happy Sam," shown here accompanying Susanna Dickinson (Joan O'Brien) and her daughter (Aissa Wayne) out of the Alamo after the battle. (United Artists, 1960) ◄

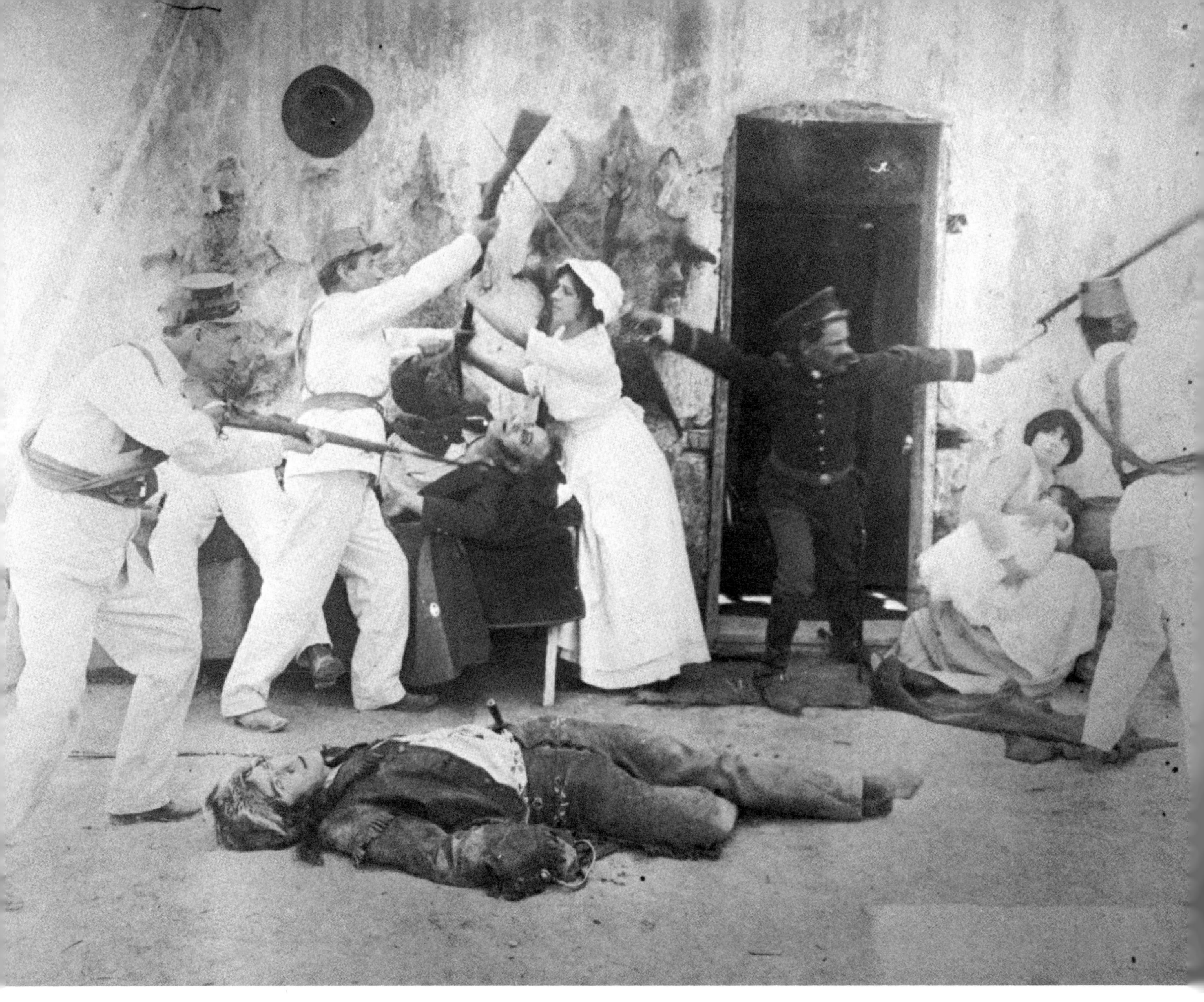

resented the only historically authentic role through which generations of subsequent Texan women could vicariously participate in the Alamo experience.

Historically, her testimony provides the principal—often the only—evidence for certain incidents of the fight: Robert Evans's unsuccessful attempt to blow up the powder magazine, Galba Fuqua's efforts to speak through shattered jaws, and the brutal bayonetings of gunner Jacob Walker and the two young Wolfe brothers, mistaken in the melee for adult soldiers. As an Anglo-American, Dickinson's testimony was held by contemporaries in higher regard than that of the other survivors—a Negro and several Tejanos.[15] Her arrival in Gonzales on March 13 was considered the first "authoritative account" of the fall, even though two Tejanos had arrived with this news two days earlier. As accounts of the battle fanned out across the countryside, Dickinson's name appeared frequently—sometimes attached to statements that seem to have been Joe's and often described as the battle's sole survivor.[16]

From a literary and dramatic standpoint, Susanna Dickinson provides an important feminine foil to the otherwise entirely male cast. She and her daughter add an element of human interest that would otherwise be lacking and by their presence give individual identity to the husband and father, Almeron Dickinson. Without them, he would probably be but one among many; with his family present, he becomes a leading character.

Susanna Dickinson's surviving statements on the battle date from many years afterward and actually reveal very little of her own activities. Although the horror of her experience is almost beyond comprehension—listening helplessly to gunfire and the clash of weapons all around, engulfed in dark and smoke, waiting in silence to be discovered, walking out amidst blood and carnage, riding miles through unsettled territory to Gonzales, tending all the while to the needs of a fifteen-month-old baby—some writers have felt compelled to embroider the story, making the Alamo's heroine still more heroic. Potter seems to have originated the rumor that she was pregnant at the time of the battle, while Barnes reported that she actually gave birth during the siege. Frank Templeton told an even more curious tale, in which the Dickinsons had two children—a boy and a girl. When the captain, manning a gun on the roof of the church, saw Evans carrying a torch toward the powder room, he "sprang for the parapet, snatching his son from a doorway as he went, and leaped for the moat below! But a volley from the enemy struck them both, and father and son fell dead in the bloody water of the ditch." Before Mrs. Dickinson even arrived in Gonzales, Houston had heard rumors of her husband's leap to death, and the story figures independently in at least two eyewitness accounts. Evi-

Alamo women resisting the final attack, scene from Gaston Melies' *The Immortal Alamo*, 1911, the first known Alamo movie. To the right, Mrs. Dickinson shields her child from an upraised Mexican bayonet. (Star Film Ranch, 1911. Courtesy Daughters of the Republic of Texas Library at the Alamo, San Antonio)

The Esparza family entering the Alamo, by Thom Ricks, ca. 1981. Enrique Esparza, eleven years old at the time of the siege, later recalled his family's arrival at the fort at twilight, only to find the gates already barred, and his mother's dauntless refusal to leave his father, Gregorio, as the siege wore on. Gregorio Esparza died at his gun, but his family survived and was released after a brief confinement and interrogation by Santa Anna. (Courtesy University of Texas Institute of Texan Cultures at San Antonio)

dently some "unfortunate father" and son did perish in this manner, but their identities remain a mystery. Mrs. Dickinson in her various interviews not only never mentioned a son but also emphatically denied the entire episode.[17]

Like the Dickinsons, several Tejano families also withdrew into the Alamo for safety when the fighting began. While the Dickinsons' heroism is legendary, however, the Tejanos' has been almost forgotten. There were at least two—possibly three—infants in the fort during the siege, but there is only one "Babe of the Alamo" Anglo-Texan Angelina Dickinson. The only Tejano women mentioned with any regularity in traditional Alamo stories are those with a significant Anglo-Texan link, the adopted sisters of Ursula de Veramendi Bowie: Juana de Navarro Alsbury and her younger sister Gertrudis de Navarro.

Madam Candelaria and the Alamo in a late-nineteenth-century cabinet photograph by San Antonio photographer Robinson. As this souvenir indicates, the century-old woman was of "considerable interest to tourists." (Photograph courtesy Daughters of the Republic of Texas Library at the Alamo, San Antonio. Quotation from Elfer, *Madam Candelaria*)

Juan Seguín and Flaca, in John Wayne's *The Alamo*. The main Tejano characters in Wayne's movie are clearly based on historical models. The middle-aged Tejano leader Juan Seguín (Joseph Calleia) is really more like his father, don Erasmo, while Graciela Carmela María "Flaca" de López y Véjar (Linda Cristal) is evidently patterned after Andrea Castañon Ramírez Villanueva—Madam Candelaria. Like Candelaria, the fictional Flaca had been born in Mexico but fled to Texas to embrace the republican cause after seeing her husband killed by Mexican armies. Unlike Candelaria, however, who would have been over fifty years old at the time of the battle, Flaca is a young Castilian beauty in the Ursula de Veramendi tradition. (United Artists, 1960)

(Also present was the former's son, Alijo Pérez.) In many accounts, Juana de Navarro, whose first and third husbands were both named Pérez, is frequently referred to simply as Mrs. Horace Alsbury (her second husband's name), with no indication of her Hispanic ancestry.[18]

The other Tejano survivors are known almost solely through the recollections of Enrique Esparza, who was but a young boy at the time of the siege. Esparza enumerated as survivors himself, his mother Anna Salazar Esparza, unnamed brothers and baby sister, an old woman named "Doña Petra [Gonzáles]," a beautiful girl named Trinidad Saucedo, the Dickinsons, the Navarros, and "several other women, young girls, and little boys." San Antonio historian Charles Stanford, writing about 1906, added several persons to this list but unfortunately failed to record his sources for their presence: Concepción Losoya, wife of Alamo defender José Toribio Losoya; their two sons and a daughter; Señora Vitono de Saline and three girls; and possibly Madam Candelaria, who claimed to have been Jim Bowie's nurse during the siege.[19]

Like Moses Rose, Candelaria does not appear in the Alamo legend until many years after the battle, and her story has been frequently discredited because of its discrepancies and lack of confirmation by other survivors. Yet there is no conclusive contradiction of her story either. Esparza did not, as Williams contended, "emphatically" deny her presence; he merely stated that "I do not remember having seen Madame Candelaria there. She may have been. . . . I did not notice the women as closely as I did the men."[20] Whether authentic or a pretender, Candelaria is easily the best-known Tejano woman associated with the Alamo. While the others left little public record of their experiences, Candelaria reminisced freely and even sat for souvenir photographs. Thus she emerged as the only viable symbolic counterpart to Anglo-Texan heroine Susanna Dickinson. Unlike Mrs. Dickinson's perpetually youthful and Madonna-like popular image, Candelaria became famous as an aged crone, suggesting the even older mythological tradition of "the eternal mother."[21]

Other Tejano heroines of the Alamo are entirely fictional and even less plausible than Candelaria. The most popular has been the beautiful young Castilian maiden—seductive, light-skinned and dark-eyed—cast in the historical shadow of Jim Bowie's renowned bride Ursula de Veramendi. Although dead of cholera over two years before the Texas revolution, Veramendi herself figures in many fictional versions of the story, "a woman of the Alamo even though in her grave." The beautiful Ursulita and her fictional descendants—Josefa in *The Grito*, 1904, Flaca in John Wayne's *Alamo* epic, or Consuela

Scene from John Wayne's *The Alamo*. A Texan raiding party returns with a herd of longhorn cattle stolen from a Mexican camp. Such provisions, which Travis had jubilantly reported "found" at the beginning of the siege, were generally confiscated from local Tejanos. (United Artists, 1960) ▶

in *The Last Command*, 1955—represent the stereotypical view of Hispanic women held by Anglo-Americans since the earliest days of cultural contact in the old Southwest. While Hispanic men were seen, in the words of one historian, as "lazy, ignorant, bigoted, superstitious, cheating, thieving, gambling, cruel, sinister, cowardly half-breeds," Hispanic women, perhaps in part because of the scarcity of white women on the frontier, were described as handsome, kind, sociable, generous, graceful, and intelligent.[22]

This prejudice against Hispanic men was evidently shared by many Anglo-Texans at the Alamo. In January 1836, the garrison elected its own delegates, Samuel Maverick and Jesse Badgett, to the convention at Washington-on-the-Brazos. Several contemporary letters attest to the Anglo-Texan soldiers' concern that the four local delegates, all Tejanos, would not adequately represent its pro-independence views. The most eloquent and influential spokesman for this prejudice was undoubtedly Travis, who remained openly distrustful of Mexican men despite considerable intimacies with local Mexican women. Travis considered his military assignment to Béxar as "going off into the enemy's country," and in contrast to his predecessors, Neill and Bowie, his personal observations there did little to reassure him. In January, Neill had predicted optimistically that "we can rely on great aid from the citizens of this town in case of an attack. They have no money here, but Don Jasper [Gaspar] Flores and Louisiano Navaro have offered us all their goods Groceries, and Beeves, for the use and support of the army." Bowie likewise believed that "the citizens of Béxar have behaved well." It is not these commendations, however, but Travis's harsh criticisms of the Tejano populace that have been popularly remembered.[23]

During the month of February, many of the Tejanos who had fought in the earlier siege of Béxar had departed with honorable discharges, and many of the townspeople had retired to outlying ranchos for safety. Travis clearly viewed these actions harshly. However, many Anglo-Texans were also discharged during this interregnum, returning after their initial period of service to tend to their families and prepare for the spring farming season. Nor were the Bexareños alone in seeking safety for their families. Among the few Anglo-Americans then resident in the city, John W. Smith made preparations to evacuate his wife, María de Jesús Curbelo, while storekeeper Nat Lewis abandoned his stock and headed east, declaring that "he was not a fighting man, he was a business man."[24]

There is considerable evidence that many Tejanos did endeavor to remain neutral in the revolutionary conflict, or at least maintained an appearance of neutrality irre-

Title page of the *Representación*, a political petition drafted by the town council, or *ayuntamiento*, of San Antonio de Béxar in December 1832. This important document, of which only two printed copies are presently known, testifies to the Tejano role in events leading to the Texas revolution. Like the Anglo-American colonists, the Tejanos expressed numerous grievances against the state government of Coahuila y Texas; unlike the former, however, the Bexareños pressed for internal reforms rather than for the complete political separation of Texas. (DeGolyer Library)

REPRESENTACION

DIRIJIDA POR EL

ILUSTRE AYUNTAMIENTO

DE LA CIUDAD DE BEXAR AL

HONORABLE CONGRESO DEL ESTADO,

MANIFESTANDO LOS MALES QUE AFLIJEN LOS PUEBLOS DE TEXAS, Y LOS AGRAVIOS QUE HAN SUFRIDO DESDE LA REUNION DE ESTOS CON COAHUILA.

AYUNTAMIENTO DE BEXAR.

Esta Corporacion penetrada en esta vez, lo mismo que otras muchas de los imponderables males que en todas épocas ha sufrido este vecindario en union de los demas Pueblos del Departamento, así por la destructora guerra de los barbaros sus implacables enemigos, como por la desatencion de nuestros gobernantes en todos tiempos, tuvo á bien acordar en sesion ordinaria de 6 del corriente, que nombrandose una comision compuesta de dos individuos de su seno, y cuatro mas de fuera de él, se ocupase en estender una muy enérgica representacion, dirijida al Honorable Con-

spective of their private loyalties. As José Rodríguez later commented, "My father was always in sympathy with the Texans, but had so far not taken up arms on either side." Many Texans, both then and later, have equated this neutrality with treason, believing with Travis that "those who have not joined us" must be against us. Travis's last letter reached the convention on March 6, as the delegates prepared to draft the new republican constitution; perhaps his exhortation that those who had not joined in the war should be forced to pay for it directly inspired the constitutional provision equating neutrality with treason: "All persons who shall leave the country for the purposes of evading a participation in the present struggle, or shall refuse to participate in it, or shall give aid or assistance to the present enemy, shall forfeit all rights of citizenship, and such lands as they may hold in the republic." Tejanos wishing to retain their property after the revolution were thus required to take an oath of allegiance to the war. Even those who had joined in the revolutionary cause, however, frequently found it difficult to secure the bounties legally due them. As Mexican-American historian David Weber has described this process of intimidation, "Since it was difficult to distinguish a loyal Mexican from a disloyal Mexican—especially for Anglo newcomers—it was expedient to assume that all Mexicans were disloyal."[25]

That many Bexareños should have remained neutral or even cooperated with the occupying forces is hardly surprising. Just three months earlier, many had seen their families endangered and their homes and possessions destroyed in house-to-house fighting during the siege of Béxar. And only two decades before, well within living memory, the city had been harshly punished for participating in an anti-Royalist uprising. Over three hundred citizens of Béxar had been executed in 1813 on the mere suspicion of republican tendencies, while several hundred women had been imprisoned and forced to grind corn and bake tortillas for General Arredondo's victorious army. Those who recalled Arredondo could hardly have expected better treatment from his former lieutenant, now His Excellency President Santa Anna.[26]

Nonetheless, many Tejanos did support the revolutionary cause. Francisco Ruiz, José Antonio Navarro, and Mexican-born patriot Lorenzo de Zavala joined in declaring the new nation's independence and in formulating its constitution. Gaspar Flores and Erasmo Seguín had also been elected to the convention and were only prevented from attending by the latter's illness and the former's untimely death. Militarily, Tejanos fought at Gonzales, Concepción, Béxar, the Alamo, and San Jacinto.[27] Several died at the Alamo. Juan Seguín's company of nine recruits apparently included Juan Abamillo, Antonio Cruz

Gregorio Esparza, painted by Cecil Lang Casebier for the 1951 Fiesta. Esparza's body was found lying near the cannon he had tended and, because his brother Francisco was serving in the Mexican army, was evidently the only one spared from the funeral pyre and allowed a Christian burial. (Courtesy The Alamo—Daughters of the Republic of Texas)

The *Veramendi Palace*, home of Jim Bowie's wife, from a painting, ca. 1900, by Tom Brown. This eighteenth-century stone house, one of early San Antonio's finest, survived until 1909 despite heavy damage suffered during the siege of Béxar. As they advanced from house to house during the siege, Texan forces dug up floors, piled furniture into barricades, and broke through walls to make portholes and passageways, while Mexican gunfire and cannonshot crashed through walls and doorways. Paul Wellman's Bowie novel, *The Iron Mistress*, evokes the resulting devastation. "The great cedar doors hung open. Bullet holes pocked the walls. At one place an ugly gap, large enough to permit the passage of men, had been torn in the side of the house. The interior, after the fighting and looting, was a chaos of wreckage." (From Barnes, *Combats and Conquests of Immortal Heroes*. DeGolyer Library) ◄

y Arocha, Juan Antonio Badillo, Gregorio Esparza, Antonio Fuentes, Alexandro de la Garza, Andrés Nava, Brigido (not José María) Guerrero, and José Toribio (not Domingo) Losoya. Seguín, Arocha, De la Garza, and Guerrero survived, the first three by being sent out as messengers. The other six members of Seguín's company fell by their weapons, as did two other young Tejanos: Carlos Espalier of Béxar, reputed to have been a protege of Jim Bowie, and Galba Fuqua of Gonzales. Anselmo Borgarra, who carried news of the fall to Houston at Gonzales, also claimed to have been inside the besieged fortress as Travis's servant.[28]

Tejanos also supported the revolutionary effort by volunteering for scouting and courier missions: José Cassiano, Blas Herrera, and others rode over the barren country between the Rio Grande and Béxar, carrying early warnings of Santa Anna's approach; Anselmo Borgarra, Andrés Barcena, and Antonio Pérez brought the first news of the fall to Anglo-Texas. In each instance, unwelcome news won the messengers scant recognition and little thanks. According to Sutherland, who was present at the Texan councils, "a majority declared that it [Herrera's report] was only the report of a Mexican, and entitled to no more consideration than many others of like character that were daily harangued throughout the country." Later Borgarra and Barcena were jailed for inciting panic in Gonzales with their "rumor" of the fall of the Alamo.[29]

Economically, the Bexareños contributed heavily to the war. For several months, both Texan and Mexican troops stationed near the city lived largely off the land, foraging for food raised by local residents. Sutherland later recalled that "their meat they obtained by driving the beef from the prairies just as they needed it." These cattle, like the "20 to 30 head of Beeves" and "80 to 90 bushels" of corn that Travis jubilantly reported "found" on the first day of the siege, were confiscated from local residents. Many families provided lodgings for the armies' officers. Others, like the Losoyas, who had been deeded old Indian houses on the Alamo grounds, were forced out of their homes for many months by military preparations and no doubt found them considerably damaged on their return. Numerous houses surrounding the Alamo were destroyed—either deliberately by raiding parties or accidentally in the course of battle. Since neither army had cash to pay for goods or services, Béxar (never a wealthy settlement) must have suffered heavy economic losses. In 1850 Gabriel Martínez submitted a claim for $170 in damages caused by the Texan's destruction of his dwelling and its contents (including corn and clothing).[30]

Quite a number of townsfolk apparently took refuge in the Alamo at the first appearance of the Mexican army but (like Nat Lewis) left before the final assault. Enrique

Most of the dwellings destroyed in the fighting around the Alamo were not expensive stone houses like the Veramendi Palace, but small *jacales* constructed of timber posts, hides, mud or clay plaster, reeds for straw thatch, and other cheap local materials. Although well adapted to the environment and the economic level of their residents, *jacales* seemed unfamiliar and primitive to Anglo-American observers. Late-nineteenth-century tourist guides and photographs, like this view by San Antonio photographer Jacobson, frequently emphasized the poverty and crudeness as "picturesque" features of Mexican life. (DeGolyer Library)

Juan Nepomuceno Seguín, on the cover of Jack Jackson's 1980 comic book *Tejano Exile*. A Texas artist credited with some of the earliest underground comics of the 1960s, Jackson uses the comic book format evocatively to portray, here and in *Recuerden El Alamo* and *Los Tejanos*, the "true story of Juan N. Seguín and the Texas Mexicans." Seguín's portrait, painted by Thomas Jefferson Wright in 1838, depicts the commandant of San Antonio in his Texas Army uniform before he resigned to serve in the Republican Senate. The original portrait now hangs in the Texas State Capitol. (Comic book, DeGolyer Library. Reproduced courtesy Jack Jackson)

Esparza maintained that they were openly offered safe passage and that those who left during this "armistice" included members of the Menchaca, Flores, Rodríguez, Ramírez, Arocha, and Silvero families. Whether open or clandestine, these departures increased Anglo-Texan resentment and provoked charges of treachery. Susanna Dickinson repeatedly asserted that a Mexican woman had deserted one night "and going over to the enemy informed them of our very inferior numbers, which Col. Travis said made them confident of success and emboldened them to make the final assault." Mexican sources confirm that information passed easily from the fort to the town throughout the siege but do not attribute this traffic to maliciousness on the part of the townspeople. They also contend that the woman informant had been purposely sent out by Travis with an offer of surrender on terms, but Texan authors have firmly rejected this possibility.[31]

The actions of Tejanos fighting for the Texan cause have been difficult for both Anglo-Americans and Hispanics to understand or accept. As Weber explains, "most Mexicans in Texas found themselves caught in a struggle between two cultures, not knowing whether to remain loyal to Mexico or become loyal to Texas—whether to be traitors to Mexico or traitors to Texas." Those who clung to old ties of family, nationality, language, religion, and tradition were branded as traitors by Anglo-Texans, while those who forsook their heritage in the name of abstract concepts such as liberty, equality, and democracy, or for more concrete advantages such as economic opportunity, ultimately found acceptance nowhere. In joining with the "Gringos," Weber argues, they became traitors to their homeland, "despised by Mexico" yet "forgotten by most Americans in Texas, who viewed all Mexicans as bad Mexicans."[32]

The best-known example of the Tejano dilemma is undoubtedly found in the life of Juan Seguín, leader of the small company of Tejanos who fought and died within the Alamo. At Stephen Austin's personal request, Seguín had in late 1835 recruited the Ninth Company, Second Regiment of Texas Volunteers. This Tejano cavalry company patrolled the countryside around Béxar, preventing Mexican reinforcements from reaching General Cos and also providing both foraging and scouting services. Seguín and his men—like the Tejano company formed by Plácido Benavides of Victoria—fought bravely beside the Anglo-Texans throughout the revolution.[33]

After the battle of San Jacinto, Seguín returned to San Antonio as military commandant. Like other landowners, both Tejano and Anglo-Texan, he found devastation in the wake of war, "their houses in ruins, their fields laid waste, and their cattle destroyed or dispersed. . . . what little was spared by the retreating enemy [Mexican] had been wasted by our own army." Worse misfortunes were yet to come. Seguín's actions as military commandant—requisitioning supplies and livestock and imposing law and order—produced resentment among both the native Tejanos and the Anglo-American immigrants who were arriving in increasing numbers. Although elected a Texas Senator in 1838 and Mayor of San Antonio three years later, Seguín faced mounting Anglo-Texan hostility after 1842, when he was suspected of collaborating with a Mexican raiding party led by General Rafael Vásquez. Seguín denied the rumors but was refused a formal court of inquiry and was forced into hiding. Feeling himself a victim of "dark intrigues" and a "foreigner in my native land," Seguín sought refuge in Mexico. When forced there to choose between prison or military service, Seguín returned to Texas as a Mexican officer under General Adrian Woll, assisted in temporarily retaking Béxar, and escorted back to Mexico numerous other Hispanic families who had found life in their homeland, now the Republic of Texas, no longer tolerable.[34] Although Seguín eventually returned to Texas, he never regained his position in society. Old Texas veterans, who had known him during the revolution, tended to be most tolerant of his personal tragedy. "Though he has since been charged with hostility to the Texan cause," wrote Sutherland, "he certainly did not manifest it at the time of which I am speaking. He manifested every desire for the success of the cause."[35]

Despite such apologies, Seguín remained largely a forgotten figure until fairly recently, and although better known today, he is still controversial. His greatest misfortune lay in his survival, which brought him into a world vastly changed and increasingly hostile, where the choices were no longer as clear or as heroic as Travis's ringing "Victory or Death!" Victory imposed an alien culture and second-class status on Seguín and his countrymen. Seguín's despair and bitterness were no doubt widely shared, but his defection had damaging implications for the entire Hispanic community in nineteenth-century Texas, for if so prominent and respected a citizen as Seguín could not be trusted, how much less could be expected of any Tejano? Nor has his conduct seemed wholly acceptable to modern Hispanics, who argue that casting Seguín as a hero represents an undesirable accommodationist approach to ethnic conflicts.[36]

Unlike Seguín, whose later conduct clouded his revolutionary heroism, the Alamo's more familiar leaders—William Barret Travis, James Bowie, and David Crockett—died at the peak of their glory, redeeming in that one moment any and all past misdeeds and eliminating the possibility of any future missteps. For most modern Americans, these three men epitomize the Alamo: Travis, the Byronic commander whose eloquent calls

Film crew shooting Alamo execution scene for Jesús S. Treviño's PBS production *Seguín*. A revisionist Chicano view of the Texas revolution, the film was shot—with intentional irony—on the set at Brackettville, Texas, built for John Wayne's "imperialist" version. Treviño's script for the execution of six defenders, seen against the wall to the left, follows Mexican accounts closely but carefully avoids the volatile question of Crockett's alleged presence among the captives. (PBS, 1982)

for aid have echoed through all of Texas history; Bowie, the Louisiana-born adventurer whose frontier exploits were already well known throughout the Southwest; Crockett, the legendary backwoods sharpshooter and former Congressman from Tennessee.

Largely because of their previous notoriety, Bowie and Crockett have long dominated popular Alamo imagery, greatly overshadowing Travis's pivotal historic role. As official commandant, Travis was the one who ultimately decided to stay and hold the fort rather than withdraw when it became evident that reinforcements would not arrive. Even more important than his military actions—for the Alamo legend and perhaps for the independence of Texas—were his ringing words: "To the People of Texas and All Americans in the world. . . . *I shall never surrender or retreat*. . . . VICTORY OR DEATH." Travis's

The only known portrait of William Barret Travis that may actually have been drawn from life. Wiley Martin's sketch appeared in Frank Templeton's 1907 novel *Margaret Ballentine.* Although dated 1835, Templeton claimed to have found the portrait "on a fly leaf of a copy of a gazetteer of Tennessee, published in 1834." The creator of the sketch, Wiley Martin, was an early Texas settler and active figure in the Anáhuac disturbances of 1832, where he may have become acquainted with Travis. (DeGolyer Library)

appeal for aid has been repeated countless times in histories, schoolbooks, poems, and other versions of the Alamo tale and is considered by Texans the "most heroic document among American historical records." Travis's letters gave voice, definition, and persuasive power to what would have otherwise been a silent and even less comprehensible sacrifice. Travis's words also helped to legitimize the Texan struggle, linking it to the American Revolution by echoing Patrick Henry's famous cry, "Liberty or Death."[37]

Unlike many of his contemporaries, Travis was a literary, well-read man, steeped in history and in the romantic ideals of his day. According to his diary, his readings in 1833–34 included novels by Sir Walter Scott, histories of England and ancient Greece, biographies of Napoleon and Josephine, and various romances of the American frontier. He was also apparently well acquainted with Lord Byron's poetry, which so vividly expressed the libertarian ideals of the romantic movement. Thus, while many other Texans could no doubt have matched Travis's steely resolve on the walls of the Alamo, few could have been so well suited to enunciate it.[38]

Despite his central role in the Alamo legend, however, Travis has rarely been the primary subject of popular fiction, children's books, adventure stories, television shows, or comic books. His popular image is, in fact, quite negative, due largely to film portrayals of him as an impetuous, hot-headed, arrogant, and slightly foppish aristocrat, antithetical to the true spirit of democracy represented by Bowie and Crockett.

Travis's words indelibly shaped the Alamo legend, yet he is rarely depicted in the act of writing them. The most popular Texan heroes have traditionally been men of action—tough, powerful fighters—rather than men of letters, and so Travis appears most frequently with sword, not pen, in hand. The most popular image of him is unquestionably that evoked by Moses Rose's tale of the line drawn in the dust. "Col. Travis then drew his sword, and with its point traced a line upon the ground, extending from the right to the left of the file. Then, resuming his position in front of the centre, he said, 'I now want every man who is determined to stay here and die with me to come across this line. Who will be first? March!' "[39]

Nineteenth-century writers greeted the story of the line, first emerging in print over a generation after its supposed occurrence, with varying degrees of credulity. The prominent poet and essayist Sidney Lanier, writing a historical sketch of San Antonio for *Southern Magazine* in 1873, popularized the tale by quoting at length William Zuber's account of the episode. Questions arose immediately. How could Rose—a Frenchman speaking only "broken English"—have understood, much less remembered Travis's

Frieze at base of San Jacinto Monument in Houston, carved by William McVey, 1936–39. (Photograph reproduced courtesy Robert Reynolds, Portland, Oregon)

"There is still time to escape! Let those who choose to stay and die with me step across this line!" —COL. WILLIAM B. TRAVIS, AT THE ALAMO, MARCH 3, 1836.

Print, ca. 1900–35, by Canadian-born illustrator Norman Price. Travis watches his men march, single file, across the famous line. (Courtesy Daughters of the Republic of Texas Library at the Alamo, San Antonio)

Fess Parker as Davy Crockett, left, and Kenneth Tobey as the ailing Jim Bowie, right. Travis (Don Megowan) draws his sword through the dust of the Alamo courtyard in a scene from Walt Disney's *Davy Crockett, King of the Wild Frontier*. (Buena Vista, 1955) ▶

lengthy oration? Zuber, the intermediary, later conceded that he had made up much of the speech himself based on information from Rose.[40]

Many later writers have argued that such a grand gesture would have been characteristic of the "inward burning" Travis. Others have disagreed violently. "No one can imagine that Travis in the presence of friends would deliver a set Ciceronian address—he was a man of deeds, not words, as all heroes are. . . . that story of the drawing of the line is too theatrical to be accepted." Others have questioned whether the haughty Travis—as he has so often been portrayed—would really have risked so much on the loyalty of the common men he was said to have scorned. A modern-day film parody suggests the risks involved, as fictional Mexican General Maximilian Rodriguez de Santos briefly retakes the Alamo in *Viva Max!*, 1969. Mistakenly using his boot heel (as he had observed an Alamo guide demonstrate earlier) to draw a line in the dust, General Max offers his men a similar choice of staying or leaving. He does not realize they stay only at the armed insistence of his aide.[41]

Despite continued challenges to its authenticity, the line persists as one of the most enduring images in all of Texas history, appearing in serious chronicles as well as paperback romances, children's books, movies, and comic strips. It is dramatically the high point of the Alamo story—the moment of destiny and decision upon which all else hinges. Thus the circumstances, characters, and specific words may vary, but the stark essence of the choice remains unchanged. Comic versions in particular may depart markedly from the established account, adjusting roles to fit the hero of the moment.

Controversy also surrounds Travis's death. His servant Joe claimed to have seen the commander shot down from the wall during the first assault. "As Travis sat wounded on the ground, General Mora . . . made a blow at him with his sword, which Travis struck up, and ran his assailant through the body, and both died on the same spot." Mexican officers also credited Travis with a hero's death, but another persistent tradition holds that he stabbed or shot himself, "to prevent himself from falling into the hands of the enemy." This story originated with the earliest reports of the fall of the Alamo, relayed to Sam Houston at Gonzales by local Tejanos. Houston repeated this secondhand information, as well as other evidently erroneous reports of suicides by Bowie and Dickinson, in various letters sent to Goliad, Nacogdoches, and Washington-on-the-Brazos. The suicide story then spread rapidly eastward in a letter written by convention delegate Andrew Briscoe, gaining credence with each newspaper printing. Joe's version of his

Avon's 1951 comic book *Davy Crockett, Frontier Fighter* depicting a fully uniformed Travis drawing an invisible line across a plank floor. Travis, like Bowie, is gravely ill, leaving Davy Crockett in effective command of the garrison. This story—appearing in numerous Davy Crockett comics—evidently derives from Constance Rourke's 1934 folklore biography of the coonskin-clad Congressman. (From the collection of Paul A. Hutton)

master's death, in contrast, did not reach Houston, the convention, or the public until after the suicide rumors.[42]

Although Joe's account of his master's heroic death is corroborated by Mexican eyewitnesses, the suicide story persists and is certainly one factor in Travis's negative image. In a mid-1970s study of Texas nationalism, Mark Nackmann accused Travis of "egocentricity and lofty self-dramatization," combining a "romantic vision . . . with suicidal impulses." Novelist James Wakefield Burke echoed this view in a fictional speech by Bowie to Travis: "You, Bill, damn you, have got some kind of death notion. You came to Texas seeking the arms of death. . . . You'll go to hell in a blaze of glory."[43]

Travis has always attracted both adamant critics and fervent apologists, for he was a man to encourage no lukewarm responses. Texan pioneer Noah Smithwick contended that "Bill Travis . . . was a good fighter; but, had not the qualities necessary to a commander, else he never would have allowed himself to be penned up in the Alamo." Most nineteenth-century chroniclers, however, disagreed. "The patriot soldier who would form himself upon the most perfect model, need not look beyond the letters and the example of Travis." More recently, popular Texas historian T. R. Fehrenbach characterized Travis as "one of those most fortunate of men; on the grim stone walls of the Alamo he had found his time and place."[44]

For Jim Bowie the Alamo was but the last in a long series of colorful frontier adventures. Growing up in the turbulent bayou country along the Mississippi River in Louisiana, Bowie earned a formidable reputation as a game hunter, fortune hunter, alligator wrestler, horse tamer, gambler, and above all, knife fighter. He moved restlessly from one adventure to the next, killing an opponent in a brutal knife fight known as the "Sandbar Duel," dabbling in some highly questionable land deals, smuggling slaves with the notorious Gold Coast pirate Jean Lafitte, searching for the famed lost silver mine of San Saba. He made and lost several fortunes but retained his reputation as a gentleman and man of honor. He reputedly spoke both French and Spanish and moved as easily through New Orleans society as through the rough settlements of the bayous or the Texas frontier. His marriage to Ursula de Veramendi, daughter of the wealthy vice-governor of Mexican Texas, brought him into close association with all the leading families of northern Mexico. He converted to Catholicism and became a Mexican citizen but continued his restless adventure-seeking. During an 1831 expedition to San Saba, he and his brother Rezin with 9 companions held off an attack by over 160 Indians, killing or wounding 70 in one of the most desperate Indian fights in Texas history.[45]

Unlike the fictional Bowie of John Wayne's *Alamo*, who urged abandoning the fort to carry out a guerilla-style harassment campaign against the Mexican army, the historical Jim Bowie was the one to make the initial decision to stay and fight. It remained largely for others to carry out this resolve, however, as Bowie fell prey to debilitating illness. Somewhat surprisingly, Bowie's conspicuous absence from the ramparts has rarely detracted from his heroism. "The very fact that Bowie was desperately ill made his death supremely courageous in the eyes of men and the manner of his death, as variously narrated, became a symbol of Texan courage. If the defenders of Texas fought from their very death beds, how could they be defeated?"[46]

Perhaps because "there is nothing colorful or romantic about [ordinary] illness," Bowie's ailment has long eluded specific identification. He is generally believed to have

Ruth Conerly Zachrisson's 1953 Fiesta painting. Zachrisson depicts the most common version of Travis's death, generally as recounted by his slave Joe: fatally wounded but with sword thrust toward his attacker, he falls back against a cannon barrel. In his head is the single bullet wound described by Francisco Ruiz, Alcalde of Béxar, who was ordered by Santa Anna to identify the dead bodies of the Texan leaders. Travis's appearance here echoes the well-known "portrait" by Henry McArdle, which was in turn a frankly idealized likeness, painted late in the nineteenth century and based on a photograph of Martin D. McHenry of Shelbyville, Kentucky, who was reputed to have been a Travis look-alike. (Courtesy The Alamo—Daughters of the Republic of Texas) ◀

Portrait of Jim Bowie, probably a nineteenth-century book illustration after an oil painting attributed to George P. A. Healy, ca. 1831–34. This portrait, probably painted on one of Bowie's trips to the East Coast, shows him fashionably attired in dark frock coat with flaring cuffs, white shirt, and dark stock. The prominent American-born artist Benjamin West, who is frequently credited with portraits of Bowie, Crockett, and other Texan heroes, actually died in England in 1820 after a sixty-year absence from the United States. The original Bowie portrait remains in family hands, although copies hang at the Alamo and the Texas State Capitol. (Courtesy Archives Division, Texas State Library)

suffered from some mysterious but deadly ailment described variously as tuberculosis, pneumonia, typhoid, or typhoid pneumonia. Dr. Sutherland, who had personally assisted Alamo surgeon Amos Pollard in caring for the garrison's sick, later commented that Bowie's disease, "being of a peculiar nature, was not to be cured by an ordinary course of treatment." Other writers have pictured Bowie as a broken man, heartsick from his wife's death and physically worn-out by years of hard drinking and hard living. Yet another popular version of Bowie's last days holds that although ill, he was removed from action only by a tragic accident, a fall from an artillery rampart that resulted in crushed ribs, punctured lungs, broken hip, or other clearly disabling injuries. This persistent story first appeared in Potter's 1860 article on the fall of the Alamo and is not corroborated by any first-person accounts. Potter later recanted the story, writing in 1878 that "Bowie was stricken by an attack of pneumonia." By then, however, the story of Bowie's fall was firmly entrenched, eliminating the need to believe that any ordinary illness could have felled so extraordinary a mortal.[47]

Even more mystery surrounds Bowie's actual moment of death. The most popular version holds that he waited in his sickbed in a small interior chamber, weapons at his side as the din outside peaked and then diminished, poised to slay the first Mexicans

Jim Bowie, The West's Greatest Fighter, a Charlton comic book of 1956. Bowie—not Bonham—dashes into the besieged fort through a stream of gunfire, and Crockett—not Bowie or Travis—commands the garrison. Many of the individual characters in this comic are closely modeled on Dell's *Walt Disney's Davy Crockett at the Alamo*, 1955. (From the collection of Paul A. Hutton)

The Death of Bowie, by Louis Betts, popular American illustrator of the early twentieth century, published in *McClure's Magazine*, January 1902. In the accompanying article, "David Crockett and the Most Desperate Defense in American History," Cyrus T. Brady describes the grim toll of Bowie's last moments: "a trail of stricken soldiers reaches from the door to the bedside. And one bolder than the rest lies on Bowie's breast, with that awful American knife buried deep in his heart." (Fondren Library, Southern Methodist University)

who burst in upon him. "Bowie, propped on his pillows, shot two soldiers who attempted to bayonet him as he lay all but helpless and plunged his terrible knife into the throat of another before they could finish him." Like his comrades on the walls, the dying Bowie was still capable of inflicting fearful casualties, climaxing in a final thrust of his famous knife.[48]

Other writers liken Bowie's death to martyrdom by emphasizing the sick man's helplessness and the brutality of his assailants. "Colonel Bowie was butchered on his bed and hoisted on the bayonets and his remains savagely mutilated," wrote William Brooker in 1897, echoing the account related years earlier by Bowie's sister-in-law Juana de Navarro Alsbury.[49] And from William Zuber, source of the Moses Rose story, came the most savage version of Bowie's death, which Zuber claimed to have heard from a former Mexican fifer named Apolinario Saldigna. After the funeral pyre had been prepared, Saldigna related, Mexican orderlies carried out the sick Bowie, untouched by the fighting. The Mexican officer in charge then berated Bowie for his betrayal of his Mexican citizenship and family, to which Bowie replied defiantly. The officer consequently "caused four of his minions to hold the sick man, while a fifth, with a sharp knife, split his mouth, cut off his tongue, and threw it upon the pile of dead men." Then, "the four soldiers who held him, lifted the writhing body of the mutilated, bleeding, tortured invalid from his cot, and pitched him alive upon the funeral pyre."[50]

Like Travis, Bowie was at first rumored to have committed suicide, and Mexican chroniclers, knowing his reputation as a fighter, scorned to find him in bed. "That perverse and haughty James Bowie died like a woman, in bed, almost hidden by covers," wrote an anonymous Mexican soldier, possibly José Juan Sánchez Navarro. These contemporary condemnations have had little effect on Bowie's popular image, however, as Dobie explains, "Imagination and patriotic sympathy rebel at the idea of Bowie's dying except in the climax of hand-to-hand combat."[51]

Although absolutely central to the Bowie legend, the "knife" is symbolically a two-edged sword. Generally described as a heavy curved blade ten inches long and two inches broad, made of the finest alloy (preferably Damascus or meteorite steel) with a hard bone or horn handle well guarded from the blade, it is perhaps the sole American equivalent of legendary swords like Arthur's "Excalibur," Siegmund's "Gram," or Roland's "Durandal."[52] To modern audiences, however, Bowie's reputation as a knife-man (perhaps, as Dobie suggests, "out of proportion to established facts") imparts strong connotations of nonrespectability. In the years after Bowie's death, pistols gradually replaced knives

Scene from John Wayne's *The Alamo*. Richard Widmark as Jim Bowie parries a Mexican bayonet with his knife as death approaches. His black servant Jethro, a fictional character freed on the battle's eve, lies already dead before his master, his body pierced by two bayonets intended for Bowie. (United Artists, 1960) ◄

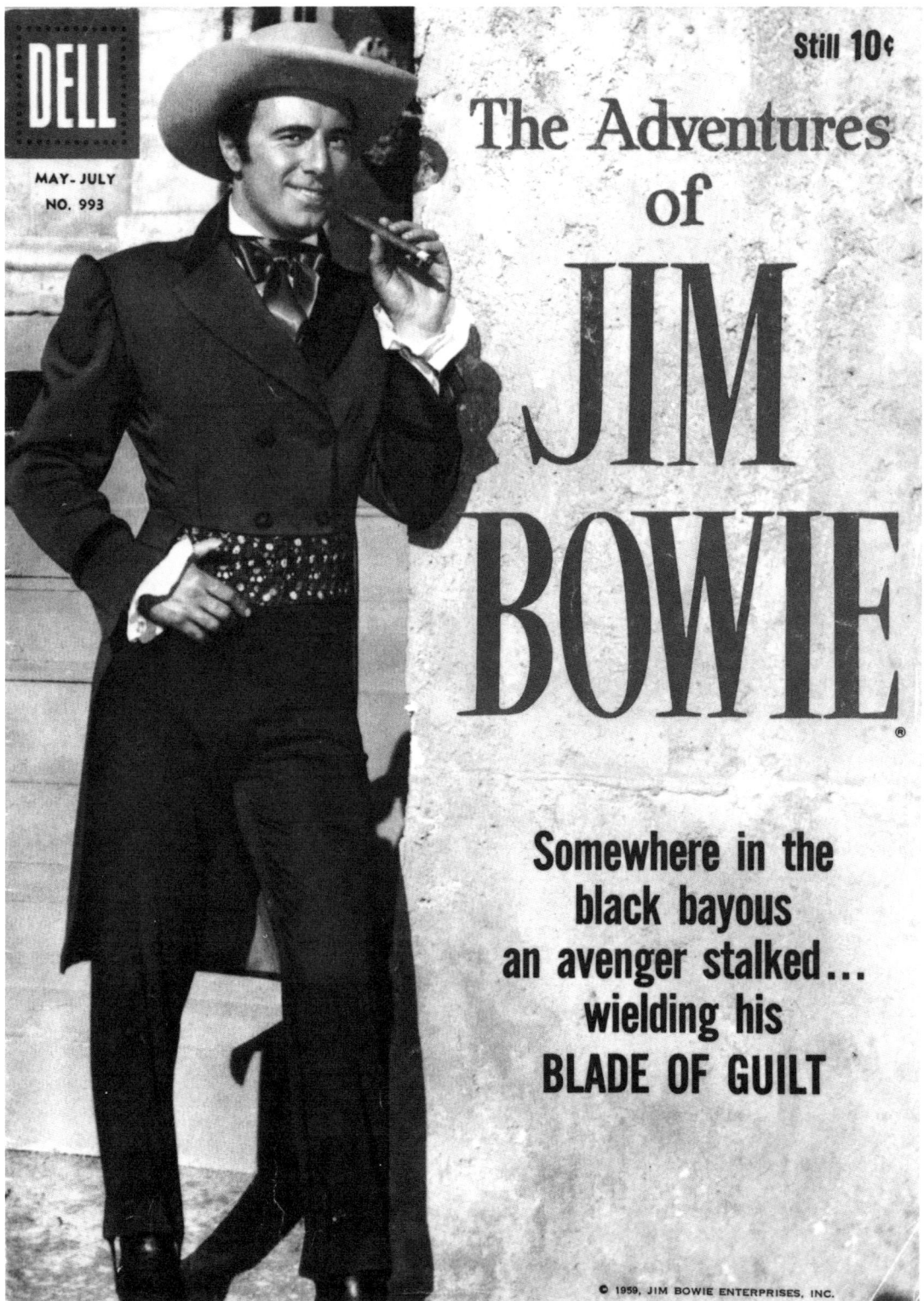

Jim Bowie, as portrayed by English actor Scott Forbes, on the cover of a 1959 Dell comic book. Forbes's short-lived ABC television series, 1956–58, failed after producers decided the Bowie knife was a bad influence on American youth. (From the collection of Paul A. Hutton)

as personal weapons, and the lethal use of knives became gradually associated with "the criminal element." Thus Bowie remains permanently an adult hero, a man's man well suited to an *Esquire* centerfold but less acceptable for juvenile audiences. A Jim Bowie television series, produced in the wake of Walt Disney's immensely popular Davy Crockett features, folded abruptly after two years when its star, Scott Forbes, resigned, complaining that "the producers and the sponsors decided it would be dangerous for kids to see a knife on T.V."[53]

The character portrayed by Forbes—like most characterizations of Bowie—was an attractive man, educated, urbane, and well mannered, yet tough and ruthless when necessary. History and legend have been kind to Bowie, and his image remains overwhelmingly positive, emerging as the leader of the Alamo band in *Last Command* and in other versions of the story. Edward Sears, one of Bowie's few critics, asserts that the lack of concrete biographical information has been a major factor in his popularity, since "it was impossible for those first biographers to learn much about Bowie, and therefore it seemed safe enough to make him the outstanding figure of the Texas Revolution." Even Dobie, one of Bowie's most sympathetic biographers, has likened him to classical heroes who chose to or were compelled to die at the right time. "No *deus ex machina* in Greek tragedy ever extricated a character from peril more neatly than the Alamo extricated Bowie from defeat in life and from tarnish of reputation. For the popular mind, particularly of posterity, the Alamo blocked out all but the heroic and noble from the records."[54]

For most modern Americans, the preeminent Alamo hero is Davy Crockett, thanks largely to a media and merchandising blitz of the mid-1950s. Sparked by a wildly popular series of Walt Disney television features, Crockett-mania swept across the country, eventually resulting in a full-length movie, hit recordings, a syndicated cartoon strip, comic books, bubblegum cards, and hundreds of thousands of spin-off products. Scores of Crockett books sold as fast as they could be rushed through the presses: reprints of the Colonel's own autobiography, adult and juvenile biographies, stampbooks and coloring books, even a "Little Golden Book" for preschoolers. Models of the Alamo proliferated in play sets, board games, and punch-outs. "Davy, Davy Crockett, king of the wild frontier," blared out over the airwaves, indelibly imprinting the television show's theme song on millions of young listeners. "Mention Davy Crockett to any person who was over three years old in 1955," comments Crockett biographer Richard Hauck, "and the automatic response will be a quick rendition of this awesome refrain." Crockett star Fess Parker, a relatively unknown young actor, suddenly found himself the nation's idol, swamped with requests for public appearances in his buckskin jacket and coonskin cap.[55]

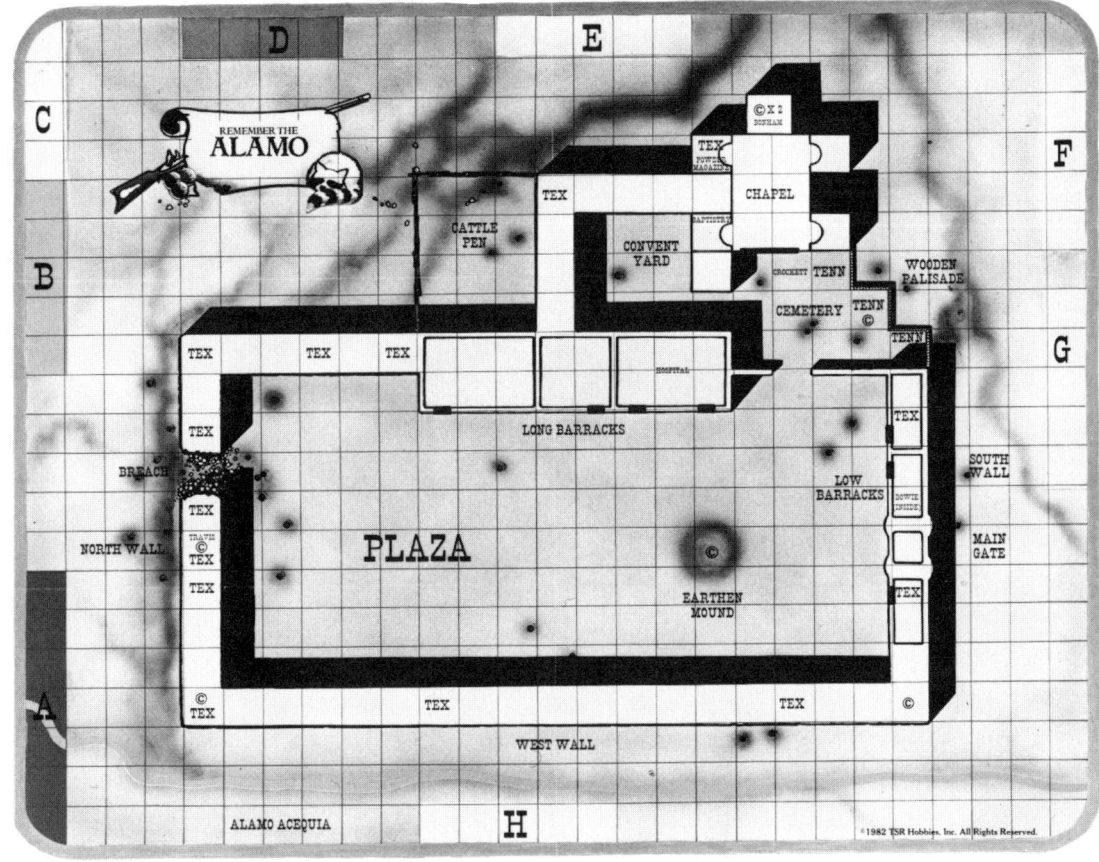

Gameboard for TSR Hobbies' "Remember the Alamo" minigame, a simplified tactical simulation designed by Kevin Hendryx, 1982. As in most Alamo games, the outcome is a foregone conclusion and the object is to attain the most glorious victory-in-defeat by prolonging the struggle. Similarly, in Harett-Gilmar's "Adventures of Davy Crockett" children's game, 1955, the winner is the first player to land in the Alamo, instead of staying in Congress as Crockett had hoped to do. (From the collection of Paul A. Hutton. Gameboard reproduced with permission of TSR, Inc., © 1982 TSR, Inc. All rights reserved)

Walt Disney's "Davy Crockett at the Alamo" play set, manufactured by Louis Marx & Co. of New York, ca. 1955. The "official" Frontierland set included a small-scale metal replica of the Alamo church (with detachable front gable), wall sections, and gates, plus plastic Texans, Mexicans, Indians, horses, campfire, well, cacti, and other accessories. In this arrangement, the figure of Fess Parker as Davy Crockett stands atop the chapel, guarding its flag. (From the collection of Paul A. Hutton. Photograph by Flying Horse Photography and Assoc.) ◄

At the time of the Texas revolution, Crockett was already an established national figure, well-known through newspaper accounts of his political career, through a series of comic almanacs bearing his name, through his popular autobiography and other books, and through a long-running stage play, *The Lion of the West*, which featured a Crockett-inspired frontier hero named Colonel Nimrod Wildfire. These literary efforts, combined with widespread "tall tales" of impossible frontier adventures, had firmly established Crockett as a legend in his own lifetime. "I'm that same David Crockett, fresh from the backwoods, half-horse, half-alligator, a little touched with the snapping-turtle; can wade the Mississippi, leap the Ohio, ride upon a streak of lightning, and slip without a scratch

Actor James Hackett as Colonel Nimrod Wildfire, the Crockett-inspired hero of *The Lion of the West*, which packed theater houses in New York, Washington, and London during the early 1830s. James K. Paulding's frontier comedy greatly popularized the emerging Crockett legend, and subsequent "portraits" of Crockett in a fur cap appear to be closely based on this likeness of Hackett, engraved after a painting by Ambrose Andrews. Crockett himself watched Hackett perform in Washington, the audience applauding wildly as the actor bowed to the Congressman and the Congressman bowed back to his image on the stage. (Courtesy Harvard Theatre Collection)

Portrait of David Crockett in hunter's garb, illustrated by D.W.C. Baker, *A Texas Scrap-Book*, 1875, in an etching by Richardson, New York, after an 1834 oil painting by John G. Chapman. Instead of the legendary buckskins and coonskin cap, he wears a cloth hunting suit and a flat-crowned, broad-brimmed hat. (DeGolyer Library)

down a honey locust; can whip my weight in wild cats, . . . hug a bear too close for comfort, and eat any man opposed to Jackson."[56]

This Crockett was both a literary and a political creation, personifying the western frontiersman: at his best, he was honest, brave, noble, resourceful, blessed with abundant "horse-sense," independent to a fault, and able to tell a good story; at his worst, uneducated, crude, violent, boastful, drunken, and even clownish. A significant portion of the Crockett legend was evidently the deliberate fabrication of Jacksonian and anti-Jacksonian politicians hoping to enlist the western vote. One faction portrayed him as a backwoods philosopher, the other as a country bumpkin. Crockett endeavored strenuously to correct the latter view, once asking two fellow Congressmen to testify to the propriety of his behavior at a White House dinner. Nonetheless, the image soon overtook the man, and historians and folklorists have been long at work to distinguish between the historical David Crockett and the legendary Davy, the "backwoods demigod, a fabulous hunter and fighter wafted to immortality in the rifle smoke of the Alamo."[57]

Even his physical appearance has been touched by legend. The historical Crockett certainly wore rough clothes for backwoods hunting, but he also took care to dress appropriately for his station as a Congressman, appearing before audiences on his 1834 tour of New England in "dark clothes," Byronic collar, and white hat—very much the fashion of the time. Surviving portraits made during his lifetime depict him primarily in urban attire. The only exception, a full-length portrait by John Gadsby Chapman, shows Crockett in hunter's garb—significantly, neither buckskins nor a coonskin cap. The legendary Davy, by contrast, is hardly ever seen without his buckskin jacket and coonskin cap, prompting humorist Richard Armour to comment, "It is assumed that he wore trousers of some sort, although they are never mentioned."[58]

Of Crockett's actual role in the siege and battle of the Alamo, little is known directly. During the initial bombardment and sallies out of the fort, Travis reported, "The Hon. David Crockett was seen at all points, animating the men to do their duty." As the siege wore on, Crockett was said by Mrs. Dickinson to have entertained the men by storytelling and playing his fiddle. When the final attack came, he and his Tennesseans are believed to have defended the weakest (and therefore, most heroic) point in the defenses, the log-and-packed-earth pallisade at the southeast corner of the main compound.[59]

In the earliest days after the battle, Crockett's name figured prominently in news reports, especially in the upper Mississippi Valley and along the East Coast, where Travis and Bowie were little known. More than any other factor, the death of the picturesque

Davy Crockett Elementary School students, San Antonio, outfitted in full buckskins, coonskin caps, and moccasins for the annual Fiesta San Jacinto pilgrimage to the Alamo, April 22, 1968. (Courtesy Express-News Corp.)

Early illustration of Crockett at the Alamo, by an unknown artist for *Ben Hardin's Crockett Almanac* of 1842. Significantly, the scene is not labeled Crockett's death, for the same almanac includes a letter purported to have come from Crockett himself, still alive and laboring in Mexican mines. Persistent rumors of Crockett's survival eventually prompted his family to contact Mexican authorities (unsuccessfully) for information on his supposed whereabouts. (DeGolyer Library)

Santa Anna inspecting the Texan dead at the conclusion of battle, in a painting entitled *The Alamo: 8 A.M.*, by prominent Mexican military artist and historian Joseph Hefter. Crockett, attired in long jacket, green vest, and light-colored breeches, lies prone atop a pile of dead bodies near the southwest corner of the chapel. (From Jerome J. Gaddy, *Texas in Revolt*. DeGolyer Library)

David Crockett leading the final resistance, near the church, in Larousse's *Histoire du Far West*, a 1980 comic book version of the Fort Alamo story, written in French by Frank Giroud and illustrated by José Bielsa. The composition of the scene, and especially Crockett's rifle-swinging pose, is apparently based on Frederick Yohn's painting *The Battle of the Alamo* (plate 9). (From the collection of Paul A. Hutton)

and popular "coonskin Congressman" galvanized national support for the Texas revolution.[60] Crockett's fame persisted through much of the nineteenth century, fanned by the continued appearance of tall tales in the almanacs and by the frequent reprinting of his books (including *Col. Crockett's Exploits and Adventures in Texas*, a spurious tale of his last days). Crockett also inspired several novels and stage plays. *The National Drama of the Fall of the Alamo, or the Death of Col. Crockett* was "patriotically revived" in Houston as early as 1845, while a later melodrama, *Davy Crockett; Or, Be Sure You're Right, Then Go Ahead*, played to packed houses in both America and England for nearly twenty-five years. Its 1878 audience in Austin, Texas, even included Alamo survivor Susanna Dickinson Hannig.[61]

By this time, however, Crockett's image as the quintessential frontiersman was about to be displaced by new heroes, representatives of a frontier even wilder and more remote—the Far West of Jesse James, Wild Bill Hickok, and Buffalo Bill Cody. By the 1920s his reputation had reached its nadir, with literary historians calling him a sloven and a wastrel who "traversed the length of Tennessee, drinking, hunting, talking, speculating, begetting children . . . living for the most part off the country . . . his last squatting place . . . as primitive as the first."[62]

Ultimately unsuccessful in both Tennessee and Washington, Crockett had resolved to start anew in Texas, and there he found the lasting glory that had previously eluded him. Although he arrived less than four months before his death, Crockett has become a Texan par excellence, and criticism of him is in many quarters tantamount to blasphemy. And yet, as with the deaths of the other Alamo heroes, differing accounts of Crockett's death appeared from the earliest days after the battle. The most popular version, that Crockett fell "fighting like a tiger," was spread by convention delegate Andrew Briscoe, who was also responsible for popularizing the tale of Travis's suicide. Although none of the Texan survivors actually saw Crockett die, both Dickinson and Joe recalled seeing his body "lying dead and mutilated," and according to the former, surrounded by twenty-four dead Mexicans. On the other hand, the first reports reaching the United States, via New Orleans and the schooner *Comanche*, suggested that Crockett had not been killed in the heat of battle but was one of seven who were found alive by the Mexicans. "[T]hese seven cried for quarter, but were told there was no mercy for them. . . . When their demand for quarter was refused, they continued fighting until all were butchered."[63]

Scene from John Wayne's *The Alamo*. John Wayne as Crockett dies at lance-point while enroute to blow up the powder magazine, a role historically attributed to Robert Evans, a lesser-known, Irish-born defender. (United Artists, 1960)

John Wayne, as Davy Crockett, meeting Travis, in an Italian comic book, *Storia del West: Alamo*, 1984, clearly based on motion picture images. (From the collection of Paul A. Hutton)

Crockett's contemporaries apparently accepted this version of his death quite matter-of-factly, but when Columbia University in 1943 published a description of Crockett's alleged surrender, the *Southwestern Historical Quarterly* objected that "the people of Tennessee and Texas will need more authority . . . than a New York publication to be convinced." In 1975 Carmen Perry received a *Texas Monthly* "Bum Steer" award for merely translating a Mexican source recounting the surrender of Crockett and several others. And so the furor over Crockett's death continues, as described more fully in the introduction to this volume. The Crockett under fire here is neither the historical man nor the literary legend but the media image created during the 1950s. Unlike the Crockett portrayed in the almanacs and other nineteenth-century sources, Disney's Crockett was specifically intended as a role model for children, someone who "proved there can be thrills and excitement in serving constructive causes." Adult critics found this Crockett "gentle, chivalrous, sensitive, eloquent, and brave" but "noble to the point of being stuffy." The rather raunchy humor of the almanacs was here "scrubbed clean" for children.[64]

To the noble frontiersman created by Disney and Fess Parker, John Wayne added the commanding force of his own personality and a new element of intense patriotism. "Republic! . . . I like the sound of the word," declares Crockett in one of the film's many monologues, giving voice to Wayne's own deeply held convictions that "the price of liberty and freedom is not cheap." Wayne's Crockett is a far more complex character than Parker's—an adult hero, once again a man's man who fights hard and plays hard, loves women and whiskey, likes to brag a bit and is not above playing a trick, but who beneath his roughness and rowdiness is honest, gallant, thoughtful, and even sentimental.[65]

Despite the towering image of Wayne as Crockett (or perhaps because Wayne remains Wayne throughout), it is Fess Parker's Crockett that dominates the collective memory of modern Americans. His clean-scrubbed and buckskin-clad image reappears continually in comic books, children's books, cartoons, and other popular media, representing, under his rough backwoods exterior, the most cherished qualities of manhood, integrity, courage, and resourcefulness. By a fascinating blend of history, legend, and marketing, the Tennessee hunter has become the epitome of Texan—and indeed American—heroism.

PLATE 1. Central panel, ninety feet high by thirty feet wide, of wall mural *Texas of History* in the Texas Hall of State, Dallas, designed and executed by Eugene Savage, Professor of Painting at Yale University, and several assistants in celebration of the Texas Centennial, 1935–36. In lower center, Travis draws his line in the dust, while a wounded Bonham, right, begins to lift the stricken Bowie across. Crockett, in his formal congressional attire, stands amongst the defenders. Above rises a "heavy pall of smoke" from the funeral pyres, supporting the symbolic female figures of the Republic of Texas and its allies, together with the apotheosized Stephen F. Austin, and simultaneously blocking from view the much-discussed Alamo parapet. (Courtesy Dallas Historical Society)

PLATE 2. Stephen F. Austin's *Map of Texas*, 1836, hand-colored, published by H. S. Tanner in Philadelphia, showing the various *empresario* grants then in existence. (DeGolyer Library)

PLATE 3. Edward Everett, *Interior View of the Church of the Alamo*, watercolor painting, 1847. Everett's romantic views are technically and artistically among the most sophisticated of the early Alamo images; this interior view in particular falls clearly within classical art traditions, echoing the many views of Roman ruins executed by eighteenth-century Italian artist Giovanni Piranesi. (Courtesy Amon Carter Museum, Fort Worth) ▶

PLATE 4. *Dawn at the Alamo*, created by Henry Arthur McArdle, one of Texas's most noted historical painters, in the years 1876 through 1883. This massive, seven-by-twelve-foot canvas oil now hangs in the Texas State Capitol Building and is a favorite image for reproduction. Originally a portrait artist, McArdle's training is quite evident in his treatment of Evans, about to ignite the powder, lower left; in the lunging figure of Bowie, lower left; in Crockett, swinging the remnants of "Old Betsy," lower right; and in Travis, manfully stomping on a wounded Mexican whilst dispatching a flag bearer. However, the most interesting face—the ultimate in perfidy—is that of the leering Mexican about to bayonet Travis in the back. Although McArdle spent much time and money collecting historical artifacts in order to make this an accurate painting, the result is a surrealistic melange reminiscent of Hieronymus Bosch's fifteenth-century visions of Hell or of Pablo Picasso's *Guernica*. The perspective is skewed, and the landscape itself warps in a Daliesque perversion of perception. (Courtesy Archives Division, Texas State Library)

PLATE 5. Robert Jenkins Onderdonk, *The Fall of the Alamo*, 1903. This famous oil painting depicts Colonel Morales' soldiers—incorrectly clad—bursting upon the defenders through the southern gate. Originally titled *Crockett's Last Stand*, the painting focuses on Crockett in his traditionally stylized pose, with his hunting rifle "Old Betsy" upraised as a club against the Mexicans. At that point in the battle, there was not much else to do. (Courtesy Archives Division, Texas State Library)

PLATE 6. Denis McLoughlin illustration for an English children's serial, *Buffalo Bill Wild West Annual*, with stories by Joan Whitford [Rex James]. This graphic portrayal of hand-to-hand fighting convincingly evokes the brutality and desperation of the final conflict. (From the collection of Paul A. Hutton)

PLATE 7. Jean Louis Theodore Gentilz, *Death of Dickinson*, painted ca. 1844 and copyrighted over a half-century later. Gentilz's small painting depicts Almeron Dickinson on bended knees before Mexican bayonets, pleading with Santa Anna to spare the life of the child he holds. Although Gentilz kept scrupulous notes of his interviews with various eyewitnesses to the siege and battle, he left no record of his source for this unusual version of the Dickinson story. The wall in the background is evidently the south end of the convent building. (Courtesy Daughters of the Republic of Texas Library at the Alamo, San Antonio) ▶

PLATE 8. Donald M. Yena, *The Alamo—March 6, 1836*. This 1967 oil painting portrays the unusual viewpoint of Mexican assault troops still outside the compound, converging in chaos on the northwest corner and advancing toward the towering outer walls through murderous gunfire. Despite some technical inaccuracies—such as an overly bright sky and the inclusion of several stereotypically sombrero-covered peasants amongst the regular Mexican troops—the painting successfully conveys the horror and heroism of the final charge. (Courtesy Texian Press) ◄

PLATE 9. *The Battle of the Alamo*, by popular early-twentieth-century illustrator Frederick C. Yohn. The print, issued ca. 1913, focuses on Crockett's last stand before the portals of the Alamo church. (Courtesy Continental Insurance)

PLATE 10. *Crockett led before Santa Anna*, frontispiece illustration by John W. Thomason, Jr., for Scribner's 1934 edition of *The Adventures of Davy Crockett, Told Mostly by Himself*. Thomason here depicts the story, related by Mexican chroniclers and widely accepted by nineteenth- and early twentieth-century Americans, of Crockett as one of several defenders who survived the combat only to be executed by Santa Anna. Elsewhere in the volume, Thomason depicts a more traditional version of Crockett's last fight, with rifle upraised and surrounded by Mexican bodies. A later edition of the autobiography, issued in the midst of the 1950s Crockett craze, omitted the now-controversial surrender scene. (DeGolyer Library. Illustrations by John W. Thomason, Jr., from *The Adventures of Davy Crockett*. Copyright 1934 Charles Scribner's Sons. Copyright renewed © 1962, Leda B. Thomason. Reproduced with the permission of Charles Scribner's Sons)

PLATE 11. Poster for Walt Disney's 1955 movie *Davy Crockett, King of the Wild Frontier*, starring Fess Parker. (From the collection of Paul A. Hutton) ▶

PLATE 12. Poster for *Heroes of the Alamo*, 1937, a low-budget, independently produced movie that focused on the tragic story of the Dickinson family instead of on the usual heroic traits of Bowie, Crockett, and Travis. (From the collection of Paul A. Hutton) ▶

Crockett led before Santa Anna.

NOW...on the MOTION
PICTURE SCREEN!
Village Drive IN
SUN. MON, + TUE.
July 3, 4, + 5
WALT DISNEY'S
DAVY CROCKETT
KING OF THE WILD FRONTIER
STARRING
FESS PARKER
BUDDY EBSEN
Directed by NORMAN FOSTER
Written by TOM BLACKBURN
Produced by BILL WALSH
Adapted from the Original "Disneyland" Television Productions
COLOR BY
TECHNICOLOR
WIDE SCREEN

A SPECTACULAR EPIC OF THE BIRTH OF TEXAS
ANTHONY J. XYDIAS
Presents
HEROES of the ALAMO
with
BRUCE WARREN · RUTH FINDLAY
LANE CHANDLER · REX LEASE
Roger WILLIAMS · Julian RIVERO
LEE VALIANOS
Screen Play by ROBY WENTZ · Directed by HARRY FRASER
Produced and Distributed by
Sunset Productions, Inc. · Hollywood, Calif.

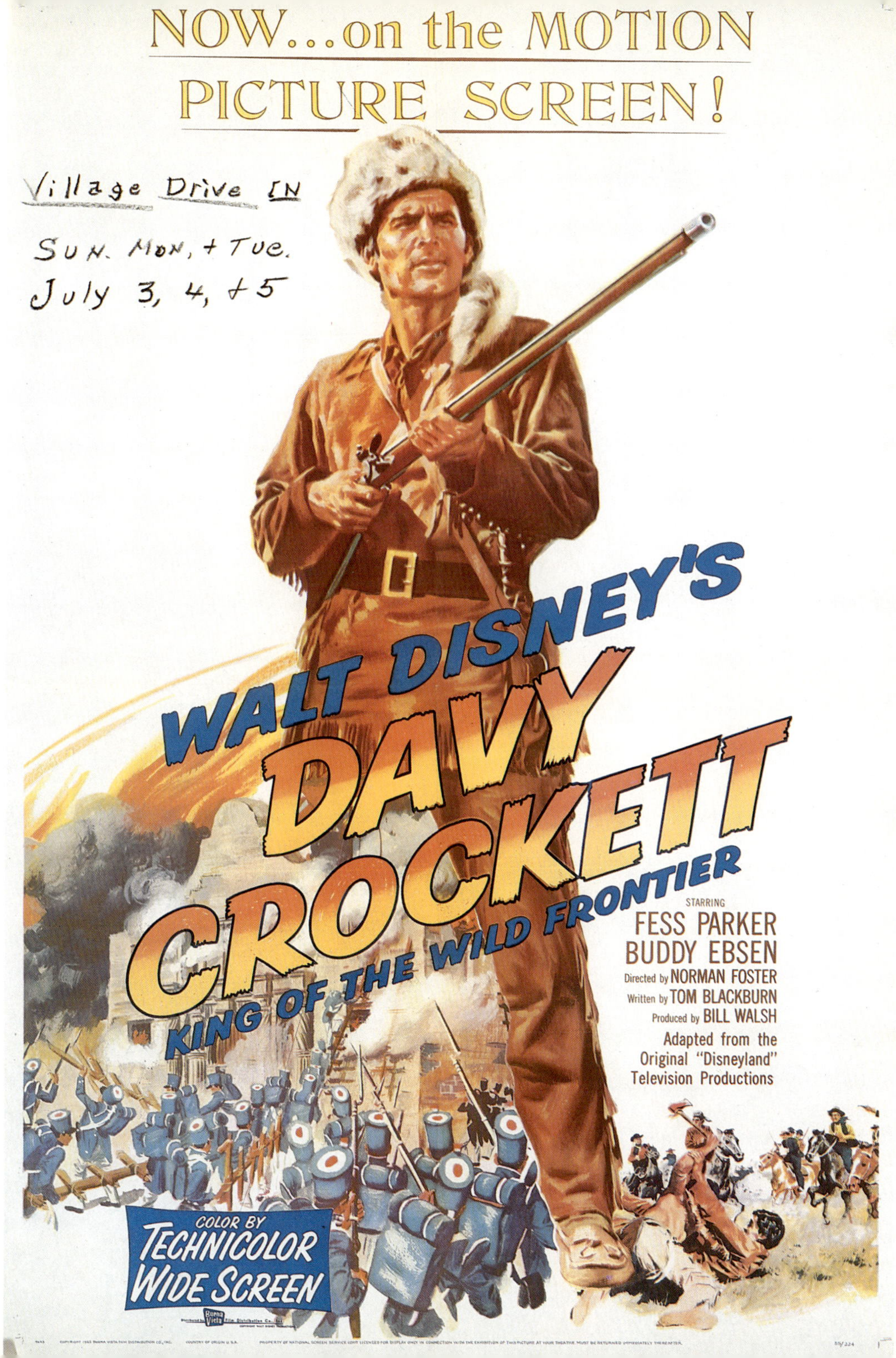

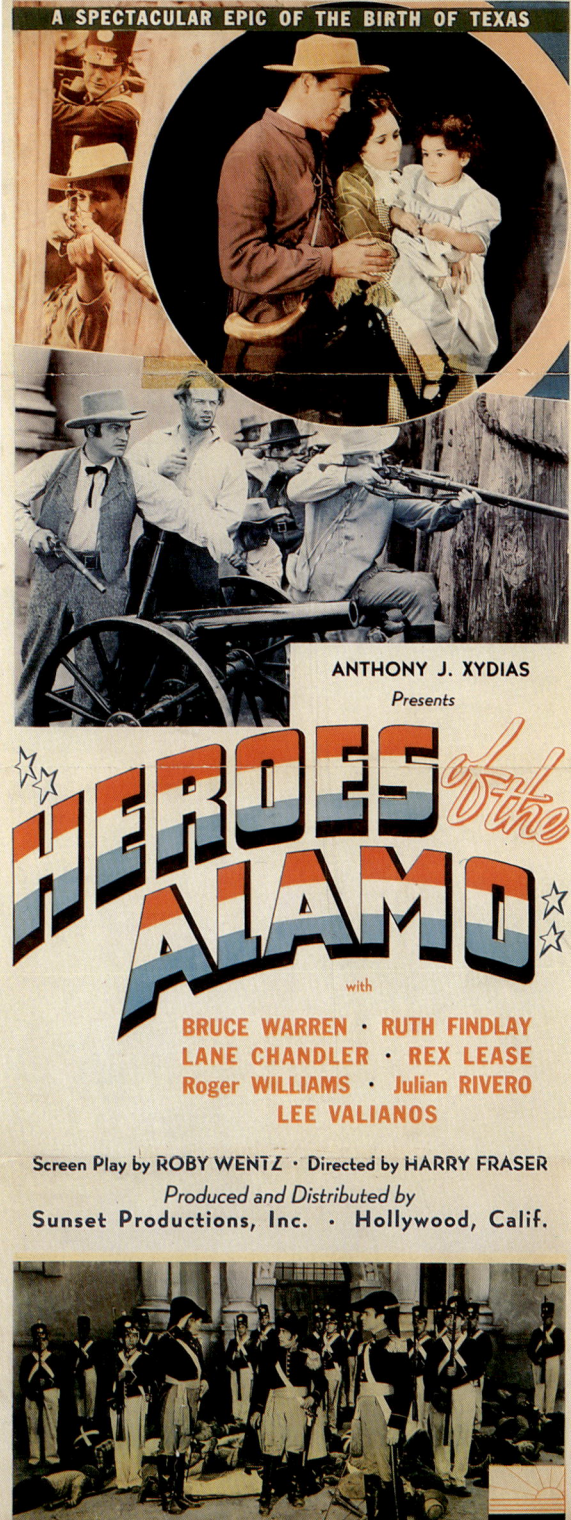

PLATE 13. Poster for *Last Command*, a 1955 Republic movie that featured Jim Bowie as the preeminent Alamo hero. Rushed into production in the wake of Disney's overwhelmingly popular *Davy Crockett*, *Last Command* was filmed from a screenplay originally commissioned by John Wayne for his own projected Alamo picture. (From the collection of Paul A. Hutton)

PLATE 14. Poster for John Wayne's epic film *The Alamo*, 1960. In the featured artwork by Reynold Brown, Wayne assumes Crockett's traditional pose but swings a lighted torch rather than the familiar long rifle. (From the collection of Paul A. Hutton)

PLATE 15. Mark Hess, cover illustration for *National Lampoon*, September 1980. (From the collection of Paul A. Hutton)

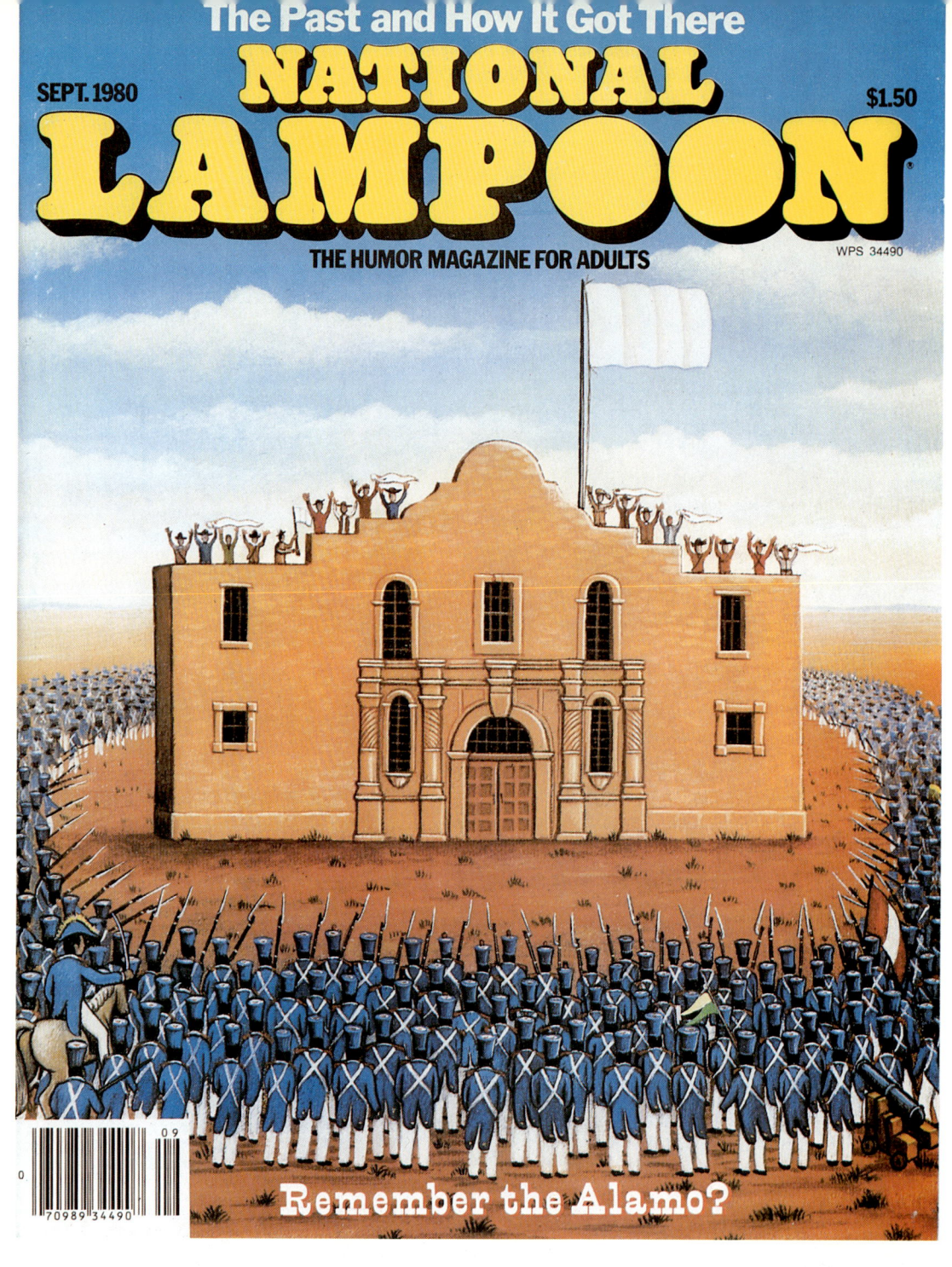

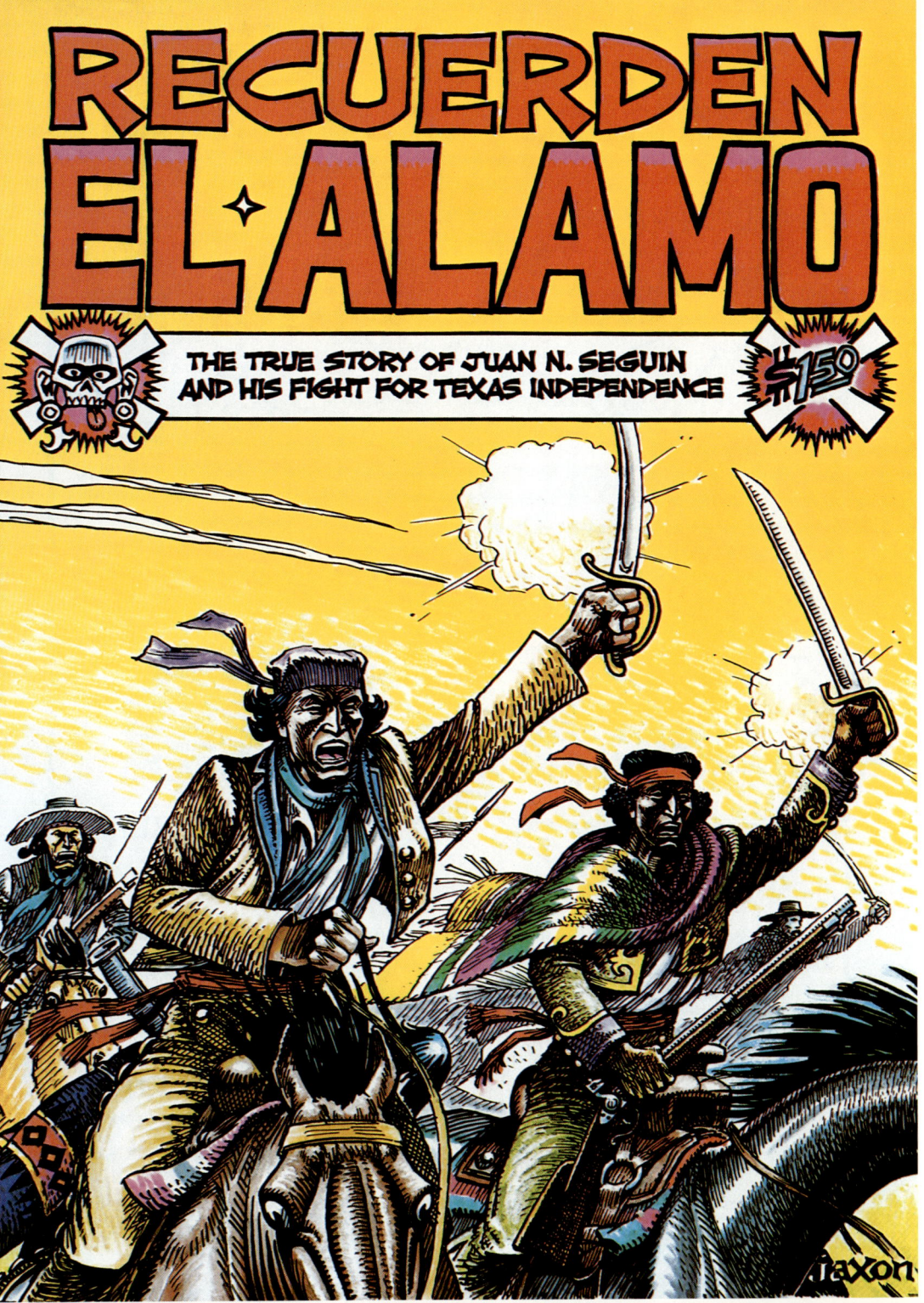

PLATE 16. Jack Jackson, cover illustration for *Recuerden El Alamo, The True Story of Juan N. Seguín And His Fight for Texas Independence*, a 1979 comic book focusing on the Tejano role in the revolution. (DeGolyer Library. Reproduced courtesy Jack Jackson, Austin)

PLATE 17. Rowland B. Wilson, cartoon published in *Esquire* magazine, March 1965. (Courtesy *Esquire*)

"Oh, stop worrying—the public has a short memory!"

Chapter 4

Memory and Mirage

by Susan Prendergast Schoelwer

Texans have never forgotten the Alamo. From the fields of San Jacinto to the gift shops of San Antonio, its memory has persisted and its image has proliferated. As one of the Republic's earliest acts, after the establishment of peace and order, Texas paid tribute to its martyred heroes. In February 1837 Colonel Juan Seguín, as military commandant of San Antonio, presided over the collection and reinterment of the ashes of the Alamo dead, accompanied by a lengthy funeral procession and orations in both Spanish and English. Although various locations have been suggested, and bones occasionally unearthed by construction workers or archaeologists, the site of this burial has never been definitely identified.

The locations of the funeral pyres and the death sites of the heroes are similarly shrouded in mystery, with various sources suggesting as many as six different places for Bowie's death and probably as many for Crockett and Travis. "If what the old residents and the historians say be true," commented the authors of *On a Mexican Mustang Through Texas*, 1905, "then there is not a spot within a quarter of a mile of the Alamo where Travis did not yield up his life." And so the quest continues, a holy mission not unlike the search for the Grail, for a shrine must have its relics, and pilgrims their holy places.[1]

For many years, controversy raged in San Antonio over what might be the most suitable memorial to the Alamo heroes. While some suggested that the thriving city was itself the most fitting monument, others replied, "Then why preserve the Alamo itself, why not tear it down and sell it and devote the proceeds to the erection of a modern, sky scraping office building and use the rents to lower the rate of taxes in Texas?" Still others warned, "Destroy the Alamo and raise no visible monument in its stead and in ten years not one child in fifty could recite the deeds, or the names of those who gave their lives that a new empire might be born."[2]

One young Texan who learned well the lessons of the Alamo was Lyndon Baines Johnson, whose troubled presidency brought the Alamo into the modern arena of national politics. Johnson had grown up steeped in Alamo lore—visiting the site many times and

Cover of Viola Berry's 1906 book of verse *The Alamo and Other Poems*, featuring a stamped design of the second Alamo monument, erected on the Capitol grounds in Austin in 1891. (DeGolyer Library)

Proposed "Alamo Heroes Monument," designed in 1912 by Alfred Giles Co., Architects, for Emil Locke of New Braunfels. Over twelve times taller than the present Alamo Cenotaph, almost half again as tall as the San Jacinto or Washington Monuments, the 802-foot Beaux Arts style tower, if erected, would have been at that time one of the tallest structures in the world. Like the San Jacinto Monument, its lower floors were to have included a Texan Museum, art gallery, and auditorium. The Alamo Shrine itself, dwarfed by the proposed monument, is visible to the far left of this artist's rendering by A. A. Brack. (Courtesy Daughters of the Republic of Texas Library at the Alamo, San Antonio)

Texas Governor Price Daniel with future U.S. Presidents John F. Kennedy and Lyndon Baines Johnson, at the Alamo during an October 1956 campaign tour. (Courtesy Express-News Corp.)

amazing interviewers years later with his ability to recite from memory a favorite Alamo ballad. Throughout his political career, he proudly recalled his father's authorship of the 1905 legislation enabling the State of Texas to purchase the long barracks. As popular opposition to the war in Vietnam mounted, critics accused the President of an "Alamo mentality" that cast any embattled military situation in the shadow of the Texas experience. In sending troops into Asia, Johnson evoked the great unspoken spectre of the Alamo—the collective guilt of Texans who had not gone riding to the rescue but had abandoned their comrades to certain death. "It's just like the Alamo," he said. "Somebody damn well needed to go to their aid." Time and again, he compared Texan heroes to

Ku Klux Klansmen at the Alamo on May Day 1982, gathered to protect the flag, the shrine, and "the white race" from anticipated Communist demonstrations. (Courtesy *San Antonio Light*)

American soldiers on the DMZ, the siege of Khe Sanh to the siege of the Alamo, and, at least by implication, himself to Travis—heroically determined to stand and fight.[3]

Johnson's close ties to the Alamo and its heroes produced, especially among those opposed to the Vietnam War, a strong anti-Alamo backlash. Critics charged that its traditional lessons of valor and patriotism were no longer relevant to a nuclear age. "If Americans must remember the Alamo," editorialized the *New York Times*, "let's remember that gallant men died needlessly in that old mission and that their sacrifice led eventually to a war that reflects little credit on the United States. . . . To persevere in folly is no virtue. To dare to retreat from error can be the highest form of courage."[4]

Loyal Texans, of course, responded angrily to such attacks on their cherished heritage, and the once-serene memorial park found itself the target of political protest. During the late 1960s and early 1970s, anti-war groups staged vigils, peace rallies, and demonstrations in front of the Alamo. In 1980, members of the Maoist Revolutionary Communist Party staged a symbolic "takeover," scaling the walls to replace the American flag with a red banner. "The Alamo itself is offensive," declared a spokeswoman, "not only to Chicano people but to people all over the world. It is a decrepit old monument . . . a symbol of oppression, not freedom; slavery, not liberation." The protestors were subsequently hauled down, arrested, and charged with "desecration of a venerated object."[5]

A much more widely publicized controversy erupted in 1969 when Commonwealth United production crews arrived in San Antonio to film scenes for *Viva Max!* The original novel, written by former Dallas newspaperman James Lehrer, was rife with political satire, including thinly disguised portraits of both Johnson and former Texas governor John Connally. DRT officials feared that the movie would show disrespect for the Alamo and the laws and honor of the State of Texas. As ersatz Mexican troops led by General Max (Peter Ustinov) prepared to retake the Alamo, ladies of the DRT rallied to its defense, locking the front doors and barricading the gates to prevent filming inside the hallowed grounds. Nothing, declared state DRT president Mrs. William L. Scarborough, could be "lower than the idea of making a comedy about a shrine where heroes died. Why couldn't they make a beautiful movie like John Wayne did?"[6]

The DRT repeatedly argued that the commercial use of Alamo images in *Viva Max!* threatened "irreparable harm to the Alamo and to the continued efforts of its custodians to make it a symbol of Texas independence and freedom." Yet commercialism has been a thriving part of the Alamo story since the 1840s, when local entrepreneurs guided visitors through the ruins and sold souvenirs made from the "true walls." Even the first

Peter Ustinov, as General Maximilian Rodriguez de Santos, posing before the Alamo chapel in a scene from the movie *Viva Max!* Vehement opposition from the Daughters of the Republic of Texas brought the film a flood of national publicity. (Commonwealth United, 1969)

First Alamo monument, carved in 1841 from stones from the Alamo by William B. Nangle, as illustrated in Baker's *Texas Scrap-Book*, 1875. This monument stood on the steps of the state capitol building from 1858 until 1881, when the building burned; a portion of the shaft survived and is still preserved in the Daughters of the Republic of Texas museum in Austin. (DeGolyer Library)

Advertisement for L & M cigarettes, part of an American bicentennial advertising campaign designed by Cunningham and Walsh and run in *Playboy* and other national magazines in March 1976. (Courtesy Liggett & Myers Tobacco Co., a division of Liggett Group Inc.)

Automobile leasing office in Plano, Texas (just north of Dallas), originally built as a game arcade. (Courtesy Larry Lange Cadillac. Photograph by Flying Horse Photography and Assoc.)

Alamo Plaza Hotel Courts, Ft. Worth Avenue, Dallas. (Courtesy Alamo Plaza Hotel Courts. Photograph by Flying Horse Photography and Assoc.)

Alamo monument was a commercial venture, marketed via an exhibition tour (twenty-five cents per view) when the state failed to purchase it immediately. At some time or other, the Alamo has appeared on virtually every sort of souvenir goods—dishes, glassware, spoons, banks, ashtrays, belt buckles, bookends and bookmarks, medals, t-shirts, frisbees—or has been used to advertise almost every sort of commercial enterprise. The authors of *On a Mexican Mustang Through Texas*, amazed at the number of commercial establishments bearing the Alamo name—ice company, drugstore, livery stable, cigar store, bakery, brewery, saloon, barbershop—wondered that any monument should be necessary "that the name and fame of the historic spot might be kept before the people."[7]

The list of Alamo enterprises is no shorter today, as evidenced by the 314 Alamo enterprises listed in a recent San Antonio telephone directory, not to mention such flourishing national businesses as Alamo car rentals or motel courts. Architectural copies likewise abound, ranging from vague allusions to the famous skyline to full-scale replicas used as private homes, reception halls, game arcades, miniature golf holes, park pavilions, lawn shrines, auto dealerships, piñatas, and boy scout projects. Nor has the commercialization of the Alamo been limited to outside entrepreneurs, for as several writers charged during the *Viva Max!* controversy, the most intense marketing occurs on the site itself. One newspaper correspondent asked, "What bigger desecration of the Alamo can be done than to turn it into a national souvenir shop for some over-priced junk?"[8]

The Alamo remains a place of strong emotions. For true believers, it is the sacred altar of Texas liberties, the holiest of holies, a "shrine to heroes' martyrdom with a stained glass window and plaques on its walls dedicated to those who shall remain immortal." For the unfortunate pilgrim not steeped in Texan lore, it is frequently a disappointment. "Most leave after spending just ten or fifteen minutes on the grounds. They . . . have their pictures taken. After that there isn't much to see or do . . . little effort is made to explain what the Alamo was and what happened there." Hispanics, whose view of the Alamo has long been ignored, are among its most outspoken critics. "The Alamo experience is an emotional experience, not a historical one," commented San Antonio historian Dr. Félix Almaráz, Jr. The Alamo image, as popularized by artists, novelists, cartoonists, and moviemakers, is grand and awe-inspiring, a "big, legendary, old mission standing out by itself in the high desert," a "lonely sentry in the desolate heat." The reality is a curious anachronism, a tiny chapel elbowed by noisy downtown traffic and dwarfed by modern skyscrapers, a Hispanic building dedicated to Anglo-Texan glories.[9]

NOTES

Chapter 1

1. Principal sources on the eighteenth- and nineteenth-century history of the site include: Carlos E. Castañeda, *Our Catholic Heritage in Texas*, 7 vols. (Austin: Von Boeckmann-Jones Co., 1936–58), vol. 3, *The Mission Era: The Missions at Work, 1731–1761*, 110-13, vol. 4, *The Mission Era: The Passing of the Missions, 1762–1782*, 4-6, vol. 5, *The Mission Era: The End of the Spanish Regime, 1780–1810*, 43-45, 199; Jack D. Eaton, *Excavations at the Alamo Shrine (Mission San Antonio de Valero)*, Special Report no. 10 (San Antonio: University of Texas at San Antonio, Center for Archaeological Research, 1980), 13-16, 52-54; Marion A. Habig, *The Alamo Mission: San Antonio de Valero, 1718–1793* (Chicago: Franciscan Herald Press, 1977); Mardith K. Schuetz, *Historic Background of the Mission San Antonio de Valero*, Archaeological Program Report no. 1 (Austin: Texas State Building Commission, 1966).

2. Castañeda, *Catholic Heritage*, 3:27-30, 92-94, 4:16-22, 237-38; Odie B. Faulk, "The Presidio: Fortress or Farce?" in *New Spain's Far Northern Frontier: Essays on Spain in the American West, 1540–1821*, ed. David J. Weber (Albuquerque: University of New Mexico Press, 1979), 67-76; T. R. Fehrenbach, *Lone Star: A History of Texas and the Texans* (New York: Macmillan Co., 1968), 45-47.

3. Zebulon M. Pike, *An Account of Expeditions to the Sources of the Mississippi . . . and a Tour Through the Interior Parts of New Spain . . . in the Year 1807* (Philadelphia: C. & A. Conrad, 1810), appendix to part 3, p. 33.

4. During the early 1800s the Alamo changed hands between local Tejano revolutionaries and Spanish royal forces in 1811 and again in 1813. The new Republic of Mexico assumed control of the site in 1821 and remained until 1835, when Texan volunteers forced the surrender of General Martín Perfecto de Cos. The Texan volunteers were soon massacred by the Mexican Army, which in turn retreated shortly after the Battle of San Jacinto in April 1836. As sporadic border warfare continued between Mexico and the Republic of Texas, Mexican troops twice occupied Béxar for brief periods in 1842. Finally, between the late 1840s and 1870s, the site served as a frontier post for both the U.S. Army and the Confederate Army. See Fehrenbach, *Lone Star*, 120-26, 261-62, 478; Gerald

Ashford, *Spanish Texas, Yesterday and Today* (Austin: Jenkins Publishing Co., 1971), 202-15; Eaton, *Excavations*, 6-7, 10; David J. Weber, *The Mexican Frontier, 1821–1846: The American Southwest Under Mexico* (Albuquerque: University of New Mexico Press, 1982), 9-10; Charles Ramsdell, *San Antonio, A Historical and Pictorial Guide* (Austin: University of Texas Press, 1968), 33, 43; Sidney Lanier, "San Antonio de Bexar," in William Corner, *San Antonio de Bexar: A Guide and History* (San Antonio: Bainbridge and Corner, 1890), 77-80, 89; Schuetz, *Historic Background*, 35-39.

5. Castañeda, *Catholic Heritage*, 5:36-42, 408-10; Oscar B. Colquitt, *Message of Governor O. B. Colquitt to the Thirty-third Legislature Relating to the Alamo Property* (Austin: Von Boeckmann-Jones Co., 1913), 20-22; Habig, *Alamo Mission*, 80-81; Schuetz, *Historic Background*, 30, 38-39; Pat Ireland Nixon, *A Century of Medicine in San Antonio: The Story of Medicine in Bexar County, Texas* (San Antonio: By the Author, 1936), 16-28.

6. Jean Louis Berlandier, *Journey to Mexico During the Years 1826 to 1834*, trans. Sheila M. Ohlendorf, Josette M. Bigelow, and Mary M. Standifer, 2 vols. (Austin: Texas State Historical Association with the University of Texas at Austin, Center for Studies in Texas History, 1980), 2:292; George W. Kendall, *Narrative of the Texan Santa Fe Expedition*, 2 vols. (New York: Harper and Bros., 1844), 1:49.

7. Carlos E. Castañeda, trans., *The Mexican Side of the Texan Revolution [1836] by the Chief Mexican Participants* (Dallas: P. L. Turner, 1928), 202, 264.

8. Joseph H. Barnard, *A Composite of Known Versions of the Journal of Dr. Joseph H. Barnard, One of the Surgeons of Fannin's Regiment, Covering the Period From December 1835 to June 5, 1836*, ed. Hobart Huson, Goliad Bicentennial ed. ([Refugio, Tex.]: n.p., 1949), 44-45.

9. *San Antonio Express*, April 9, 1905, in Donald E. Everett, *San Antonio: The Flavor of Its Past, 1845–1898* (San Antonio: Trinity University Press, 1975), 18; William Brooker, *Texas: An Epitome of Texas History. . . .* (Columbus, Ohio: Nitschke Bros., 1897), 12.

10. Adina De Zavala, *History and Legends of the Alamo and Other Missions In and Around San Antonio* (San Antonio: By the Author, 1917), 54-68.

11. William Bollaert, *William Bollaert's Texas*, ed. W. Eugene Hollon and Ruth Lapham (Norman: University of Oklahoma Press with The Newberry Library, 1956), 222-24; Marilyn McAdams Sibley, *Travelers in Texas, 1761–1860* (Austin: University of Texas Press, 1967), 65; Ione W. T. Wright, *Our Living Alamo, Mission San Antonio de Valero* (Dallas: Banks Upshaw and Co., 1937), 83-84; Colquitt, *Message*, 51.

12. Francis Baylies, *A Narrative of Major General Wool's Campaign in Mexico, in the Years 1846, 1847, & 1848* (Albany: Little and Co., 1851), 11; George W. Hughes, *Memoir Descriptive of the March of a Division of the United States Army Under the Command of Brigadier General John E. Wool, from San Antonio de Bexar in Texas to Saltillo, in Mexico . . . in 1846* (U.S. Congress, Senate, 31st Cong., 1st sess., Senate exec. doc. no. 32, 1850), 10.

13. "Rendering the Alamo," *American Heritage* 30 (October/November 1979): 50; Records of the Office of the Quartermaster General (RG92), Consolidated Correspondence File, 1794–1915, files on the Alamo, Edwin B. Babbitt, and San Antonio; Records of the Office of Chief of Engineers (RG77); National Archives, Washington, D.C., photocopies on file at the Daughters of the Republic of Texas Library at the Alamo, San Antonio (hereafter cited as DRT Library at the Alamo).

14. Colquitt, *Message*, 6-9, 15-16, 50-53.

15. Rena Maverick Green, ed., *Samuel Maverick, Texan: 1803–1870, A Collection of Letters, Journals and Memoirs* (San Antonio: By the Author, 1952), 323-25; Colquitt, *Message*, 22-23.

16. Corner, *San Antonio*, 11.

17. "Rendering the Alamo," 50; Charles M. Barnes, *Combats and Conquests of Immortal Heroes, Sung in Song and Told in Story* (San Antonio: Guessaz & Ferlet Co., 1910), 47-48, 248-49, 262-63; Lucy Buss and Ron Bechtol, "Besieged by the Alamo," *SA: The Magazine of San Antonio* 3 (October 1979): 71-73; Ramsdell, *San Antonio*, 77; Kevin R. Young, "Major Babbitt and the Alamo 'Hump,'" *Military Images* 6 (July–August 1984): 16-17.

18. John M. Odin, Bishop of Galveston, to Captain James H. Ralston, Assistant Quartermaster, U.S. Army at San Antonio, Galveston, April 30, 1847, fair copy; contract for lease of Alamo property, January 1, 1850; Records of the Office of the Quartermaster General (RG92); National Archives, photocopies on file at DRT Library at the Alamo.

19. Colquitt, *Message*, 5.

20. *Archdiocese of San Antonio, 1874–1974* (San Antonio: The Archdiocese, 1974), 6-7.

21. Corner, *San Antonio*, 9-12; Henry Ryder-Taylor, *History of the Alamo and of the Local Franciscan Missions* (San Antonio: Nic Tengg, [1906]), 96; De Zavala, *History and Legends*, 45; Cecilia Steinfeldt, *San Antonio Was: Seen Through a Magic Lantern, Views From the Slide Collection of Albert Steves, Sr.* (San Antonio: San Antonio Museum

Association, 1978), 28-32; Mary Ann Noonan Guerra, *The Alamo* (San Antonio: Alamo Press, 1983); picture files, DRT Library at the Alamo.

22. Colquitt, *Message*, 38-42, 54-55; Leonora Bennett, *Historical Sketch and Guide to the Alamo* (San Antonio: By the Author, 1902), 85.

23. Colquitt, *Message*, 17, 140; Reuben M. Potter, "The Fall of the Alamo," *Magazine of American History* 2 (January 1878): 12; Corner, *San Antonio*, 9-11; Steinfeldt, *San Antonio Was*, 50-56; picture files, DRT Library at the Alamo.

24. Harriet P. Spofford, "San Antonio de Bexar," *Harper's New Monthly Magazine* (July 1877): 831-50, as quoted in Galveston, Harrisburg and San Antonio Railway Company, *The "Star and Crescent" and "Sunset" Route* [Houston: Southern Pacific, 1882], 36; Alexander E. Sweet and J. Armoy Knox, *On a Mexican Mustang Through Texas: From the Gulf to the Rio Grande*, rev. ed. (London: Chatto & Windus, 1905), 288-91; Sam Woolford and Bess Woolford, *The San Antonio Story* (Austin: Joske's, 1950), picture caption, n.p.

25. Ryder-Taylor, *History of the Alamo*, 72.

26. De Zavala, *History and Legends*, 18-19, 33-34, 45; Colquitt, *Message*, 133-38. Adina Emily De Zavala (1861–1955) was the eldest child of Augustine and Julia Tyrell de Zavala; Augustine was, in turn, Lorenzo de Zavala's son by his second marriage, to Emily West. Although Adina De Zavala was thus no more than half Hispanic in ancestry, she seems to have identified closely with Tejano perspectives. See Lorenzo de Zavala, *Journey to the United States of North America*, trans. Wallace Woolsey (Austin: Shoal Creek Publishers, 1980), xi, xv; L. Robert Ables, "The Second Battle for the Alamo," *Southwestern Historical Quarterly* 70 (January 1967): 373.

27. Principal sources for the DRT controversy include: Ables, "Second Battle," 372-413; Colquitt, *Message*, 131-40; De Zavala, *History and Legends*, 47-50, 215-19; Peter Molyneaux, "How the Alamo Was Saved," *Bunker's Monthly, The Magazine of Texas* 1 (March 1928): 419-32; Martha Anna Turner, *Clara Driscoll, An American Tradition* (Austin: Madrona Press, 1979), 16-29; Daughters of the Republic of Texas, *Fifty Years of Achievement: History of the Daughters of the Republic of Texas* (Dallas: Banks Upshaw and Co., 1942), 181-217.

28. Colquitt, *Message*, 133-40, 156-57.

29. Colquitt, *Message*, 136; Steinfeldt, *San Antonio Was*, 31-32; Ables, "Second Battle," 411-12.

30. Fehrenbach, *Lone Star*, 285.

31. De Zavala, *History and Legends*, 55-56.

32. Charles B. Hosmer, Jr., *Presence of the Past: A History of the Preservation Movement in the United States Before Williamsburg* (New York: G. P. Putnam's Sons, 1965).

33. William B. Rhoads, *The Colonial Revival* (New York: Garland Publishing, 1977); Susan Prendergast Schoelwer, "Curious Relics and Quaint Scenes: The Colonial Revival at Chicago's Great Fair," in *The Colonial Revival in America*, ed. Alan Axelrod, A Winterthur Book (New York: W. W. Norton & Co., 1985), 210-14.

34. De Zavala, *History and Legends*, 47-50, 215; DRT, *Fifty Years*, 201-12.

35. DRT, *Fifty Years*, 183-85, 227-35; Commission of Control for Texas Centennial Celebrations, *Monuments Erected by the State of Texas to Commemorate the Centenary of Texas Independence* (Austin: Steck Co., 1938), 28, 40-41; Wright, *Our Living Alamo*, 84-87.

36. *San Antonio Express*, April 29, 1900, as quoted in Ables, "Second Battle," 379.

37. Daniel E. Fox, *Traces of Texas History, Archaeological Evidence of the Past 450 Years* (San Antonio: Corona Publishing Co., 1983), 120-21; Eaton, *Excavations*, 17-19.

38. Jesse Luna, "Alamo Contributions Recalled," *San Antonio News*, June 16, 1981; Marguerite Routledge, "The Restoration of the Alamo: Governor Colquitt's Project That Has the Hearty Approval of Texas," *Texas Magazine* 5 (April 1912): 42.

39. Ford, Powell, and Carson, "The Alamo: Master Plan Report Prepared for the Daughters of the Republic of Texas," 1979, DRT Library at the Alamo; David McLemore, "Battle Stations!" *Dallas Morning News*, November 18, 1984; tablet installed on reconstructed walls of the Alamo compound's "Southwestern Room."

40. Gary L. Foreman, *Remembering the Alamo* (San Antonio: By the Author, 1983).

Chapter 2

1. John H. Jenkins, ed., *The Papers of the Texas Revolution, 1835–1836*, 10 vols. (Austin: Presidial Press, 1973), 4:160-64, 186-88, 317-22, 333-35, 388-92, and *passim*. Other discussions of the campaign may be found in Eugene C. Barker, ed., *History of Texas* (Dallas: Turner Co., 1929), 221-33; Castañeda, *Catholic Heritage*, vol. 6, *Transition Period: The Fight for Freedom, 1810–1836*, 267-81; Vito Alessio Robles, *Coahuila y Texas, Desde la Consumación de la Independencia Hasta el Tratado de Palde Guadalupe Hidalgo*, 2 vols. (Mexico, 1945–46), 2:57-82, as trans. David Glenn Hunt (master's thesis, Southern Methodist University, 1950), 56-86.

2. Robles, *Coahuila y Texas*, Hunt trans., 78-80; Eaton, *Excavations*, 7; Ford, Powell, and Carson, "Master Plan," 9-10, 31; De Zavala, *History and Legends*, 23-30.

3. Bowie's source of rank has been a recurring question. He was a colonel in the "rangers" against the Indians before the Texas revolution, but documentation of his Texan army rank is missing. On October 9, 1835, Bowie wrote a letter of resignation to General Stephen F. Austin but made no mention of the rank he was resigning. By October 22, however, Austin had assigned him troops to command and addressed him as Colonel Bowie, as did Fannin by October 24. Traditionally, an address of rank by a commanding general carries the weight of an official commission, particularly in such a politically unstable situation as a revolution. Travis had resigned his commission as a captain on November 6, 1835, but on November 11 Austin was still addressing him by that rank. That he left the siege is certain, for his letter to the Council on December 3, 1835, in which he hoped for a lieutenant-colonelcy of cavalry, was sent from San Felipe de Austin. On December 17, he was at Mill Creek, where he resigned the pro-offered rank of major in the artillery, until appointed as colonel, First Regiment of Infantry, by Houston on the 23rd. This was superceded by his appointment the next day by Henry Smith as "Lieutenant Colonel in the Legion of Cavalry of the Army of Texas," just as he had wanted all along. See Jenkins, *Papers*, 2:75, 187-88, 210, 341, 376-77, 3:91-92, 241-42, 301, 310.

4. Jenkins, *Papers*, 4:236-38.

5. In her landmark work on the Alamo, Amelia W. Williams speculated:

The place, moreover, seemed to cast some sort of spell over the Texan leaders. However indifferent or reluctant a man might be before going to Bexar, once there, he was soon writing to the Governor, the Council, the Commander-in-Chief, anybody that had any authority to give aid, saying, "Bexar is the key to the situation, public safety demands our lives rather than surrender it into the hands of the enemy." And so the decision was made to hold the place against all odds, and a small band of resolute men was assembled for its defense.

Amelia W. Williams, "A Critical Study of the Siege of the Alamo and of the Personnel of its Defenders," *Southwestern Historical Quarterly* 36 (April 1933): 266. Williams's study was published in five parts by the *Southwestern Historical Quarterly*: chapter I, vol. 36 (April 1933): 251-87; chapter II, vol. 37 (July 1933): 1-44; chapter III, vol. 37 (October 1933): 79-115; chapter IV, vol. 37 (January 1934): 157-84; chapter V, vol. 37 (April 1934): 237-312. (Hereafter only volume and page numbers will be cited.)

6. Ibid.; further discussion of the religious and cultural conflicts may be found in

William H. Goetzmann, *When the Eagle Screamed: The Romantic Horizon in American Diplomacy, 1800–1860* (New York: John Wiley and Sons, 1966); Samuel H. Lowrie, *Culture Conflict in Texas, 1821–1835* (New York: Columbia University Press, 1932); Eugene C. Barker, *Mexico and Texas 1821–1835* (Dallas: P. L. Turner, 1928); George C. Rives, *The United States and Mexico, 1821–1848*, 2 vols. (New York: Charles Scribner's Sons, 1913); David J. Weber, ed., *Foreigners in Their Native Land: Historic Roots of the Mexican Americans* (Albuquerque: University of New Mexico Press, 1973).

7. Jenkins, *Papers*, 3:278-79, 4:58-61, 303, 352-53.

8. Ibid.; Eaton, *Excavations*, 8-10; Ford, Powell, and Carson, "Master Plan," 10, B2-B11; Williams, "Critical Study," 37:17-19; Amelia W. Williams, "A Critical Study of the Siege of the Alamo and the Personnel of its Defenders" (Ph.D. diss., University of Texas, 1931), 395-414.

9. Jenkins, *Papers*, 4:58-60, 88, 127, 137, 153-55, 159, 160, 176-77, 185, 236-38, 303, 317-19, 320-21, 327-28, 339, 414, 415.

10. Antonio López de Santa Anna, *The Eagle: The Autobiography of Santa Anna*, ed. Ann Fears Crawford, trans. Sam Guyler and Jaime Platon (Austin: Pemberton Press, 1967); Clarence R. Wharton, *El Presidente: A Sketch of the Life of General Santa Anna* (Houston: C. C. Young Printing Co., 1924); Wilfrid Hardy Callcott, *Santa Anna: The Story of an Enigma Who Once Was Mexico* (Norman: University of Oklahoma Press, 1936); Oakah L. Jones, Jr., *Santa Anna* (New York: Twayne Publishers, 1968); Frank C. Hanighen, *Santa Anna: The Napoleon of the West* (New York: Coward-McCann, 1934); José Fuentes Mares, *Santa Anna: Aurora y Ocaso de un Comediante* (Mexico City: Editorial "Mexico Nuevo," 1937).

11. Richard G. Santos, *Santa Anna's Campaign Against Texas, 1835–1836, Featuring the Field Commands Issued to Major General Vicente Filisola*, 2nd ed., rev. (Salisbury, N.C.: Documentary Publications, [1981]), 40-59; Carlos Sánchez-Navarro, ed., *La Guerra de Tejas: Memorias de un Soldado* (Mexico City: Editorial Polis, 1938), 75-81; Castañeda, trans., *Mexican Side*, 2-13, 97-100, 165-71, 211-16.

12. Castañeda, trans., *Mexican Side*, 13, *passim*; Santos, *Santa Anna's Campaign*, 1-39; Carlos Pereyra, *Tejas, La Primera Desmembración de Méjico* (Madrid: Editorial-America, [1917]), as trans. Ernest R. Ochoa (master's thesis, Southern Methodist University, 1948), 66-69; James Presley, "Santa Anna in Texas: A Mexican Viewpoint," *Southwestern Historical Quarterly* 62 (April 1959): 490-506.

13. Santos, *Santa Anna's Campaign*, 60-61; Samuel E. Asbury, ed., "The Private

Journal of Juan Nepomuceno Almonte, February 1–April 16, 1836," *Southwestern Historical Quarterly* 48 (July 1944): 16-17; Castañeda, trans., *Mexican Side*, 13; José Enrique de la Peña, *With Santa Anna in Texas: A Personal Narrative of the Revolution*, trans. and ed. Carmen Perry (College Station: Texas A&M University Press, 1975), 38.

14. Presley, "Santa Anna," 504-5; Santos, *Santa Anna's Campaign*, 9-13, 67-68.

15. The majority of reports of the Alamo's water supply rely on inferences from Jameson's letters that the aqueducts were used, but the only known mention of water by an Alamo defender, Dr. John Sutherland (*Dallas News*, February 12, 1911), states that the defenders used only the well inside the walls. This suggests that many of Jameson's projected improvements were never completed. See also Williams, "Critical Study," 37:19; John Sutherland, *The Fall of the Alamo* (San Antonio: Naylor Co., 1936), 21-22.

16. Jenkins, *Papers*, 3:112-14, 379-80, 4:414-15, 433-34, 501.

17. Williams, "Critical Study," 37:20-32, 163-65; Jenkins, *Papers*, 4:502-5; Walter Lord, *A Time to Stand* (New York: Harper & Bros., 1961), 107-8.

18. Lord, *Time*, 107-8, 117, 195; Williams, "Critical Study," 37:271; J. M. Morphis, *History of Texas, from Its Discovery and Settlement. . . .* (New York: United States Publishing, 1874), 174-75. The "Alamo Piper" evidently first appeared in Williams's dissertation resulting from an interview with Susanna Dickinson's granddaughter, as one of the stories she used to be told.

19. Lord, *Time*, 165-66; Morphis, *History*, 168; Williams, "Critical Study," 37:42-43, 258.

20. Sánchez-Navarro, ed., *La Guerra*, map opposite 96; Lord, *Time*, 70, 72, 106, 108, 114, 138, 143-46; Santos, *Santa Anna's Campaign*, 14-17, 63-75, 83; Williams, "Critical Study," 37:18; De la Peña, *With Santa Anna*, 33, 38-39, 42, 46-47.

21. Patrick Ireland Nixon, *The Medical Story of Early Texas, 1528–1853* (Lancaster, Pa: Lancaster Press, 1946), 181-88; Nixon, *Century of Medicine*, 50-61; Williams, "Critical Study," 37:157-58.

22. Jenkins, *Papers*, 4:518-19.

23. Williams, "Critical Study," 37:34-44, 181-83; Santos, *Santa Anna's Campaign*, 36, 74; Lord, *Time*, 159, tenth page of illustration insert; De la Peña, *With Santa Anna*, 46-47; Castañeda, trans., *Mexican Side*, 14-15, 102-3.

24. Lord, *Time*, 161; Asbury, ed., "Journal," 23. One of the problems with Lord's eminently readable work is his lack of documentation. Backtracking sources in his bibliography is frustrating because he does not specify which sources supplied which data.

His main concern appeared to be writing an entertaining story, with as much accuracy as this would permit.

25. De la Peña, *With Santa Anna*, 51-54; Santos, *Santa Anna's Campaign*, 75-76; Castañeda, trans., *Mexican Side*, 103-4; Dan Kilgore, *How Did Davy Die?* (College Station: Texas A&M University Press, 1978), *passim*; Francisco Becerra, *A Mexican Sergeant's Recollections of the Alamo and San Jacinto . . . as Told to John S. Ford in 1875* (Austin: Jenkins Publishing Co., 1980), 22-24; Miguel A. Sánchez Lamego, *The Siege and Taking of the Alamo*, trans. Consuelo Velasco (Santa Fe: Press of the Territorian, 1968), 50-53; Asbury, ed., "Journal," 23.

26. José María Tornel, *Secretaria de Guerra y Marina. El Exma Sr. Presidente interino de la República Mexicana, á los habitantes de ella, sabed: . . . "Para recompensar las acciones distinguidas del ejército y de la marina de guerra, se establece una Legion militar"* (Mexico, April 27, 1836), 7. Original pamphlet, announcing the creation of a Mexican Legion of Honor, in the Jenkins Garrett Library, University of Texas at Arlington.

Chapter 3

1. Williams, "Critical Study," 37:22-27; Jan Isbelle Fortune, "Why Bonham Chose to Die with Travis," *Dallas Morning News*, March 8, 1931; Walter Lord, "Myths and Realities of the Alamo," in *The Republic of Texas*, ed. Stephen B. Oates (Palo Alto, Calif.: American West Publishing Co. and Texas State Historical Association, 1968), 18-25; A. Garland Adair and M. H. Crockett, Sr., eds., *Heroes of the Alamo*, 2nd ed. (New York: Exposition Press, 1957), 40-45; Milledge L. Bonham, Jr., "James Butler Bonham: A Consistent Rebel," *Southwestern Historical Quarterly* 35 (October 1931): 124-36. Recent historians have found little verification for the tradition that Bonham and Travis were close boyhood friends in South Carolina. Perhaps Travis had instead become familiar with Bonham's name through his readings on the 1832 Nullification Crisis, in which Bonham had played a key role. See Travis's diary entry for December 27, 1833, in Robert E. Davis, ed., *The Diary of William Barret Travis* (Waco, Tex.: Texian Press, 1966), 93.

2. Ramsey Yelvington, *A Cloud of Witnesses: The Drama of the Alamo* (Austin: University of Texas Press, 1959); Lord, *Time*, 123-31. Dr. Sutherland's memoirs, written in 1860 in response to "several conflicting reports" that had recently appeared (possibly those published by Potter, Henderson Yoakum, or *The Texas Almanac* for 1860), remained in manuscript form well into the present century; see *Dallas News*, February 5 and 12, 1911; James T. DeShields, *Tall Men with Long Rifles* (San Antonio: Naylor Co., 1935), 34-50; Sutherland, *Fall of the Alamo*, 5-7, 23-26.

3. Lord, *Time*, 11, 43, 143.

4. Williams, "Critical Study," Ph.D. diss., 237-66, 280-90; Lord, *Time*, 213-19.

5. Christopher Bryant, *The Bee Hunter* (New York: Pageant Press, 1966); Marvel Comics Group, *Two-Gun Kid, "Remember the Alamo!"* (New York: Non-Pareil, 1965); James Warren, "The Rook: Man Whom Time Forgot," *Eerie* 82 (March 1977): 5-24; Rick Yager, "The Imaginary Adventures of Little Orvy," comic strip (Field Enterprises, January 29, 1961); A. H. Palacios, *Le Drame de Fort Alamo: La Légende de Manos Kelly* (Paris: Humanoides Associes, 1980).

6. Williams, "Critical Study," 37:303-10; Lord, *Time*, 204-5.

7. Frederick C. Chabot, *With the Makers of San Antonio* (San Antonio: By the Author, 1937), 274; Sutherland, *Fall, passim*; Juan N. Seguín, *Personal Memoirs of John N. Seguín. . . .* (San Antonio: Ledger Book and Job Office, 1858), 8-9, in *Northern Mexico on the Eve of the United States Invasion*, ed. David J. Weber (New York: Arno, 1976); Potter, "Fall," *passim*; Jean Louis Theodore Gentilz, "Relation de Anto Cruz Arocha," notes, ca. 1843–44, Gentilz-Frételliére Collections, DRT Library at the Alamo.

8. Potter, "Fall," 8; Williams, "Critical Study," 37:307-8; Evelyn Brogan, *James Bowie: A Hero of the Alamo* (San Antonio: Theodore Kunzman, 1922), 10.

9. Lord, *Time*, 207-9, 213; Jake Ivey, "The Problem of the Two Guerreros," *Alamo Lore and Myth Organization (ALAMO) Newsletter* 4 (March 1982): 10-12.

10. Lord, *Time*, 176-77, 207-8, 228-29; William T. Gray, *From Virginia to Texas, 1835* (Houston: Gray, Dillaye, 1909), 136-38; David Drake, "Joe, Alamo Hero," *Negro History Bulletin* 44 (April–June 1981): 34-35; Williams, "Critical Study," 37:285-86, 298.

11. W. P. Zuber, "An Escape from the Alamo," *Texas Almanac for 1873*, pp. 80-85; Llerena Friend, "Historiography of the Account of Moses Rose and the Line that Travis Drew," in William P. Zuber, *My Eighty Years in Texas*, ed. Janis B. Mayfield (Austin: University of Texas, 1971), 255-62; Williams, "Critical Study," 37:31; J. Frank Dobie, W. P. Zuber, and R. B. Blake, "Rose and His Story of the Alamo," in *In The Shadow of History*, ed. J. Frank Dobie, Mody C. Boatright, and Harry H. Ransom (Austin: Texas Folklore Society, 1939), 9-41.

12. The only known firsthand corroboration of Travis's famous line comes from a statement made by Alamo survivor Susanna Dickinson to the Texas Adjutant General three years after the Rose story appeared in print. See Lord, *Time*, 202-3, 228.

13. Maury Maverick, "Critics Can't Dim Alamo Symbolism," *San Antonio Express News*, April 22, 1979; Russell Birdwell, *A News Release: John Wayne's "The Alamo"*

(New York: Russell Birdwell, 1960), 77. An unusual illustration, of two boys and an "old frontiersman" slipping through a trapdoor into long-forgotten tunnels below the Alamo, appears in Edward Stratemeyer [Ralph Bonehill], *For the Liberty of Texas* (Boston: Dana Estes and Co., 1900), opp. 258.

14. Ronnie Dugger, *The Politician, The Life and Times of Lyndon Johnson: The Drive for Power, From the Frontier to Master of the Senate* (New York: W. W. Norton, 1982), 35; Barnes, *Combats*, 33-34; Robert Penn Warren, *Remember the Alamo!* (New York: Random House, 1958), 129-30, apparently takes this explanation from F. Templeton, *Margaret Ballentine, or the Fall of the Alamo* (Houston: State Printing, 1907), 174.

15. C. Richard King, *Susanna Dickinson, Messenger of the Alamo* (Austin: Shoal Creek Publishers, 1976), 30-36. For accounts of Dickinson's various interviews see Lord, *Time*, 95; Morphis, *History of Texas*, 174-77; Andrew Jackson Sowell, *Rangers and Pioneers of Texas* (San Antonio: Shepard, 1884), 138-39; Charles W. Evers, interview with Susanna Dickinson, ca. 1878, reprinted in *San Antonio Express*, February 24, 1929; "The Survivor of the Alamo," *San Antonio Express*, April 28, 1881.

16. Henderson K. Yoakum, *History of Texas from its First Settlement to its Annexation to the United States in 1846*, 2 vols. (New York: Redfield, 1856), 2:104-6; Ruth Pittman, "One Did Survive!" *Elks Magazine* (May 1982), as reprinted in *ALAMO Newsletter* 4 (September 1982): 14.

17. Potter, "Fall," 14-15; Barnes, *Combats*, 31-32. The story of the alleged jump appears in Templeton, *Margaret Ballentine*, 185; Sam Houston, *The Writings of Sam Houston*, 1813–1863, ed. Amelia W. Williams and Eugene C. Barker, 8 vols. (Austin: University of Texas, 1938–43), 1:362–65; De la Peña, *With Santa Anna*, 52; Lord, *Time*, 165. Dickinson denied this rumor in her 1878 interview with Evers, see *San Antonio Express*, February 24, 1929.

18. On the Navarro sisters see Lord, *Time*, 95, 164-65, 176, 208; Williams, "Critical Study," 37:169; Chabot, *Makers of San Antonio*, 244; Mary A. Maverick, "Fall of the Alamo," 1889, in Green, ed., *Samuel Maverick*, 55-56. The age of Navarro's son is given variously as eighteen months to eight years.

19. Esparza's recollections appeared originally in two newspaper articles by Charles Merritt Barnes, *San Antonio Express*, May 12 and 19, 1907. Charles H. Stanford, "The Story of the Alamo," in Ryder-Taylor, *History of the Alamo*, 58.

20. Esparza interview, *San Antonio Express*, May 12, 1907; see also Lord, *Time*, 208; Williams, "Critical Study," 37:169-70. The section on Madam Candelaria in a recent juvenile publication—*Our Mexican Ancestors*, by D. Jeanne Callihan (San Antonio: University of Texas Institute of Texan Cultures, 1981), 107-10—is very carefully worded to present Candelaria's story without either confirming or denying it.

21. Maurice Elfer, *Madam Candelaria: Unsung Heroine of the Alamo* (Houston: Rein Co., 1933). While Señora Esparza is known only through the testimony of her son Enrique, Juana de Navarro spoke of her experiences to at least two contemporaries: Mary A. Maverick (see note 18 above) and John S. Ford. Her statement to Ford remains in the Ford papers at the University of Texas Archives but has apparently never been published. Navarro lived until 1880 (see her obituary in the *San Antonio Express*, March 7, 1880) but had been almost forgotten twenty years later, when an Alamo guidebook informed readers, "What became of Mrs. Alsbury and sister [Gertrudis de Navarro] history has not recorded." See Bennett, *Guide to the Alamo*, 100. On Candelaria, see also Corner, *San Antonio*, 117-19; Daniel James Kubiak, *Ten Tall Texans*, rev. ed. (San Antonio: Naylor Co., 1970), 71-82.

22. Birdwell, *News Release*, 64; Moncure Lyne, *The Grito, or, From the Alamo to San Jacinto* (New York: Neale Publishing Co., 1904). "Ursulita" appears as a beautiful apparition in Franklin Y. Martin's play *Death Comes to the Alamo* (Dallas: Tardy Publishing Co., 1935). For further discussion of Anglo-American stereotypes of Hispanics see Weber, ed., *Foreigners*, 60-61; Weber, " 'Scarce more than apes,' Historical Roots of Anglo-American Stereotypes of Mexicans in the Border Region," in *New Spain's Far Northern Frontier*, 296-97; Arnoldo De León, *They Called Them Greasers: Anglo Attitudes Toward Mexicans in Texas, 1821–1900* (Austin: University of Texas Press, 1983), 9-10, 39-43; James M. Lacy, "New Mexican Women in Early American Writings," *New Mexico Historical Review* 34 (January 1959): 41-51.

23. Williams, "Critical Study," 36:268-69, 270-71, 37:22-24. Travis's diary contains numerous references to liaisons with local Hispanic women, see Davis, ed., *Diary*, passim.

24. James P. Newcomb, ed., "The Memoirs of Captain Menchaca," *The Passing Show*, July 20, 1907; José M. Rodríguez, *Rodríguez Memoirs of Early Texas*, 2nd ed. (San Antonio: Standard Printing Co., 1961), 8-9; Esparza interview, *San Antonio Express*, May 12, 1907; Lord, *Time*, 92; Williams, "Critical Study," 37:10-11; Yoakum, *Texas from its First Settlement*, 2:104-6; Houston, *Writings*, 1:364.

25. Rodríguez, *Memoirs*, 8; Constitution of the Republic of Texas, March 17, 1836, General Provisions, Section 8, in Jenkins, ed., *Papers*, 5:113; Weber, ed., *Foreigners*, 145.

26. Ashford, *Spanish Texas*, 202-15; Weber, *Mexican Frontier*, 9-10.

27. George O. Coalson, "Texas Mexicans in the Texas Revolution," in *The American West: Essays in Honor of W. Eugene Hollon*, ed. Ronald Lora (Toledo, Ohio: University of Toledo, 1980), 209-30; Institute of Texan Cultures, *The Mexican Texans* (San Antonio: University of Texas Institute of Texan Cultures, 1971), 10-18; Weber, ed., *Foreigners*, 91-93; Thomas Lloyd Miller, "Mexican Texans in the Texas Revolution," *Journal of Mexican American History* 3 (1973): 105-30.

28. Williams, "Critical Study," 37:242-44, 254-58, 263, 269, 273; Lord, *Time*, 208, 213-19; Weber, ed., *Foreigners*, 91; Thomas Lloyd Miller, "The Roll of the Alamo," *Texana* 2 (Spring 1964): 54-64; Thomas Lloyd Miller, "Mexican-Texans at the Alamo," *Journal of Mexican American History* 2 (Fall 1971): 33-44. Both Lord and Miller conclude that Domingo Losoya did not die at the Alamo; however, more recent evidence uncovered by University of Texas at San Antonio archaeologist Jake Ivey (who directed excavation of the Losoya family home) suggests that Domingo's nephew José Toribio Losoya did fight and die in the Alamo, see Jake Ivey, "The Losoyas and the Texas Revolution," *ALAMO Newsletter* 4 (March 1982): 12-13.

29. Sutherland, *Fall*, 14-15; Lord, *Time*, 74, 78, 87; Williams, "Critical Study," 36:260-61, 268, 271, 275-77, 287, 37:10-11.

30. Sutherland, *Fall*, 21; Williams, "Critical Study," 36:268-69, 37:14, 27-29; claim by Gabriel Martínez, June 1, 1850, file box 60, memorial no. 39, State Department of the State of Texas, cited by Williams, "Critical Study," 37:27.

31. Lord, *Time*, 107-8, 111, 137, 145, 161; Maverick, "Fall of the Alamo," 55-56; Esparza interview, *San Antonio Express*, May 12, 1907; Morphis, *History of Texas*, 175; Williams, "Critical Study," 37:32; De la Peña, *With Santa Anna*, 44.

32. Weber, ed., *Foreigners*, 93.

33. Seguín, *Personal Memoirs*; Chabot, *Makers of San Antonio*, 118-28; Walter Prescott Webb, ed., *The Handbook of Texas*, 2 vols. (Austin: Texas State Historical Association, 1952), 2:589-91; Matt S. Meier and Feliciano Rivera, *Dictionary of Mexican American History* (Westport, Conn.: Greenwood Press, 1981), 325.

34. Seguín, *Memoirs*, iv, 16-18, 26-27.

35. Sutherland, *Fall*, 13; also Potter, "Fall," 21.

36. Paul A. Hutton, "The Celluloid Alamo: A Look at Alamo Films," paper delivered at Eighty-Ninth Annual Meeting of the Texas State Historical Association, Fort Worth, March 2, 1985, pp. 18-19; Don Graham, *Cowboys and Cadillacs: How Hollywood Looks at Texas* (Austin: Texas Monthly Press, 1983), 49-50.

37. Williams, "Critical Study," 37:14; G. P. Stephens, *Texas, A Contest of Civilizations* (Boston: Houghton, Mifflin, 1903), 207.

38. Davis, ed., *Diary*, passim; Virgil E. Baugh, *Rendezvous at the Alamo: Highlights in the Lives of Bowie, Crockett, and Travis* (New York: Pageant Press, 1960), 170-71; Lon Tinkle, *Thirteen Days to Glory: The Siege of the Alamo* (New York: McGraw-Hill Book Co., 1958), 95.

39. Zuber, "Escape," 82.

40. Zuber, "Escape," 80; J. Frank Dobie, "The Line that Travis Drew," in Dobie, Boatright, and Ransom, eds., *In the Shadow of History*, 10, 28; Lord, *Time*, 201-4; Lord, "Myths and Realities," 22-23.

41. Dobie, "The Line," 14; Stanford, "Story of the Alamo," 40-41.

42. Gray, *Virginia to Texas*, 131, 136-38. For Mexican accounts see De la Peña, *With Santa Anna*, 50; Helen Hunnicott, ed., "A Mexican View of the Texas War: Memoirs of a Veteran of the Two Battles of the Alamo," *Library Chronicle of the University of Texas* 4 (Summer 1951): 63, 72. For early reports of Travis's suicide see Jenkins, *Papers*, 5:45-46, 48-49, 51-54, 71-72; Williams, "Critical Study," 37:41-42; Lord, *Time*, 206; Lord, "Myths and Realities," 23-24.

43. Mark E. Nackmann, *A Nation within a Nation: The Rise of Texas Nationalism* (Port Washington, N.Y.: Kennikat Press, 1975), 56-57; James W. Burke, "Death over the Alamo—the Bloody Birth of Texas Independence," in *Missions of Old Texas* (South Brunswick and New York: A. S. Barnes, 1971), 155.

44. Noah Smithwick, *The Evolution of a State; or, Recollections of Old Texas Days*, comp. Norma S. Donaldson (Austin: Gammel Book Co., 1900), 138; John M. Niles, *History of South America and Mexico; . . . To which is Annexed, A Geographical and Historical View of Texas. . . .* (Hartford: H. Huntington, Jun., 1838), 325; Fehrenbach, *Lone Star*, 208.

45. Biographical information on Bowie is drawn primarily from the following sources: J. Frank Dobie, "James Bowie, Big Dealer," *Southwestern Historical Quarterly* 60 (January 1957): 337-57; Dobie, "James Bowie," in *Heroes of Texas* (Waco, Tex.: Texian Press, 1964), 33-53; Williams, "Critical Study," 37:90-115.

46. Edward G. Rohrbough, "How Jim Bowie Died," in Dobie, Boatright, and Ransom, eds., *In the Shadow of History*, 48.

47. Ibid.; Sutherland, *Fall*, 12-13; Potter, "Fall," 8; Lord, *Time*, 199-200; Nixon, *Medical Story*, 181-82.

48. E. Alexander Powell, *The Road to Glory* (New York: Charles Scribner's Sons, 1915), 177.

49. Brooker, *Texas*, 64; Sutherland, *Fall*, 40; Maverick, "Fall of the Alamo," 56; Sowell, *Rangers and Pioneers*, 146-49.

50. Rohrbough, "How Jim Bowie Died," 48-53.

51. Williams, "Critical Study," 37:35-36; Dobie, "James Bowie," *Heroes*, 45; Jenkins, *Papers*, 5:71.

52. J. Frank Dobie, "James Bowie and the Bowie Knife," *Stories of Christmas and the Bowie Knife* (Albuquerque: University of New Mexico Press, 1948), 33-34, 44.

53. Dobie, "James Bowie," *Heroes*, 38; "Use of His Bowie Knife Barred, Star Quits Show," *San Antonio News*, May 1, 1958; "There Was a Man: James Bowie," *Esquire* 32 (November 1949): 67.

54. Edward S. Sears, "The Low Down on Jim Bowie," in *From Hell to Breakfast*, ed. Mody C. Boatright and Donald Day (Austin and Dallas: Texas Folk-Lore Society and University Press, 1944), 199; Dobie, "James Bowie," *Heroes*, 49.

55. Richard B. Hauck, *Crockett: A Bio-Bibliography* (Westport, Conn.: Greenwood Press, 1982), 91-93; "Folk Hero and Fad: The Legend of Davy Crockett," *Disneyland Line* 14 (August 19, 1982).

56. Hauck, *Bio-Bibliography*, 45-47, 67-74. Other sources on Crockett and the Crockett legend include: James Atkins Shackford, *David Crockett: The Man and the Legend*, 2nd ed. (Austin: Pemberton Press, 1968); Constance Rourke, *Davy Crockett* (New York: Harcourt, Brace and Co., 1934); Walter Blair, "Six Davy Crocketts," *Southwest Review* 25 (July 1940): 443-62.

57. Blair, "Six Davy Crocketts," 444, 453.

58. Ibid., 456; Richard Armour, *It All Started With Columbus*. . . . (New York: Bantam Books, 1965), 65; Hauck, *Bio-Bibliography*, 60-62, 107-13, 140-41; Shackford, *David Crockett*, 281-91.

59. Williams, "Critical Study," 37:28-29; Morphis, *History of Texas*, 174-75.

60. Lord, *Time*, 169-74.

61. William Ransom Hogan, "The Theater in the Republic of Texas," *Southwest Review* 19 (July 1934): 390-91; King, *Susanna Dickinson*, 108-11.

62. Vernon L. Parrington, *Main Currents in American Thought, An Interpretation of American Literature from the Beginnings to 1920*, 3 vols. (New York: Harcourt, Brace, 1927), 2:172-79.

63. Lord, "Myths and Realities," 24; Lord, *Time*, 206-7; Jerry J. Gaddy, comp., *Texas in Revolt: Contemporary Newspaper Accounts of the Texas Revolution* (Fort Collins, Colo.: Old Army Press, 1973), 47; Morphis, *History of Texas*, 177; Mary Austin Holley, *Texas* (Lexington, Va.: J. Clarke, 1836), 354.

64. Lord, "Myths and Realities," 24; Kent Biffle, "Surrender? Davy's Fans Never Will," *Dallas Morning News*, January 31, 1985; Kilgore, *How Did Davy Die?*; Hauck, *Bio-Bibliography*, 92-95; "Folk Hero and Fad."

65. *The Alamo*, souvenir book (Hollywood: Sovereign Publications, 1960); Hauck, *Bio-Bibliography*, 95-96.

Chapter 4

1. Sweet and Knox, *On a Mexican Mustang*, 291.

2. William T. Hefley, comp., *In Memory of the Heroes of the Alamo and to Give the Facts of History as to the Resting Place of Their Ashes* ([Cameron, Tex.]: By the Author, 1913).

3. Dugger, *The Politician*, 28-35, 407-9; Hugh Sidey, "Deep Grow the Roots of the Alamo," *Life* 64 (May 31, 1968): 32; Dick McMurray, "Saving the Alamo 'By Law,'" *Austin American Statesman*, December 2, 1968.

4. "Remembering the Alamo," *New York Times*, March 3, 1968, sec. 4, p. 12E.

5. *San Antonio Light*, June 17, 1980.

6. Porter Sparkman, "DRT Girds for Battle Against Filming Alamo," *San Antonio Express*, March 26, 1969.

7. Joe Davenport, "DRT Seeking Injunction," *San Antonio Express*, April 9, 1969; Sweet and Knox, *On a Mexican Mustang*, 286-87; J. Frank Dobie, "The Alamo's Immortalization of Words," *Southwest Review* 27 (Summer 1942): 402-10.

8. Mrs. Jack Trudeau, "Plenty of Embarrassment," *San Antonio Express*, March 28, 1969; Buss and Bechtol, "Besieged by the Alamo," 71-73; Ned Huthmacher, "Another Alamo Filler," *Alamo News* (newsletter of Alamo International) 33 (July 1983); "Alamo Replica Going to Capitol," *San Antonio Express*, June 18, 1937.

9. William H. Goetzmann, "Anglo-American Dreams: Keep the White Lights Shining," *Texas Humanist* 7 (January–February 1985): 30-31; Gregory Curtis, "Behind the Lines," *Texas Monthly* (February 1984): 5; Alvarez quoted in Fred Bonavita, "The Battle Rages on for the Alamo," *Houston Post Sunday Magazine* (August 19, 1984): 17; Bob Greene, "Remember the Alamo?" *Esquire* 101 (April 1984): 12.

Selected Bibliography

The Alamo of History and Imagination

by Paul Andrew Hutton

Historical Background

* Items marked with asterisk are represented in the exhibition and are from the collections of the DeGolyer Library, Southern Methodist University.
† Items marked with dagger are represented in the exhibition and are from the collection of Paul A. Hutton.
‡ Items marked with double dagger are represented in the exhibition and are from other collections as indicated.

Baker, Karle W. "Trailing the New Orleans Greys." *Southwest Review* 22 (April 1937).
* Bennett, Leonora. *Historical Sketch and Guide to the Alamo.* San Antonio: By the Author, 1902.
Binkley, William C. *The Texas Revolution.* Baton Rouge: Louisiana State University Press, 1952.
> The author was chairman of the history department at Vanderbilt University when he gave a series of four lectures at Louisiana State University that were compiled into this little volume. Binkley made no pretense of writing a history of the revolution but instead presented an interpretive overview. His brief book remains the best on this much neglected topic. There is still no solid monograph giving an overview of the revolution.

Castañeda, Carlos E. *Our Catholic Heritage in Texas, 1519–1936.* 7 vols. Austin: Von Boeckmann-Jones Co., 1936–58.
* Chabot, Frederick C. *The Alamo, Altar of Texas Liberty.* [San Antonio]: By the Author, 1931.
——. *The Alamo: Mission, Fortress, and Shrine.* San Antonio: By the Author, 1937.
* Corner, William. *San Antonio de Bexar: A Guide and History.* San Antonio: Bainbridge and Corner, 1890.
* De León, Arnoldo. *They Called Them Greasers: Anglo Attitudes Toward Mexicans in Texas, 1821–1900.* Austin: University of Texas Press, 1983.
* DeShields, James T. *Tall Men With Long Rifles: The Glamorous Story of the Texas Revolution, As Told by Captain Creed Taylor.* . . . San Antonio: Naylor Co., 1935.

* De Zavala, Adina. *History and Legends of the Alamo and Other Missions In and Around San Antonio.* San Antonio: By the Author, 1917.
    * Reprinted in abridged form in 1956 by the Naylor Company as *The Alamo: Where the Last Man Died.*
* Driscoll, Clara. *In the Shadow of the Alamo.* New York: G. P. Putnam's Sons, 1906.
    This collection of stories includes the author's memoir on how she saved the Alamo, a history of the Alamo shrine, and a short fictional tale.
* Eaton, Jack D. *Excavations at the Alamo Shrine (Mission San Antonio de Valero).* San Antonio: University of Texas at San Antonio, Center for Archaeological Research, 1980.

Fehrenbach, T. R. *Lone Star: A History of Texas and the Texans.* New York: Macmillan Co., 1968.

* Ford, John S. *Origin and Fall of the Alamo: March 6, 1836.* San Antonio: Johnson Brothers Printing Co., 1901.

Fox, Anne A., Feris A. Bass, Jr., and Thomas R. Hester. *The Archaeology and History of Alamo Plaza.* San Antonio: Center for Archaeological Research, University of Texas at San Antonio, 1976.

* Frantz, Joe B. "The Alamo." *Battles of Texas.* Waco, Tex.: Texian Press, 1967.
    An excellent color painting of the battle by Donald Yena illustrates the essay.
* Gaddy, Jerry J., comp. *Texas in Revolt: Contemporary Newspaper Accounts of the Texas Revolution.* Fort Collins, Colo.: Old Army Press, 1973.
    These newspaper excerpts, although unfortunately undated, are nicely complemented by color reproductions of paintings by Joseph Hefter, three of which concern the Alamo.

Guerra, Mary Ann Noonan. *The Alamo.* San Antonio: Alamo Press, 1983.

Haley, J. Evetts. *The Alamo Mission Bell.* Austin: Encino Press, 1974.

Houston, Andrew Jackson. *Texas Independence.* Houston: Anson Jones Press, 1938.

Leclerc, Frédéric. *Texas and Its Revolution.* Houston: Anson Jones Press, 1950.
    Translated by James L. Shepherd III from the 1840 French edition.

* Lord, Walter. *A Time to Stand.* New York: Harper & Bros., 1961.
    This is the best book on the battle. Authoritative as well as eminently readable, it reflects the skills of this professional writer on historical topics. Unlike many writers, Lord attempts to place the battle within a larger, national context. Nevertheless, the documentation is hard to follow and the book will not satisfy scholars. It is, however, the book to begin with when studying the Alamo.

———. "Myths and Realities of the Alamo." In *The Republic of Texas*, edited by Stephen B. Oates. Palo Alto, Calif.: American West Publishing Co. and Texas State Historical Association, 1968.

    Lord here addresses several key controversies that surround the Alamo story.

McWilliams, Perry. "The Alamo Story: From Fact to Fable." *Journal of the Folklore Institute* 15 (September-December 1978).

Maillard, N. Doran. *The History of the Republic of Texas....* London: Smith, Elder and Co., 1942.

* Myers, John M. *The Alamo*. New York: E. P. Dutton and Co., 1948.

    Nicely done popular history that focuses on key personalities to present the heroic, traditional version of the story. This book has often been reprinted in paperback format and has thus had a wide reading audience for over thirty years.

Nevin, David. *The Texans*. New York: Time-Life Books, 1975.

    Excellent pictorial history.

Newell, Rev. C. *History of the Revolution in Texas, particularly in the War of 1835 and '36....* New York: Wiley and Putnam, 1838.

Potter, Reuben M. *The Fall of the Alamo: A Reminiscence of the Revolution of Texas*. San Antonio: Herald Steam Press, 1860.

    * Also see *Magazine of American History* 2 (January 1878).

* Sutherland, John. *The Fall of the Alamo*. San Antonio: Naylor Co., 1936.

    First modern reprint of Dr. Sutherland's 1860 memoir. The pamphlet includes a sketch of Sutherland's life by his granddaughter, Annie B. Sutherland, as well as Sutherland's rough drawing of the Alamo grounds.

* Tinkle, Lon. *Thirteen Days to Glory: The Siege of the Alamo*. New York: McGraw-Hill Book Co., 1958.

    A professor at Southern Methodist University, the author painstakingly researched the battle but nevertheless emphasized narrative and drama over analysis and scholarship. Although good popular history for a general audience, it will not satisfy the serious student of the battle.

Vigness, David M. *The Revolutionary Decades: The Saga of Texas, 1810–1836*. Austin: Steck Vaughn Co., 1965.

Weber, David J. *The Mexican Frontier, 1821–1846: The American Southwest Under Mexico*. Albuquerque: University of New Mexico Press, 1982.

    A superb overview of Mexico's northern frontier during the era of the Texas War for Independence. This book provides the essential background to the Alamo story.

Wharton, Clarence R. *The Republic of Texas: A Brief History.* . . . Houston: C. C. Young Printing Company, 1922.

Williams, Alfred M. *Sam Houston and the War of Independence in Texas.* Boston: Houghton, Mifflin and Co., 1895.

Williams, Amelia W. "A Critical Study of the Siege of the Alamo and of the Personnel of Its Defenders." Ph.D. diss., University of Texas, 1931.

    Published in part in the *Southwestern Historical Quarterly* 36 (1932–33) and 37 (1933–34). Williams's work, long considered the standard academic reference on the battle, is of stunningly poor quality.

* Yoakum, Henderson K. *History of Texas from its First Settlement to its Annexation to the United States in 1846.* New York: Redfield, 1856. Vol. 2 of 2.

Young, Kevin R. "Major Babbitt and the Alamo 'Hump.' " *Military Images* 6 (July-August 1984).

    The reconstruction of the Alamo by the U.S. Army.

The Texans

Adair, A. Garland, and M. H. Crockett, Sr., eds. *Heroes of the Alamo: Accounts and Documents of William B. Travis, James Bowie, James B. Bonham and David Crockett, and Their Texas Memorials.* 2nd ed. New York: Exposition Press, 1957.

    Essentially a reprint of the January 1956 issue of *Under Texas Skies*.

Baugh, Virgil E. *Rendezvous at the Alamo: Highlights in the Lives of Bowie, Crockett, and Travis.* New York: Pageant Press, 1960.

Blair, Walter. "Six Davy Crocketts." *Southwest Review* 25 (July 1940).

Burke, James W. *David Crockett: The Man Behind the Myth.* Austin: Eakin Press, 1984.

* Butterfield, Jack C. *Men of the Alamo, Goliad and San Jacinto: An Analysis of the Motives and Actions of the Heroes of the Texas Revolution.* San Antonio: Naylor Co., 1936.

Canales, José Thomas, ed. *Bits of Texas History in the Melting Pot of America: Native Latin American Contribution to the Colonization and Independence of Texas.* San Antonio: Artes Graficas, 1957.

* [Crockett, David]. *The Adventures of Davy Crockett, Told Mostly by Himself.* New York: Charles Scribner's Sons, 1934.

    This book contains both the authentic 1834 *A Narrative of the Life of Davy*

Crockett of the State of Tennessee and the spurious 1836 *Col. Crockett's Exploits and Adventures in Texas*. What makes this a particularly desirable edition of Crockett's autobiography is the wonderful illustrations, in both color and black-and-white, by noted Texas artist John W. Thomason, Jr. In the 1955 reprint of this book, Thomason's color frontispiece depicting Crockett as a prisoner being led before Santa Anna was dropped from the volume.

* Davis, Robert E., ed. *The Diary of William Barret Travis: August 30, 1833–June 26, 1834*. Waco, Tex.: Texian Press, 1966.

* Dobie, J. Frank. *Stories of Christmas and the Bowie Knife*. Austin: Steck Co., 1953.

———. *James Bowie, Big Dealer*. Austin: By the Author, 1957.

> The author sent out this pamphlet as a Christmas greeting with a printed dedication that reads: "Neither Jim Bowie nor anything that could be truthfully written about him signifies Christmas. But we send this booklet with good hearts, and while wishing you all a Merry Christmas wish for Texas a nobler set of heroes." Dobie contributed an essay entitled "Bowie and the Bowie Knife" to the *Southwest Review* in 1931 and published the article from which this pamphlet was reprinted in the January 1957 issue of the *Southwestern Historical Quarterly*. A similar Bowie piece is in Dobie's *Tales of Old-Time Texas* (Boston: Little, Brown and Co., 1955).

Dobie, J. Frank, Mody C. Boatright, and Harry H. Ransom, eds. *In the Shadow of History*. Dallas: Southern Methodist University Press, 1980.

> First published by the Texas Folklore Society in 1939 and now available in a facsimile reprint from SMU Press, this volume contains essays by J. Frank Dobie on Travis's line, by Edward G. Rohrbough on the numerous versions of Jim Bowie's death, and reprint essays on Louis Rose by W. P. Zuber and R. B. Blake.

Dorson, Richard M., ed. *Davy Crockett: American Comic Legend*. New York: Rockland Editions, 1939.

> Reprints many of the tall tales and original illustrations from the Crockett Almanacs published from 1835 to 1856.

* Douglas, Claude L. *James Bowie, The Life of a Bravo*. Dallas: Banks Upshaw and Co., 1944.

> This is the best biography of Bowie, although that is not saying much for it.

Elfer, Maurice. *Madam Candelaria: Unsung Heroine of the Alamo*. Houston: Rein Co., 1933.

> This pamphlet presents Candelaria's rather imaginative and supposedly eyewitness account of the battle.

Ellis, Edward S. *The Life of Colonel David Crockett*. Philadelphia: Porter and Coates, 1884.
> The author was a prolific writer of historical fiction and popular history in the nineteenth century. This biography of Crockett went through numerous editions and was a popular book for generations of young Americans. Ellis also authored at least four fictional works on Crockett.

Hauck, Richard B. *Crockett: A Bio-Bibliography*. Westport, Conn.: Greenwood Press, 1982.
> This volume in Greenwood Press's popular culture series addresses the evolution of the Crockett legend.

* *Heroes of Texas*. Waco, Tex.: Texian Press, 1964.
> This anthology features "James Butler Bonham" by Ben Proctor, "James Bowie" by J. Frank Dobie, "David Crockett" by H. Bailey Carroll, and "William B. Travis" by Joe B. Frantz. Portraits of each hero by C. B. Normann are featured.

* Kilgore, Dan. *How Did Davy Die?* College Station: Texas A&M University Press, 1978.
> Careful research led the author to conclude that Crockett did indeed surrender and was executed on the order of Santa Anna. This little book originated as Kilgore's presidential address before the Texas State Historical Association in 1977. Despite the author's solid research and balanced perspective, the book continues to be the subject of controversy.

Kilpatrick, Dr. "Early Life in the Southwest—The Bowies." *DeBow's Review* 13 (October 1852).

* King, C. Richard. *Susanna Dickinson, Messenger of the Alamo*. Austin: Shoal Creek Publishers, 1976.

King, Margaret Jane. "The Davy Crockett Craze: A Case Study in Popular Culture." Ph.D. diss., University of Hawaii, 1976.

Leach, Joseph. *The Typical Texan: Biography of an American Myth*. Dallas: Southern Methodist University Press, 1952.
> An excellent exploration of the evolution of the Texan persona with much on Davy Crockett and the Alamo.

Lodge, Henry Cabot, and Theodore Roosevelt. *Hero Tales from American History*. New York: Century Co., 1895.

* Contains Roosevelt's essay "Remember the Alamo"; reissued in 1909 as Roosevelt's *Stories of the Great West*.

McDonald, Archie P. *Travis*. Austin: Jenkins Publishing Co., 1976.

Meine, Franklin J., ed. *The Crockett Almanacks: Nashville Series, 1835–1838*. Chicago: Caxton Club, 1955.

Mixon, Ruby. "William Barret Travis: His Life and Letters." Master's thesis, University of Texas, 1930.

Rourke, Constance. *Davy Crockett*. New York: Harcourt, Brace and Co., 1934.

———. "Davy Crockett: Forgotten Facts and Legends." *Southwest Review* 19 (January 1934).

* Ryan, William M. *Shamrock and Cactus: The Story of the Catholic Heroes of Texas Independence*. San Antonio: Southern Literary Institute, 1936.

Seguín, Juan N. *Personal Memoirs of John N. Seguín, From the Year 1834 to the Retreat of General Woll From the City of San Antonio 1842*. San Antonio: Ledger Book and Job Office, 1858.

* Reprinted in David J. Weber, *Northern Mexico on the Eve of the United States Invasion* (New York: Arno Press, 1976).

Shackford, James Atkins. *David Crockett: The Man and the Legend*. Chapel Hill: University of North Carolina Press, 1956.

Reissued by Pemberton Press, Austin, 1968, this is the best biography of Crockett available, although it is by no means definitive. The author was stricken with an incapacitating illness, which eventually took his life, and could not finish the book. The final editing and writing was done by his brother, John B. Shackford.

Shackford, James A., and Stanley J. Folmsbee, eds. *A Narrative of the Life of David Crockett of the State of Tennessee by David Crockett*. Knoxville: University of Tennessee Press, 1973.

This is the definitive edition of Crockett's autobiography with excellent annotations by the editors. It is based on James Atkins Shackford's 1948 doctoral dissertation at Vanderbilt University.

* Thorp, Raymond W. *Bowie Knife*. Albuquerque: University of New Mexico Press, 1948.
This is still the best book on Bowie and his knife.

Turner, Martha Anne. *William Barret Travis: His Sword and His Pen*. Waco, Tex.: Texian Press, 1972.

Wellman, Paul I. *Good Soldiers Do Die*. Dallas: Times Herald, 1951.

> Brief pamphlet on Jim Bowie and the Alamo by the distinguished novelist.

Williams, Robert H. "Travis—A Potential Sam Houston." *Southwestern Historical Quarterly* 40 (October 1936).

The Mexicans

Alessio Robles, Vito. *Coahuila y Texas desde la Consumación de la Independencia hasta el Tratado de Paz de Guadalupe Hidalgo*. México: n.p., 1945–46.

> Translated by David Glenn Hunt (master's thesis, Southern Methodist University, 1950) and Laron D. Jorda (master's thesis, Southern Methodist University, 1950).

Asbury, Samuel E., ed. "The Private Journal of Juan Nepomuceno Almonte, February 1–April 16, 1836." *Southwestern Historical Quarterly* 48 (July 1944).

Becerra, Francisco. *A Mexican Sergeant's Recollections of the Alamo and San Jacinto . . . as Told to John S. Ford in 1875*. Austin: Jenkins Publishing Co., 1980.

> This memoir, first published in 1882, is rather imaginative but still contains some valuable information. Dan Kilgore wrote an introduction to this edition.

Callcott, Wilfrid Hardy. *Santa Anna: The Story of an Enigma Who Once Was Mexico*. Norman: University of Oklahoma Press, 1936.

* Castañeda, Carlos E., trans. *The Mexican Side of the Texan Revolution [1836] by the Chief Mexican Participants*. Dallas: P. L. Turner, 1928.

> This is a key source for the Alamo, although the memoirs are often self-serving and must be read with caution.

Crawford, Ann Fears, ed. *The Eagle: The Autobiography of Santa Anna*. Austin: Pemberton Press, 1967.

* De la Peña, José Enrique. *With Santa Anna in Texas: A Personal Narrative of the Revolution*. Translated and edited by Carmen Perry. College Station: Texas A&M University Press, 1975.

> The publication of this excellent narrative by one of Santa Anna's staff officers caused considerable controversy because it asserts that Davy Crockett surrendered and was executed. The editor, the former director of the Daughters of the Republic of Texas Library at the Alamo, was bitterly criticized by fanatical defenders of the heroic Crockett legend.

* Filisola, Vicente. *Representacion Dirigida al Supremo Gobierno . . . en Defensa de su Honor y Aclaracion de sus Operaciones. . . .* Mexico: I. Cumplido, 1836.

———. *Memorias Para la Historia de la Guerra de Tejas*. 2 vols. Mexico City: Tipografia de R. Rafael, 1848.

Fuentes Mares, José. *Santa Anna: Aurora y Ocaso de un Comediante*. Mexico City: Editorial Jus, 1956.

* Hanighen, Frank C. *Santa Anna: The Napoleon of the West*. New York: Coward-McCann, 1934.

> Popular history. The dust jacket for the book features a depiction of the battle of the Alamo. Although the battle was but a minor episode in Santa Anna's eventful life, the publishers well knew how to instantly identify the General to the book-buying public.

Jones, Oakah L., Jr. *Santa Anna*. New York: Twayne Publishers, 1968.

Muñoz, Rafael F. *Santa Anna*. Mexico City: Editorial "Mexico Nuevo," 1937.

Pereyra, Carlos. *Tejas, La Primera Desmembración de Méjico*. Madrid: Editorial-America, [1917].

Sánchez Lamego, Miguel A. *The Siege and Taking of the Alamo*. Santa Fe, N.M.: Press of the Territorian, 1968.

> * A modern Mexican general's viewpoint on the battle, translated by Consuelo Velasco from the author's *Sitio y Toma del Alamo*, 1966.

* Sánchez-Navarro, Carlos, ed. *La Guerra de Tejas: Memorias de un Soldado*. Mexico City: Editorial Polis, 1938.

Santa Anna, Antonio López de. *Manifiesto Que de sus Operaciones en la Campaña de Tejas*. . . . Vera Cruz: Imprenta Liberal a cargo de Antonio María Valdes, 1837.

Santos, Richard G. *Santa Anna's Campaign Against Texas, 1835–1836, Featuring the Field Commands Issued to Major General Vicente Filisola*. 2nd ed., rev. Salisbury, N.C.: Documentary Publications, [1981].

> Invaluable source for the official Mexican military record of the Texas revolution.

* Trujillo Herrera, Rafael. *Olvidate de "El Alamo": Ensayo Historico*. Mexico City: Populibros la Prensa, 1965.

> The modern Mexican viewpoint, "Forget the Alamo."

Valades, Jose C. *Santa Anna y la Guerra de Texas*. Mexico City: Imprenta Mundial, 1936.

Wharton, Clarence R. *El Presidente: A Sketch of the Life of General Santa Anna*. Houston: C. C. Young Printing Co., 1924.

Fiction

Acheson, Sam. "We Are Besieged." *Southwest Review* 47 (Autumn 1941).
> * Alamo play, performed by the Little Theater of Dallas with set design by Jerry Bywaters and Lester E. Lang; also published in *Three Southwest Plays*, 1941.

* Armour, Richard. *It All Started with Columbus. . . .* New York: Bantam Books, 1965.
> Noted humorist includes small section on "The Winning of Texas."

Baker, Karle W. *Star of the Wilderness*. New York: Coward-McCann, 1942.
> Novel based on the career of Dr. James Grant, a leader of the Matamoros expedition.

† Barr, Amelia E. *Remember the Alamo*. New York: Dodd, Mead and Co., 1888.

* Barrett, Monte. *The Tempered Blade*. Indianapolis: Bobbs-Merrill Co., 1946.
> The 1950s television series on Jim Bowie was based on this novel.

Bennett, Johonnas. *La Belle San Antone*. New York: Neale Publishing Co., 1909.

* Berry, Viola R. *The Alamo and Other Poems*. Denton, Texas: News Publishing Co., 1906.
> Sixty-four-page poem on the battle.

* Birdwell, Russell. *A News Release: John Wayne's "The Alamo."* New York: Russell Birdwell, 1960.
> This 183-page book on the film contains publicity photographs and news releases.

Blalock, Robert, and Clinton Giddings Brown. *Ramrod Jones, Hunter and Patriot: A Tale of the Texas Revolution against Mexico*. Akron, Ohio: Saalfield Publishing Co., 1905.

* Blandin, Isabella M. E. *From Gonzales to San Jacinto . . . A Historical Drama of the Texas Revolution*. Houston: Dealey and Baker, 1897.

* Bowman, Jonathan. *The Alamo: The Cradle of Texas Liberty*. San Antonio: Maverick-Clarke Litho. Co., 1897. (Poem)

Brogan, Evelyn. *James Bowie: A Hero of the Alamo*. San Antonio: Theodore Kunzman, 1922.

† Brown, Dee. *Wave High the Banner: A Novel Based on the Life of Davy Crockett*. Philadelphia: Macrae-Smith-Co., 1942.

Brown, Kitt. *Texas Wildflower*. New York: Fawcett Gold Medal Books, 1982.

Bryan, J. Y. *Come to the Bower*. New York: Viking Press, 1963.

Bryant, Christopher, *The Bee Hunter*. New York: Pageant Press, 1966.
> Novel based on the character in *Col. Crockett's Exploits and Adventures in Texas*, 1836.

* Burke, James W. *The Blazing Dawn*. New York: Pyramid Books, 1975.

Calkins, William H. *Sung at the Alamo*. Dallas: Mathis, Van Nort and Co., 1937.

Clemens, Jeremiah. *Bernard Lile; an Historical Romance.* . . . Philadelphia: J. B. Lippincott and Co., 1856.

    This early novel contains a chapter on the Alamo. The hero escapes the fortress as a courier to Fannin.

Crozier, D. D. *Golden Rule: A Tale of Texas*. Richmond, Va.: Whittet and Shepperson, Printers, 1900.

† Culp, John H. *The Men of Gonzales*. New York: William Sloane Associates, 1960.

Davis, J. Frank. *The Road to San Jacinto*. Indianapolis: Bobbs-Merrill Co., 1936.

Edson, J. T. *The Quest for Bowie's Blade*. London: Transworld Publishers, 1974.

———. *Ole Devil at San Jacinto*. London: Transworld Publishers, 1977.

Evans, Augusta J. *Inez: A Tale of the Alamo*. New York: G. W. Carleton and Co., Publishers, 1871.

    † Also issued in serial format in paper wrappers, n.d.

Fairman, Paula, *Wild Hearts*. New York: Pinnacle Books, 1984.

    Modern romance novel that uses the Alamo as a setting. The Alamo has proven quite popular with the authors of these paperback romances. Other Alamo romance novels are Ann Forman Barron, *Banner Bold and Beautiful* (Greenwich, Conn.: Fawcett, 1975); Shana Carrol, *Yellow Rose* (New York: Jove Publications, 1982); Rebecca Drury, *Wives and Widows* (New York: Dell Publishing Co., 1982); Corrine Johnston, *The Texan Women* (New York: Jove Publications, 1977); Elinor Lockwood, *Miranda* (New York: Leisure Books, 1977); Willo Davis Roberts, *Victoria* (New York: Scholastic Books, 1985).

† Fletcher, Farris. *Remember the Alamo*. New York: Dell Publishing Co., 1982.

Foreman, L. L. *The Road to San Jacinto*. New York: E. P. Dutton and Co., 1943.

Frazee, Steve. *The Alamo*. New York: Avon Book Division, 1960.

    Paperback novel tie-in for the John Wayne film.

* Ganilh, Anthony [A. T. Myrthe]. *Ambrosio de Letinez, or the First Texian Novel.* . . . 2 vols. New York: Charles Francis and Co., 1842.

    Issued under the pseudonym A. T. Myrthe and first published in 1838 under the title *Mexico Versus Texas, A Descriptive Novel.* . . . (Philadelphia: N. Siegfried).

Gilliam, David Tod. *The Rose Croix*. Akron, Ohio: Saalfield Publishing Co., 1906.

Gorman, Herbert. *The Wine of San Lorenzo*. New York: Farrer and Rinehart, 1945.

A young boy survives the battle of the Alamo and is adopted as the ward of Santa Anna.

Gray, Edward McQueen. *Alamo and Other Verses*. Florence, N.M.: By the Author, 1898.

† Hartman, Dane. *Dirty Harry: Duel for Cannons*. New York: Warner Books, 1981.
Modern detective novel with the climactic final shootout at the Alamo.

* Heavenhill, William S. *Siege of the Alamo: A Mexico-Texan Tale*. San Antonio: Schulz and Schott, 1888. (Poetry)

Hunter, Theresa M. *Romantic Interludes: Love Stories of Texas Heroes*. San Antonio: Naylor Co., 1936.
Includes stories on Bowie and Travis.

Jakes, John. *The Furies*. Garden City, N.Y.: Nelson Doubleday, 1976.
Volume four of the highly successful Kent family novels. Only the first part of the book concerns the Alamo.

Kelton, Elmer. *Massacre at Goliad*. New York: Ballantine Books, 1965.

Knaggs, John R. *The Bugles Are Silent: A Novel of the Texas Revolution*. Austin: Shoal Creek Publishers, 1977.

Knapp, George L. *The Lone Star of Courage*. New York: Dodd, Mead and Co., 1931.

Krey, Laura. *On the Long Tide*. Boston: Houghton Mifflin Co., 1940.

* Lehrer, James. *Viva Max!* New York: Duell, Sloan and Pearce, 1966.
Satirical novel upon which the Peter Ustinov film was based.

Lyle, Eugene P., Jr. *The Lone Star*. New York: Doubleday, Page and Co., 1907.

† Lyne, Moncure. *The Grito, or, From the Alamo to San Jacinto*. New York: Neale Publishing Co., 1904.

* McLane, Hiram H. *The Capture of the Alamo: A Historical Tragedy, in Four Acts, with Prologue*. San Antonio: San Antonio Printing Co., 1886.

Martin, Franklin Y. *Death Comes to the Alamo: The Last Hours of Travis and his Immortals*. Dallas: Tardy Publishing Co., 1935. (Play)

Mayer, Edwin Justus. *Sunrise in My Pocket or The Last Days of Davy Crockett: An American Saga*. New York: Julian Messner, 1941.
A play based on the last three months of Crockett's life. The author presented his play as a reminder that the struggle then going on against Hitler was not without parallel.

* Nona, Francis. *The Fall of the Alamo, An Historical Drama in Four Acts. . . .* New York: G. P. Putnam's Sons, 1879.

* Another booklet, *Patriotic Texan Hymns from the Fall of the Alamo*, was published in conjunction with Nona's play.
* Porter, Jenny L. *The Siege of the Alamo*. Los Angeles: Pepperdine University Press, 1981.
    Epic poem, with illustrations by David Damm.
* Read, Opie. *In the Alamo*. Chicago: Rand, McNally and Co., 1900.

Roark, Garland, and Charles Thomas. *Hellfire Jackson*. Garden City, N.Y.: Doubleday and Co., 1966.

Satterfield, Mabel Sturdivant. *The Lone Star Rises*. Dallas: Story Book Press, 1936.

† Stoddard, William O. *The Lost Gold of the Montezumas: A Story of the Alamo*. Philadelphia: J. B. Lippincott, 1898.
    Jim Bowie finds the San Saba mine, but the secret dies with him in the Alamo.

* Templeton, Frank. *Margaret Ballentine, or the Fall of the Alamo*. Houston: State Printing Co., 1907.

Venable, Clarke. *All the Brave Rifles*. Chicago: Reilly and Lee Co., 1929.

Vernon-Cole, Willis. *The Star of the Alamo*. New York: Writer's Guild, 1926.

Watts, Morton S. *The Maid of the Alamo, or the Incarnation of Chivalry: A Story of the Texas Revolution*. Mineral Wells, Tex.: n.p., 1913. (Poetry)

* Wellman, Paul I. *The Iron Mistress*. Garden City, N.Y.: Doubleday and Co., 1951.
    This novel, based on the career of Jim Bowie, is probably the best of the Alamo fiction.

† Yelvington, Ramsey. *A Cloud of Witnesses: The Drama of the Alamo*. Austin: University of Texas Press, 1959.
    This play was performed in San Antonio in 1958 by the Baylor Theatre group.

Children's Books
(Fiction, unless otherwise noted)

Allen, Edward. *Heroes of Texas*. New York: Julian Messner, 1970. (History)

Altsheler, Joseph A. *The Texan Scouts: A Story of the Alamo and Goliad*. New York: D. Appleton and Co., 1913.
    The author wrote a three-novel series on the Texas revolution for young boys. *The Texan Star*, 1912, and *The Texan Triumph*, 1913, were the other volumes.

‡ Baker, Karle W. *Texas Flag Primer*. Yonkers-on-Hudson: World Book Co., 1926. Loaned by Susan Wheeler.
    Elementary reader illustrated by Rodney Thomson.

Beals, Frank L. *Davy Crockett*. Evanston, Ill.: Row, Peterson and Co., 1941.
    Fictionalized biography.

Beecher, Elizabeth. *Walt Disney's Davy Crockett King of the Wild Frontier.* New York: Simon and Schuster, 1955.

    This was the large-format "Big Golden Book" tie-in with the Disney television show and film.

Bosworth, Allan R. *Ladd of the Lone Star.* New York: Aladdin Books, 1952.

Brady, Cyrus Townsend. *Border Fights and Fighters.* Garden City, N.Y.: Doubleday, Page and Co., 1916.

    ‡ This history of the early frontier contains "David Crockett and the Most Desperate Defense in American History," which also appeared in *McClures Magazine* 17 (January 1902). Fondren Library, SMU.

Burton, Ardis E. *Walt Disney Legends of Davy Crockett.* Racine, Wis.: Whitman Publishing Co., 1955.

    Adaptation of the Disney television programs.

* Callihan, D. Jeanne. *Our Mexican Ancestors.* Stories for Young Readers, vol. 1. San Antonio: University of Texas Institute of Texan Cultures, 1981.

    This history reflects the new emphasis on ethnic pluralism in the Texas heritage. It includes chapters on Juan Seguín, Madame Candelaria, Enrique Esparza, and Juan Martín de Veramendi and his friendship with Jim Bowie.

* Casad, Mary B. *Bluebonnet at the Alamo.* Austin: Eakin Press, 1984.

    Delightful story concerning the visit of Bluebonnet the armadillo to the Alamo, where she helps retrieve Jim Bowie's knife. Illustrated by Pat Binder.

* *Cobblestone* 3 (March 1982).

    Special issue devoted to the Alamo; includes non-fiction and fiction.

* Cousins, Margaret. *We Were There at the Battle of the Alamo.* New York: Grosset and Dunlap, 1958.

    Excellent historical fiction for children, with wonderful illustrations by Nicholas Eggenhoffer.

Crownfield, Gertrude. *Lone Star Rising.* New York: Thomas Y. Crowell Co., 1940.

Davis, Hazal H. *Davy Crockett: Frontiersman and Indian Scout.* New York: Random House, 1955.

    Biography for young children, profusely illustrated by William Moyers.

Downey, Fairfax. *Texas and the War with Mexico.* New York: American Heritage Publishing Co., 1961.

    Excellent history.

Ellis, Edward S. *"Remember the Alamo."* Philadelphia: John C. Winston Co., 1914.

Flynn, Jean. *Jim Bowie: A Texas Legend*. Burnet, Tex.: Eakin Press, 1980.
    Fictionalized biography.
———. *William Barret Travis*. Austin: Eakin Press, 1982.
    Fictionalized biography.
† Ford, Anne. *Davy Crockett*. A See and Read Biography. New York: G. P. Putnam's Sons, 1961.
    Juvenile biography, illustrated by Leonard Vosburgh.
Garst, Shannon. *James Bowie and His Famous Knife*. New York: Julian Messner, 1955.
    This volume in the popular Messner juvenile biography series went through nine editions.
Hall-Quest, Olga W. *Shrine of Liberty: The Alamo*. New York: E. P. Dutton and Co., 1948. (History)
Hoff, Carol. *Johnny Texas*. Chicago: Follett Publishing Co., 1950.
    This award-winning children's novel concerns events before and during the Texas revolution.
Holbrook, Stewart H. *Davy Crockett: From the Backwoods of Tennessee to the Alamo*. New York: Random House, 1955.
    Standard juvenile biography in the famous Landmark Books series.
Johnson, William Weber. *The Birth of Texas*. Boston: Houghton Mifflin Co., 1960.
    This juvenile history often crosses over into fiction with invented dialogue, rather standard for this type of book. The illustrator, Herb Mott, shows the Alamo defenders armed with six-shooter revolvers.
Kerr, Rita. *Girl of the Alamo*. Austin: Eakin Press, 1984.
    Fiction concerning Susanna Dickinson.
Lenvers, Léo. *Davy Crockett; Le Coureur des Bois*. [France]: Fernand Nathan, 1984.
    French juvenile biography illustrated by Jean Marcellin.
Lockwood, Myna. *Up with Your Banner*. New York: E. P. Dutton and Co., 1946.
McCaleb, Walter F. *The Alamo*. San Antonio: Naylor Co., 1956. (History)
* ———. *William Barret Travis*. San Antonio: Naylor Co., 1957. (Biography)
† McIntyre, John T. *In Texas With Davy Crockett*. Philadelphia: Penn Publishing Co., 1926.
* McNeil, Everett. *In Texas with Davy Crockett: A Story of the Texas War of Independence*. 6th printing. New York: E. P. Dutton and Co., 1931.
    First published in 1908.

* McSpadden, J. Walker. *Texas, A Romantic Story for Young People*. New York: J. H. Sears and Co., 1927.
>Illustrated by Howard L. Hastings.

Meadowcroft, Enid L. *The Story of Davy Crockett*. New York: Grosset and Dunlap, 1952.
>A volume in the famous "Signature Books" series of juvenile biographies.

† Miers, Earl S. *The Rainbow Book of American History*. Cleveland: World Publishing Co., 1955.
>History, illustrated by James Daugherty.

† Munroe, Kirk. *With Crockett and Bowie, or Fighting for the Lone-Star Flag*. New York: Charles Scribner's Sons, 1905.

† Murphy, Keith. *Battle of the Alamo*. Milwaukee: Raintree Publishers, 1979.
>Nonfiction dealing mostly with Davy Crockett.

Parks, Aileen Wells. *Davy Crockett: Young Rifleman*. Indianapolis: Bobbs-Merrill Co., 1949.
>This volume in the "Childhood of Famous Americans" series is still in print.

Patten, Lewis B. *The Adventures of Jim Bowie*. Racine, Wis.: Whitman Publishing Co., 1958.
>Fiction based on the Jim Bowie television series starring Scott Forbes.

* Pennybacker, Anna J. *A New History of Texas for Schools*. . . . Tyler, Texas, 1888. (School text)

* ———. *A History of Texas for Schools*. . . . Rev. ed. Austin: By the Author, 1924. (School text)

Richards, Norman. *The Story of the Alamo*. Chicago: Childrens Press, 1970.
>History with nice illustrations by Tom Dunnington.

Richey, Dorothy H. *Road to San Jacinto*. San Antonio: Naylor Co., 1961.

Sabin, Edwin L. *With Sam Houston in Texas*. Philadelphia: J. B. Lippincott Co., 1916.

Shapiro, Irving. *Yankee Thunder: The Legendary Life of Davy Crockett*. New York: Julian Messner, 1944.
>The author based his book around the Davy Crockett of the Crockett Almanacs, not the real frontiersman, so the Alamo is not an important part of this fine children's book. The text is complemented by wonderful James Daugherty illustrations.

† ———. *Walt Disney's Davy Crockett King of the Wild Frontier*. New York: Simon and Schuster, 1955.

The "Little Golden Book" tie-in to the Disney film.

† ———. *Walt Disney's Davy Crockett Stamp Book.* New York: Simon and Schuster, 1955.

Staffelbach, E. H. *For Texas and Freedom.* San Francisco: Harr Wagner Publishing Co., 1953.

* Stratemeyer, Edward [Ralph Bonehill]. *For the Liberty of Texas.* Boston: Dana Estes and Co., 1900.

    Stratemeyer was a prolific author of juvenile historical fiction and often wrote under the pen name of Captain Ralph Bonehill.

Templeton, R. L. *Cannon Boy of the Alamo.* Quanah, Tex.: Nortex Press, 1975.

———. *Alamo Soldier: The Story of Peaceful Mitchell.* Quanah, Tex.: Nortex Press, 1976.

† Tinkle, Lon. *The Valiant Few: Crisis at the Alamo.* New York: Macmillan Co., 1964.

    Nicely illustrated history.

* Warren, Robert Penn. *Remember the Alamo!* New York: Random House, 1958.

† Whitford, Joan [Rex James]. *Buffalo Bill Wild West Annual No. 8.* London: Popular Press for T. V. Boardman Co., [1956].

    Contains a twelve-page story "Bravest of the Brave" on the Alamo, with color illustrations by Denis McLoughlin, a famous British comic book artist. This popular series of British children's books was written under the pseudonym Rex James.

Winders, Gertrude Hecker. *Jim Bowie: Boy with a Hunting Knife.* Indianapolis: Bobbs-Merrill Co., 1953.

    A volume in the "Childhood of Famous Americans" series.

Comic Books and Cartoons

The Adventures of Jim Bowie, no. 893 (1958) and no. 993 (1959). New York: Dell Publishing Co. † No. 993.

    Tie-in with the television series. There were only two issues of this comic, and neither concerned the Alamo.

Blazing the Trails West, no. 144A (June 1958). New York: Gilberton Co.

    This special issue by the "Classics Illustrated" publisher was part of a three-part series on frontier history. It contains an excellent thirteen-page story "Texas and the Alamo," with artwork by John Severin.

Cheyenne Kid, no. 28 (May 1961). Derby, Conn.: Charlton Comics Group.

In "Remember the Alamo" the Cheyenne Kid and George Kimbell lead the thirty-two from Gonzales into the Alamo. The hero escapes the battle by carrying out Travis's last message.

Cowboy Picture Library, no. 299 (1959). London: Amalgamated Press.

This issue of the British comic book is devoted to Davy Crockett.

† *Davy Crockett*, no. 129 (September 1966). New York: Gilberton Co.

The "Classics Illustrated" version of Crockett's life, based on the autobiography.

Davy Crockett, no. 34 (March 1970). Milan, Italy: Editoriale Cepim/Daim Press.

An Italian version of the pre-Alamo exploits of Crockett. Another issue was published in April 1970 (*Davy Crockett in Attaco Notturno*), and both were reprints of comics first done in 1957 by G. Bonelli.

Davy Crockett, no. 12 (1977). New York: King Features Syndicate.

This American edition of a Spanish comic book features some particularly fascinating graphics as the artist presents a European version of the Alamo. There was only one issue.

Davy Crockett Frontier Fighter, no. 1 (August 1955). Derby, Conn.: Charlton Comics Group.

There were eight issues of this comic book published between 1955 and 1957.

Dead-Eye Western, no. 1 (November–December 1948). New York: Hillman Periodicals.

"The Bowie Knife and the Alamo" features an amazingly negative depiction of the Mexicans.

Eerie, no. 82 (March 1977). New York: Warren Publishing Co.

This issue introduced the science fiction hero "Rook," who uses his time machine to return to the Alamo to try and rescue his great-great-grandfather. Nice artwork by Luis Bermejo.

Farr, Naunerle C. *Davy Crockett/Daniel Boone*. West Haven, Conn.: Pendulum Press, 1979.

Pendulum Press published this paperback book as part of an educational comic book series for use in the schools. It contains excellent graphics by Fred Carrillo.

† *Frontier Fighter Davy Crockett*, no. 1 (1951). New York: Avon Periodicals.

This version of the Alamo has Crockett killed as he attempts to blow up the powder magazine. There was only one issue of this comic book.

† Hess, Mark. "Remember the Alamo?" Cover illustration, *National Lampoon* 2 (September 1980).

† *Histoire du Far West: Une Bande Dessinée Larousse.* Paris, France: Librairie Larousse, 1980.

    French hardback comic book on the history of the frontier. "Fort Alamo" by Frank Giroud is one of three historical stories in the book. Excellent artwork by José Bielsa.

Jace Pearson's Tales of the Texas Rangers, no. 18 (December–February 1958). New York: Dell Publishing Co.

    This issue includes a four-page story "Famous Texans: William Barrett Travis."

* Jackson, Jack. *Recuerden El Alamo: The True Story of Juan N. Seguín and His Fight for Texas Independence.* Berkeley, Calif.: Last Gasp, 1979.

* ———. *Tejano Exile: The True Story of Juan N. Seguín and the Texas-Mexicans after San Jacinto.* San Francisco: Last Gasp, 1980.

* ———. *Los Tejanos: The True Story of Juan N. Seguín and the Texas-Mexicans During the Rising of the Lone Star.* Stamford, Conn.: Fantagraphics Books, 1982.

    Superb black-and-white comic book rendering of the story of Juan Seguín with an excellent color cover depicting Seguín at the Alamo. The 136-page book combines wonderful graphics with accurate history. First published in two separate comic books.

† *Jim Bowie,* no. 16 (September 1956). Derby, Conn.: Charlton Comics Group.

    This issue of the Charlton Jim Bowie series does the Alamo story, which is copied almost panel by panel from the Dell comic *Davy Crockett at the Alamo.* In this comic it is Bowie who dashes into the Alamo with reinforcements and then later dies, like Disney's Crockett, swinging his rifle at the swarming Mexicans. Despite the demise of the hero, the Jim Bowie comic book series went on for three more issues.

† Palacios, Antonio Hernández. *Le Drame de Fort Alamo: La Légende de Manos Kelly.* Paris: Humanoides Associes, 1980.

    French hardback comic book concerning a fictional Alamo survivor. Nice color graphics by Palacios.

* Patton, Jack, and John Rosenfield, Jr. *Texas History Movies.* Dallas: Southwest Press, 1928.

———. *Texas History Movies: Four Hundred Years of History and Industrial Development . . . Compliments of Magnolia Petroleum Company,* rev. ed. [Dallas]: Turner Co., 1935.

These wonderfully witty, and unfortunately racist, comic strips ran in the *Dallas News* beginning in the fall of 1926. They covered all of Texas history from the Spanish explorers to Reconstruction, emphasizing the colorful and dramatic aspects of the story. Naturally the Alamo formed a large part of the tale. The strips were gathered together in a hardback volume in 1928 and were later reissued by the Magnolia Petroleum Company (now Mobil) in paperback format for use in the public schools. Over the years numerous paperback editions, often abridged, were issued by the oil company to the delight of generations of Texas school children. In 1974 the Texas State Historical Association published a new abridged version with more text and fewer pictures and with insults to various ethnic groups removed. Also gone was much of the humor and verve of the original.

* Ray, Frederic. *The Story of the Alamo*. N.P.: By the Author, 1955.

Excellent artwork marks this illustrated rendering of the Alamo tale, which for years has been sold at the DRT Alamo giftshop.

Schaare, C. Richard. *The Life of Davy Crockett in Picture and Story*. New York: Cupples and Leon Co., Publishers, 1935.

This was one of four pictorial biographies that Schaare did on famous frontiersmen. They were later combined into *Pioneer Stories for Boys*. The author has Crockett surrender only to be executed by order of Santa Anna.

Siegel, Larry, and Mort Drucker. "Mad Visits John Wayde on the Set of 'At the Alamo,' " *Mad* 63 (June 1961). New York: E. C. Publications.

Satirical comic-book version of the John Wayne movie.

† Smith, Bradford. "The American Adventure: Remember the Alamo." Comic Strip, Lafave Newspaper Features, ca. 1955.

Star Spangled War, no. 172 (August 1973). New York: National Periodical Publications. (DC)

The saga of Jim Bonham's ride is told in the story "Decision."

Storia del West, no. 3 (August 1967). Milan, Italy: Editoriale Cepim/Daim Press. † 1984 reprint.

This Italian series, under the editorship of Sergio Bonelli, covers the entire span of frontier history from Lewis and Clark to Wounded Knee. Each paperback copy runs ninety-eight pages, with a color cover and black-and-white comic panels. This issue concerns the Alamo and is marked by superior artwork and considerable attention to historical accuracy. In 1984 Daim Press began to reprint the series.

Tex Granger, no. 20 (January 1949). Chicago: Commended Comics, Parents Magazine.

Three-page story "Davy Crockett's Last Fight." In early comic books like this one, Crockett's image is based on contemporary portraits of him. After 1955, however, most Crockett images reflect the influence of Fess Parker's portrayal in the Disney film.

† "True Comics: Davy Crockett—At the Height of the Battle." *Chicago Sun*, ca. 1949.

Two-Fisted Tales, no. 28 (July–August 1952). New York: Fables Publishing Co. (EC)

† Reprint ed., vol. 2 (West Plains, Mo.: Russ Cochran, Publisher, 1980).

The six-page story "Alamo" is perhaps the best of the Alamo comics. With excellent artwork by John Severin, one of the most highly regarded comic book artists, the story is told from the viewpoint of a Mexican soldier who must unwillingly participate in the firing squad that shoots the last five Alamo defenders. This is one of the most expensive Alamo comics for the collector, but it has been reprinted in volume two of Cochran's four-volume reprint of EC's *Two-Fisted Tales* series.

Two-Gun Kid, no. 75 (May 1965). New York: Marvel Comics Group.

"Remember the Alamo!" is the feature story in this issue of the long-running western hero comic book. The Two-Gun Kid attempts to rescue his friend Jim Bowie at the Alamo.

† *Walt Disney's Davy Crockett at the Alamo*, no. 639 (1955). New York: Dell Publishing Co.

This ninety-eight-page color comic book is a tie-in with the Disney television shows and movies. It features a text story on the Alamo and a picture biography of Jim Bowie, as well as various Crockett tales. A nice collector's piece.

Western Gunfighters, no. 1 (August 1970). New York: Marvel Comics Group.

In the story "Renegades," four men are sent by Travis to bring back reinforcements and are unfairly branded as cowards for missing the battle.

‡ Wilson, Rowland B. "Oh, stop worrying—the public has a short memory!" *Esquire* 63 (March 1965). Fondren Library, SMU.

World Famous Heroes Magazine, no. 1 (October 1941). New York: Comic Corporation of America.

Exhibition Checklist

Items Not Illustrated in Catalog

by Susan Prendergast Schoelwer
with Tom W. Gläser

Books, Pamphlets, Serials

Additional exhibition items in this category are listed in the bibliography. Except as noted, the following are from the collections of the DeGolyer Library, Fikes Hall of Special Collections, Southern Methodist University.

Almonte, Juan N. *Noticia Estadistica sobre Tejas.* Mexico: I. Cumplido, 1835.

Chabot, Frederick C. *With the Makers of San Antonio.* San Antonio: By the Author, 1937.

Cisneros, José. "Riders of the Border." *Southwestern Studies*, Monograph no. 30. El Paso, Tex.: Texas Western Press, 1971.

Coahuila y Texas. *Constitutión Politica del Estado Libre de Coahuila y Tejas . . . 1827.* Ciudad de Leona Vicario: J. M. Bangs, 1829.

Coahuila y Texas. *Nota Estadistica Remitida . . . con Arreglo al Articulo 161, Numero 8, de al Constitución Federal . . . de 1826.* Mexico: En la Impr. del Aguila, 1826.

[Crockett, David]. *Life of David Crockett, The Original Humorist and Irrepressible Backwoodsman. . . .* New York: Lovell, Coryell and Co., [1865].

———. *Pictorial Life and Adventures of Davy Crockett.* Philadelphia: T. B. Peterson and Brothers, n.d.

De Zavala, Adina. "The Story of the Siege and Fall of the Alamo." From the Archives. A Resume. 1911. [Bryan, Tex.: Frederick S. White, 1984.]

Galveston, Harrisburg and San Antonio Railway Company. *Eden: An Excursion from New Orleans to the Pacific by Rail, Through Texas and Mexico via the "Star and Crescent" and "Sunset" Route.* [Houston: Southern Pacific, 1882.]

Goetzmann, William H. *When the Eagle Screamed: The Romantic Horizon in American Diplomacy, 1800–1860.* New York: John Wiley and Sons, 1966.

Hallenbeck, Cleve. *Spanish Missions of the Old Southwest.* Garden City, N.Y.: Doubleday, Page, and Co., 1926.

Houston, Sam. *Documents of Major General Sam Houston . . . Containing a Detailed Account of the Battle of San Jacinto.* New Orleans: John Cox, 1836.

"How the Alamo Really Looked." *San Antonio Express*, September 28, 1913. Photographic reproduction courtesy *San Antonio Express.*

Howe, Henry. *Historical Collections of the Great West. . . .* Cincinnati: By the Author, 1856. Vol. 1 of 2.

Hunt, Lenoir. *Bluebonnets and Blood: The Romance of "Tejas."* Houston: Texas Books, 1938.

Katz, Harvey. *Shadow on the Alamo: New Heroes Fight Old Corruption in Texas Politics.* Garden City, N.Y.: Doubleday and Co., 1972.

Lowman, Al., ed. *This Bitterly Beautiful Land: A Texas Commonplace Book.* Austin: Roger Beacham, Publisher, 1972.

Lowman, Shepard C. *"The Siege and Fall of the Alamo."* N.P.: The Sons of the Republic of Texas, 1942.

Lundy, Benjamin. *The War in Texas.* . . . Philadelphia: Merrihew and Gunn, 1836.

Mexico. *Diario del Gobierno de la Republica Mexicana*, Supplement for March 21, 1836. Photographic reproduction courtesy Daughters of the Republic of Texas Library at the Alamo.

Phillips, Alfred A., ed. *The Forget-me-not: A Gift for 1846.* New York: Nafis and Cornish, 1845.

Rodríguez, José M. *Rodríguez Memoirs of Early Texas.* 2nd ed. San Antonio: Standard Printing, 1961.

Ruiz, Antonio Francisco. "Fall of the Alamo." *Texas Almanac for 1860.* Galveston: Galveston News Steam Printing Co., [1859].

San Antonio de Béxar, Ayuntamiento de. *Ordnanzas Municipales.* . . . Ciudad de Leona Vicario: J. M. Bangs, 1829.

San Antonio Illustrated. New York: Albertype Co., 1893.

San Antonio Traction Company. *Souvenir of the Picturesque Alamo City.* San Antonio: Ebers and Wurtz, 1907.

Santos, Richard G. "Proposed View of Mission San Antonio de Valero circa 1790." *Texana* 3 (Fall 1965).

Smith, Richard P. *Col. Crockett's Exploits and Adventures in Texas, Written by Himself.* Philadelphia: T. K. and P. G. Collins, 1836.

Sweet, Alexander E., and J. Armoy Knox. *On a Mexican Mustang Through Texas: From the Gulf to the Rio Grande.* London: Chatto & Windus, 1905.

Telegraph and Texas Register. March 24, 1836. Photographic reproduction courtesy Barker Texas History Center, The University of Texas at Austin.

"Texas and the Oregon Territory." *Illustrated London News* 3:4 (June 15, 1844). Fondren Library, SMU.

Texas Commission of Control for Texas Centennial Celebrations. *Monuments Erected by the State of Texas to Commemorate the Centenary of Texas Independence.* Austin: Steck Co., 1938.

Tornel, José María. *Secretaria de Guerra y Marina. El Exma Sr. Presidente . . . "Para recompensar las acciones distinguidas del ejército y de la marina de guerra, se establece una Legion militar."* Mexico: April 27, 1836. From the Jenkins Garrett Library, University of Texas at Arlington.

True West 21:1 (September–October, 1973). Cover illustration by Joe Ruiz Grandee.

Wall, Bernhardt. *Following General Sam Houston, 1793–1863.* Lime Rock, Conn.: By the Author, 1935.

Zamacois, Niceto de. *Historia de Méjico. . . .* Mexico: J. F. Parres and Co., 1880. Vol. 12 of 18.

Zuber, William P. "An Escape from the Alamo." *Texas Almanac for 1873.* Galveston: Galveston News Steam Printing Co., [1872].

Art

Except as noted, artworks are represented by photographic reproductions.

Bissett, William. *The Alamo.* Watercolor copy, 1912, by V. Chafsky, after painting by Bissett, 1838–39. DRT Library at the Alamo.

Callcott, Frank. *The Alamo, Midnight, March 6, 1936.* Facsimile ed., 1978, of lithograph, 1936–38. DeGolyer Library.

DeYoung, Harry. *Mrs. Almeron Dickinson.* Oil painting, 1941. The Alamo—DRT.

Eastman, Seth. *Plaza at San Antonio.* Sketch, 1849. Bushnell Collection, Peabody Museum, Harvard University.

Everett, Edward. *Ruins of the Church of the Alamo, San Antonio de Bexar.* Watercolor, 1846–47. Amon Carter Museum, Fort Worth.

Eyth, Louis. *Death of Bowie: A Command from the Mexicans that He Be Killed.* Drawing, ca. 1878. Original not located; photograph, DRT Library at the Alamo.

Frazer, James L. *Green B. Jameson.* Oil painting, 1952. The Alamo—DRT.

Lee, Arthur T. *Alamo, San Antonio.* Watercolor, ca. 1848. Rochester Historical Society, Rochester, N.Y.

Marshall, Bruce. *Flag of the Louisiana Volunteers: The New Orleans Grey Flag.* Color print after painting, ca. 1975. Original, collection of Paul A. Hutton.

Onderdonk, Robert Julian. *Christmas at the Alamo.* Oil painting, ca. 1910–20. Collection of Mrs. William C. Clegg, San Antonio.

Pentenrieder, Erhard. *San Antonio Scenes*. Engraved stationery, ca. 1856. Amon Carter Museum, Fort Worth.

Unknown artist. *Alamo Church*. Painting, prob. 19th century. Original not located; photograph, DRT Library at the Alamo.

Unknown artist. *Battle of the Alamo*. Painting [?], prob. 19th century. The Bettmann Archive, New York.

Unknown artist. *Lorenzo de Zavala*. Oil painting, ca. 1820–36. Archives Division, Texas State Library.

Unknown artist. *Stephen F. Austin*. Oil painting, ca. 1830. Archives Division, Texas State Library.

Artifacts and Ephemera

Except as noted, the following are from the collection of Paul A. Hutton.

Belt buckle with design of Texas Centennial postage stamp. Pewter. Dory, ca. 1936.

Bookmark. "The Alamo" souvenir. Silverplate, ca. 1890–1910.

Card. "Hon. David Crockett 'Davy Crockett.'" Men of History, 2nd series. Pan Handle Scrap [Chewing Tobacco] and Royal Bengal Little Cigars [Co.], New Jersey, ca. 1860–1900.

Collector's bottle. "David Crockett." Americana Porcelain. McCormick Distillery Co., Weston, Mo., ca. 1975.

Collector's bottle. "Jim Bowie." Americana Porcelain. McCormick Distillery Co., Weston, Mo., ca. 1975.

Collector's bottle. "The Alamo." By Laurence H. Butcher. Americana Collection of Great Moments in History, no. 2. Glass with paper label. J.W. Dant Distillery Co., Louisville, Ky., 1969.

Cream Pitcher. Texas Centennial souvenir. Glazed porcelain with view of Alamo. Japan, ca. 1935–36.

Game. "Battle of the Alamo." Solodar Co., San Antonio, 1966.

Greeting card. ". . . Davey Crockett's hat went on to become the Alamo's only survivor." By J. C. Duffy. Kersten Bros. Co., Scottsdale, Ariz., 1981.

Letter opener. "The Alamo" souvenir. Brass, ca. 1910–30.

Neckerchief. "Davey Crockett Sharpshooter/Remember the Alamo" souvenir, ca. 1955.

Playset. Alamo model. Plastic and metal, ca. 1955.

Playset. "The Alamo." Paper punch-out. Golden Press, 1960.

Playset. "Davy Crockett Far-West Story." *Eroi del West* series. Plastic figures, HO scale. Atlantic, Italy, ca. 1970–75.

Postcard. "Night View of the Alamo." Texas Postcard Co., Plano, Tex., 1984. DeGolyer Library.
Puzzle. "James Bowie." Action Classics, 1979.
Toy. Davy Crockett Frontier Money, ca. 1955.

Broadsides

The following are from the collections of the DeGolyer Library.

Coahuila y Texas. "El Gobernador del Estado de Coahuila y Tejas.... Se accede a los solicitudes de los empresarios, Lorenzo de Zavala y Juan Macmulen...." Monclova, January 27, 1834.
Felix Huston. "Texas. The people of Mississippi and Louisiana are called on to afford prompt and efficient aid to the people of Texas...." Natchez, Miss., April 25, 1836.
Muzquiz, Melchor. "El Ciudadano Melchor Muzquiz, Coronel de Ejército.... Queda para siempre prohibido en el territorio de los Estadios Unidos Mexicanos, el commercio y trafico de esclavos...." Mexico, July 23, 1824.
Texas, Republic of. "Unanimous Declaration of Independence...." San Felipe de Austin: Baker and Bordens, 1836.

Manuscripts

The following are from the collections of the DeGolyer Library.

Austin, Stephen F. Deed to James T. Long, San Felipe de Austin, January 26, 1826. Document signed "Estevan F. Austin."
Navarro, José Antonio. Autograph on José Antonio Salinas, statement of indebtedness, Béxar, August 17, 1839.
Santa Anna, Antonio López de, to Agustín de Iturbide, Jalapa, Mexico, February 29, 1822. Letter signed.
Seguín, Erasmo. Autograph on John W. Smith, sworn statement as administrator of Eugenio Navarro estate, [Béxar], May 16, 1838.
Seguín, Juan N. Statement to Béxar County Court as administrator of Jim Bowie estate, Béxar, [ca. 1840]. Autograph document signed.
Travis, William Barret. Autograph as witness to promissory note of Susan Ann Robinson Mosely, Robert J. Mosely, and James Wright to James B. Miller, Alfred, Texas, December 18, 1833.

Maps

DeGolyer, Homer. [The Mexican Army's March into Texas.] Manuscript map, n.d. DeGolyer Library.
Labastida, Ygnacio de. "Plan of the City of San Antonio de Béxar and Fortification of the

Alamo. . . ." Manuscript map, March 1836. Photographic reproduction courtesy Barker Texas History Center, The University of Texas at Austin.

Sánchez Navarro, José Juan. "Fort San Antonio de Valero, commonly called the Alamo." Manuscript map, 1836. Photographic reproduction courtesy Barker Texas History Center, The University of Texas at Austin.

Motion Picture Materials

Except as noted, the following are from the collection of Paul A. Hutton.

The Alamo. United Artists, 1960.
Advertisement. "There Were No Ghost Writers at the Alamo." By Russell Birdwell. *Life*, July 4, 1960.
Record jacket. "Ballad of the Alamo." Sung by The Sons of Texas. [New York]: A. A. Records, 1960.
Souvenir book. Hollywood: Sovereign Publications, 1960.
Still photographs:
    Alamo defenders raising 1824 Mexican flag. (DRT Library at the Alamo.)
    Bowie, Crockett, and Travis.
    Bowie arriving with men.
    Bowie with black servant.
    Mexican troops advancing inside Alamo compound during assault.
    Mexican troops climbing Alamo walls in assault scene.
    Travis and Bowie.
    Travis at the Alamo stockade.
    Travis dueling with two Mexican soldiers during melee.

Heroes of the Alamo. Sunset, 1937.
Still photographs:
    Bowie's death scene.
    Crockett's death scene.
    Dickinson with wife.
    Rex Lease as Travis.

The Immortal Alamo. Star Film Ranch, 1911.
Still photograph. Davy Crockett. (DRT Library at the Alamo.)

The Iron Mistress. Warner Brothers, 1952.
Lobby card. Bowie in duel.

The Last Command. Republic, 1955.
Lobby cards:
    John Russell as Almeron Dickinson.
    Santa Anna and troops surveying battlefield.
Still photograph. Alamo defenders.

The Man From the Alamo. Universal-International, 1953.
Still photograph. Alamo defenders discussing their fate.

The Martyrs of the Alamo. Triangle Film Corp., 1915.
Still photograph. Alamo defenders in coonskin caps.

San Antonio. Warner Brothers, 1945.
Still photograph. Errol Flynn dueling inside moonlit Alamo ruins.

Seguín. PBS, 1982.
Script. By Jesús Salvador Treviño.
Still photograph. The Seguín family.

Viva Max! Commonwealth United Entertainment, 1969.
Poster.
Press book.

Walt Disney's Davy Crockett, King of the Wild Frontier. Buena Vista, 1955.
Still photographs:
    Bowie, Crockett, and Travis.
    Mexican troops scaling walls in the final assault.

Alamo Cenotaph, San Antonio. William Barret Travis sculpted by Pompeo Coppini, 1936–37. Photograph by Parrish Photography, San Antonio.
"Alamo Church Restored," ca. 1900. Retouched photograph with mss. annotations by Adina De Zavala. Original, DRT Library at the Alamo.
Alamo, construction of new roof, ca. 1920. DRT Library at the Alamo.
Alamo, decorated for the Battle of Flowers, 1896. DRT Library at the Alamo.
Alamo facade, with mist in doorway. DeGolyer Library.
Alamo monument bas relief. State Capitol grounds, Austin. Photograph by Paul A. Hutton.

Photographs

Except as noted, historical photographs are represented by copy prints.

Alamo monument from Japan, Alamo grounds. DRT Library at the Alamo.
Alamo piñata, ca. 1978. Photograph by Ron Bechtol, San Antonio.
Alamo replica at Fair Park, Dallas, 1909–34. DRT Library at the Alamo.
De Zavala, Adina. Autographed portrait, ca. 1935. DRT Library at the Alamo.
Driscoll, Clara, ca. 1900. DRT Library at the Alamo.
Mission of Nuestra Señora de la Concepción la Purisima de Acuña, 1886. Original cabinet photograph, DeGolyer Library.

Index

Page numbers in italics refer to illustrations

Abamillo, Juan, 125
Acuña, Rudy, 7
Alamo, the,
  archaeological excavations of, 22, 59-60
  comic books on, *68, 109, 130, 140, 144, 148, 158, 161,* 206-10
  commercialization of, 3, 29, 168, 171-73
  descriptions of, 24, 26-32, 33-36, 38, 39, 40-41, 58
  fiction works on, 41, 62, 89, 99, 104, 108, 109, 115, 117, 121, 127, 140, 159, 168, 199-206. *See also* Bowie, James, television series on
  Hispanic views of, 7, 9-10, 15, 18, 132, 133, 173
  legends of, 29, 52
  monuments to, 5, *71, 136,* 163-65, 173
  movies on. *See* individual titles
  name of, 24
  ownership of, 32-33, 36-39, 43-47
  parts of: church, 18, *19, 20,* 22-23, 24, 26, *27, 28, 29, 30,* 33-36, *37,* 38-39, 41-48, *49, 50, 53, 54,* 56-59, *110, 155,* pl. 3; convent (long barracks): 20, 23, 24, 25, 26, 28, 29, *34,* 37, 38-39, 41-51; plaza, 18, *20, 21,* 37, 38, 39, *40, 52, 57,* 58-59
  pictorial works of, *27, 42, 53, 62, 68, 70, 89, 96, 98, 99, 113, 144, 163, 171,* pls. 1, 4, 5, 15, 17. *See also under* Alamo, Siege and Battle of the, pictorial works of
  preservation of, 18, 36-39, 43-60, 163
  repairs of, 26, 32, 33-36, 38-39, 43
  as symbol, 3, 4, 6, 9, 10, 11, 12, 17, 18, 168, 173
  and uses of the site, 22, 39; as hospital, 18, 26; as living quarters, 18, 22, 23, 24, 25, 26, 31, 33, 35, 39, 59; as military post, 18, 22, 23-26, 32-38, 56, 174-75; as mission, 18-24, 32, 56; as museum, 38-39; as retail store, 22, 38, 51; as shrine, 3, 5, 9, 18, *39*

The Alamo (movie, 1960), 7, 11, 14, 16, 55, 56, 76, 77, 85, *100,* 101, 105, *114,* 115, *120,* 121, 122, *123, 141, 146,* 147, *160, 161,* 168; pl. 14

Alamo, Second Battle of the, 18, 47-51, 56-58

Alamo, Siege and Battle of the, 80-103; blacks in, 104, 112, 117; children in, 97, 101, 104, 109, 115-21; couriers in, 6, 12, 81, 82, 104, 105-8, 109-12, 128; final assault of, 88-97; flags of, 8, 17, 81, 94; fortifications of, 68-69, *70, 71, 72;* funeral pyre of, 97-98, *101,* 127, 142, 163, pl. 1; pictorial works of, *ii, vi, 42, 89, 92, 93, 95, 96, 98, 99, 157,* pls. 1, 4, 5, 6, 7, 8, 9, 10; powder magazine in, 14, 16-17, 83, 117, 160, pl. 4; reinforcements for, Mexican, 88; reinforcements for, Texan, 82, 104-8; Santa Anna's plan for, 85, 86, 88-91, 92; survivors of, battle, 97, 112, 115-21; survivors of, siege, 109-12, 128-29; women in, 101, 104, 109, *114,* 115-22, 185

Alfred Giles Co., Architects, *165*
Allen, James, 12, 109
Almaráz, Félix, Jr., 173
Alsbury, Horace, 29
Alsbury, Juana de Navarro. *See* Navarro, Juana de
Andrews, Ambrose, 152
Armies. *See* names of individual armies
Arocha family, 131
Arredondo, Gen. Joaquín de, 73, 125
Austin, Stephen F., 63, 179; pl. 2
Autry, Micajah, 108, *110*

Babbitt, Bruce, 9-10
Babbitt, Capt. Edwin B., 32
"Babe of the Alamo." *See* Dickinson, Angelina
Badgett, Jesse, 122
Badillo, Juan Antonio, 128
Barcena, Andrés, 128
Barnard, Dr. Joseph Henry, 27
Beckmann, John Antonio, *50,* 55
Beckmann, John Conrad, 50
Belgin, Harvey, 20
Ben (Almonte's cook), 112
Benavides, Plácido, 131

219

Berlandier, Jean Louis, 25-26
Betts, Louis, 145
Béxar. *See* San Antonio
Béxar, Siege of, 63, 66, 125, 127
Bissett, William, 44
Blake, Jacob Edmund, 29, *34*, 50
Blake, R. B., 39
Bollaert, William, 29, 32, *33*, 44, *45*, 50
Bonham, James Butler, 10, 80, 104, *106*, 108, 182; pl. 1
Bonilla, Ruben, 9-10
Borgarra, Anselmo, 128
Bowie, James, 3, 5, 10, 63, 66-67, 69, 71, 73, 81, *96*, 97, *105*, 122, 132-33, 135, 138, *139*, 141-49, pls. 1, 4, 13; death of, 71, 138, 144-47, 163; illness of, 69-73, 141-44; television series on, *148*, 149
Bowie knife, 147-49
Brack, A. A., *165*
Brackettville, Texas, *55, 56, 133*
Brady, Cyrus T., 145
Briscoe, Andrew, 138, 159
Brown, John Henry, 104
Brown, Reynold, pl. 14
Brown, Tom, *127*
Burdillón (Mexican general), 13
Burial, of Alamo dead, 163
Burleson, Gen. Edward, 63

Candelaria, Madam, 119-21
Caro, Ramón Martínez, 88
Casebier, Cecil Lang, 127
Cassiano, José, 128
Castrillón, Gen. Manuel Fernández, 13, 14-15, 76, 94, 97
Catholic Church, 20, 32, 36, 38, 67
Chabot, Frederick, 44
Chafsky, V., 44

Chapman, John Gadsby, *153*, 154
Cisneros, José, *101*
Cloud, Daniel, 108
Coahuila–Texas Civil Militia, *65*
Colquitt, Oscar B., 34, 48, 51
Confederate Army, 26, *32*, 174
Cook, Howard, 105
Coppini, Pompeo, *20*
Corner, William, 20, 33
Cos, Gen. Martín Perfecto de, 7, 33-34, 61, 63, 66, 67, 71, 73, 81, 90, 94, 174
Crockett, Davy, 3, 5, 69, 80, 83, 86, 94, 97, *105*, 132-33, 135, *139*, *140*, 144, 149-62, pls. 1, 4, 5, 9, 10, 14; death of, 12-16, 17, 133, 156, 159-62, 163, pls. 4, 5, 9, 10, 14; as folk hero, 151-54; media image of, 161-62
Crockett-mania, 13-14, 149, 150-51, 155
Cruz y Arocha, Antonio, 7, 109, 125, 128
Curbelo, María de Jesús, 122

Darst, Jacob, 111
Daughters of the Republic of Texas, 10, 15, 16, 43, 47-48, 51-53, 56, 58-59, 168, 169
Davy Crockett, King of the Wild Frontier. *See* Walt Disney's *Davy Crockett, King of the Wild Frontier*
De la Garza, Alexandro, 109, 128
De la Peña, Lt. Col. José Enrique, 14, 97
De Labastida, Col. Ygnacio, 25-26, *72, 73*
De Sauque, Francis, 112
De Zavala, Adina, 24, 39, 43, 47-48, *49*, 52, 56, 58, 177
De Zavala, Lorenzo. *See* Zavala, Lorenzo de
"Death Line." *See under* Travis, William Barret, and "Line in the dust"
Degüello, 91, 94

Dexter, W. W., *99*
DeYoung, Harry Anthony, *106, 111*
Dickinson, Capt. Almeron, 94, 115, 117, 138; pls. 7, 12
Dickinson, Angelina, *114*, 115, 117-18, 121; pl. 12
Dickinson, Susanna, 12, 112, *114*, 115-18, 121, 131, 159, 183
Dobie, J. Frank, 11, 12, 149
Driscoll, Clara, 43, 47-48, 56, 58-59
DRT. *See* Daughters of the Republic of Texas
Duque, Col. Francisco, 90, 92, 94

Eastman, Capt. Seth, 29, *31*
Eaton, Jack D., *23*
Eckerskorn, J., *50*
Ellis, Edward S., 13
Emmrich, James, *36*
Escopetas, 85-86
Espalier, Carlos, 128
Esparza, Anna Salazar (Mrs. Gregorio), *118*, 121
Esparza, Enrique, *118*, 121, 131
Esparza, Francisco, 127
Esparza, Gregorio, 97, 118, *127*, 128
Evans, Robert, 14, 101, 111, 117, 160; pl. 4
Everett, Lt. Edward, 22, 29, 32, 34, 36, *46*, 47; pl. 3

Falconer, Thomas, 29, *30*
Fannin, Col. James Walker, 7, 10, 88, 97, 179
Filisola, Gen. Vicente, 27, 76
Flores, Gaspar, 122, 125
Flores family, 131
Forbes, Scott, *148*, 149
Ford, Powell and Carson Architects, 59

Foreman, Gary L., 17, 60
Franciscans, the, 20, 22, 23, 26
Fries, John, 35
Fuentes, Antonio, 128
Fuqua, Galba, 105, 117, 128

Gaona, Gen. Antonio, 76, 88
Garza, Alexandro de la. *See* De la Garza, Alexandro
Gentilz, Jean Louis Theodore, 29, *89*; pl. 7
Giesecke, F. E., 51
Giles (Alfred) Co., Architects. *See* Alfred Giles Co., Architects
Goldbeck, Eugene O., *52, 58*
Goliad, Texas, 66, 81, 88, 102
Gonzáles, José María, 91
Gonzáles, Petra, 121
Gonzales, Texas, men from. *See* "Immortal Thirty-Two"
Graham, C. B., 46
Grandee, Joe Ruiz, *113*
Grant, Dr. James A., 66, 81
Green, Thomas Jefferson, 5
Grenet, Hugo, 38, *39*, 43, 48, 50
The Grito (movie, 1904), 121
Guerrero, Brigido, 6, 112, 128

Harris, Ethel, *53*
Hastings, Howard L., 78
Healy, George P. A., *143*
Hefter, Joseph, *65, 157*
Heroes of the Alamo (movie, 1937), 106, *107*; pl. 12
Herrera, Blas, 128
Hess, Mark, pl. 15
Highsmith, Benjamin, 109
Historic American Buildings Survey, *36*
Holland, Tapley, 111

Houston, Col. Andrew Jackson, 27
Houston, Gen. Sam, 66, 67, 70, 82-83, 138
Hughes, Capt. George W., 32
Hugo & Schmeltzer, mercantilists, 38, 43, 47, 51, 58

Ikin, Arthur, *44*
The Immortal Alamo (movie, 1911), *116*, 117
"Immortal Thirty-Two," 82, 104-9

Jacales, 23, *129*
Jackson, Jack, 7, *68, 130*; pl. 16
Jacobson (San Antonio photographer), *129*
Jameson, Green B., 68-69, *70*, 81, 94, 111, 181
Jiménez, José, *36*
Joe (Travis's slave), 92, 112, *114*, 115, 138, 140, 143, 159
John (De Sauque's slave), 112
John, Ida, 44
Johnson (courier), 109
Johnson, Col. Frank, 66, 81
Johnson, Lyndon Baines, 163, 166, 168

Kendall, George, 26
Kilgore, Dan, 16-17
King, William P., 105
Ku Klux Klan, 10, *167*

Lanier, Sidney, 135
The Last Command (movie, 1955), 11, 14, *84*, 85, 121-22, 149
Lewis, John Francis, *110*
Lewis, Nat, 122, 128
"Line in the dust." *See under* Travis, and "Line in the dust"

Lion of the West (stage play, 1830s), 151, *152*
Locke, Emil, *165*
Lord, Walter, 4, 12, 14
Losoya, Concepción, 121
Losoya, Domingo, 186
Losoya, José Toribio. *See* Toribio Losoya, José
Losoya family, 59-60, 128
Luna, José, 59
Lungkwitz, Hermann, *35*

McArdle, Henry Arthur, 143; pl. 4
McBarron, H. Charles, *97*
McGregor, John, 83
McHenry, Martin D., 143
McLane, Hiram, *62*, 89
McLoughlin, Denis, pl. 6
McSpadden, J. Walker, 78
McVey, William, *136*
Man from the Alamo (movie, 1953), 115
Markos, Lajos, 94, *95*
Martin, Albert, 81
Martin, Wiley, *134*
Martínez, Gabriel, 128
Matamoros Expedition, 66
Maverick, Mary Ann Adams, *28*, 29, 185
Maverick, Samuel A., 29, 31, 32-33, 39, 50, 122
Menchaca family, 131
Mexican-American War, 32
Mexican Army, 26, 61, 63, *64*, *65*, 66, 67, 69, 73-76, *77*, 78, 79, 80-81, 85-88, 90-92, 94, *95*, 97, 174; at the Alamo, 80-97, pls. 4, 5, 6, 7, 8, 9, 10, 17; march of, to San Antonio, 76, 79, 80; at siege of Béxar, 61, 63, 66; weaponry of, 82, 85-88
Mier y Terán, José Manuel, 25, 26

Milam, Benjamin, 63, 66
Millsaps, Isaac, 105
Mission San Antonio de Valero. *See under* Alamo, and uses of the site, as mission
Moore, Francis, Jr., 44
Mora (Mexican general), 138
Morales, Col. Juan, 89, 90, 94, 97; pl. 5
Movimiento Estudiantil Chicanos de Aztlan, 15
Mueller, C. H., 89

Nangle, William B., 170
Nava, Andrés, 128
Navarro, Gertrudis de, 118, 121, 185
Navarro, Jose Antonio, 125
Navarro, Juana de, 29, 118, 121, 147, 185
Navarro, Louisiano, 122
Neill, Col. James C., 66, 69, 122
New Orleans Greys, the, 8, 17, 94
Niles, John M., *ii*, iv

Odin, John M., 36
Olmos, James Edward, *75*
Onderdonk, Robert Jenkins, pl. 5
Ortiz, Father Francisco Xavier, 22

Parker, Fess, 13, 138, *139*, 149, *151*, 162; pl. 11
Patton, Jack, *42*, *92*
Peña, José Enrique de la. *See* De la Peña, José Enrique
Pennybacker, Anna J. Hardwicke, 11
Pentenreider, Erhard, 54
Peréz, Alijo, 121
Peréz, Antonio, 128
Perry, Carmen, 14-16, 17, 161
Phelps, Henry T., 59
Pike, Zebulon M., 24

Pollard, Dr. Amos, *111*, 144
Potter, Reuben M., 8, 39, 41, 112, 115, 144
Prejudice, Anglo, 6, 10, 17, 67, 92, 122, 125, 128, 131, 132
Presidios, 23
Price, Norman, *137*

Raba, Ernst, *36*
Ramírez family, 131
Ramírez y Sesma, Gen. Joaquín, 73, 90
Ray, Frederic, *21*
Richardson (etcher), *153*
Ricks, Thom, *118*
Robinson (San Antonio photographer), *119*
Rodríquez family, 125, 131
Roman Catholic Church. *See* Catholic Church
Romano, Mariano, 33
Romero, Col. José María, 90, 92, 94
Rose, Louis "Moses," 11, 12, 115, 135
Rose, N. H., *36*
Rosenfield, John, Jr., *42*, *92*
Ruiz, Francisco, 125, 143
Russi, David, 35

Saldigna, Apolinario, 147
Saline, Vitono de, 121
San Antonio, 10, 23, 32, 38-39, 40, 52, 59-60, 61, 66, 67, 80, 124
San Antonio, Siege of. *See* Béxar, Siege of
San Fernando Church, 80, 81
San Jacinto, Battle of, 27, 82-83, 102, 174
Sánchez Estrada, Juan José, 25
Sánchez Navarro, Capt. José Juan, *25*, 26, 56, *71*, 147
Sánchez y Tapia, José María, 25
Sánchez y Tapia, Lino, 26, *64*

Santa Anna, Gen. Antonio Lopez de, 8, 12, 13, 14-15, 67, 69, 73-75, 76, 79, 80-83, 85, 86, 88-91, 92, 94, 97-98, *100*, 101, 102, *110*, *157*; pl. 7
Saucedo, Trinidad, 121
Savage, Eugene, pl. 1
Schiwetz, Edward Muegge (Buck), *19*
Schmeltzer, Gustav, 43
Second Battle of the Alamo. *See* Alamo, Second Battle of the
Seguín (television movie, 1982), 7, *75*, *133*
Seguín, Erasmo, 6-7, *120*, 125
Seguín, Juan N., 6-8, 9, 10, 68, 108, 109, 112, 120, 125, 128, *130*, 131-32, 163; pl. 16
Sesma, Gen. Joaquín Ramírez y. *See* Ramírez y Sesma, Gen. Joaquín
Severin, John, *92*
Sevier, Clara Driscoll. *See* Driscoll, Clara
Silvero family, 131
Smith, Gov. Henry, 67, 70, 179
Smith, John W., 12, 80, 105, 108, 109, 122
Smithers, Launcelot, 109
Soldaderas, 79, 91
Souvenirs. *See* Crockett-mania
Spanish Army, 24, 26, 174
Sutherland, Dr. John, 80, 108, 109, 128, 144, 181

Taylor, Rolla, *24*
Tejanos: at the Alamo, 6, 7, 8-9, 10, 88, 97, 104, 108, 109, 112, 117, 118, 120, 121, 125, 128, 131; in San Antonio, 6, 29, 59, 67, 79, 80, 122, 124, 125, 128, 131, 174; in the Texas Revolution, 6-7, 8, 9, 10, 79, 122, 125, 128, 131, pl. 16
Texan Army, 26, 61, 63, 66-69, 79-80,

81-83, 85, 86, 88, 91, 94, *111*; at the Alamo, 66-97, 104, 108, 109; at siege of Béxar, 61, 63, 66; weaponry of, 69, 82-83, 85-86
Texas Dragoons, *65*
Texas Sesquicentennial, 17
Thermopylae, 3, 5-6, 61
Thomason, John W., Jr., pl. 10
Thrall, Homer, 74
Toribio Losoya, José, 121, 128, 186
Tornel y Mendivil, José María, 102
Torres, Lt. José María, 94
Travis, William Barret, 3, 5, 6, 8, 10, 13, 63, *68*, 69, 71, 80, 81, 85, 94, *95*, *105*, 108, 112, 122, 125, 131, 132-41, *142*, 143, 182, pls. 1, 4; death of, 13, 71, *95*, 138, 140, *142*, 143, 163; and "Line in the dust," 10-12, 115, 135, *137*, 138, *139*, *140*, 183, pl. 1

United States Army, 26, 32-33, 34, 36, 38, 43, 54

Urrea, Gen. José, 81
Ustinov, Peter, *169*

Veramendi, Juan Martín de, 69
Veramendi, Ursula de, 69, 120, 121, *127*, 141
Veramendi Palace, 25, 66, *127*, 129
Vietnam War, 166, 168
Viva Max! (movie, 1969), 26, 138, 168, *169*
Von Schmidt, Eric, *vi*, 17
Vosburgh, Leonard, *27*

Walker, Jacob, 117
Walt Disney's *Davy Crockett, King of the Wild Frontier* (television series, 1955), 13-14, 138, *139*, 149, 151, 162; pl. 11
Warnell, Henry, 112
Wayne, John, 16, *55*, *101*, *160*, *161*, 162; pl. 14
Weber, David J., 7

Wedemeyer, Henry, *53*
Welcker, Armand, *99*
Wharton, Clarence, 11
Williams, Amelia W., 4, 11-12, 112, 179
Wilson, Rowland B., pl. 17
Wolfe brothers, 117
Woll, Gen. Adrian, 76
Wool, Brig. Gen. John E., 32
Wright, Thomas Jefferson, *130*

Ybarra, Alfred, *55*
Yena, Donald M., pl. 8
Yoakum, Henderson, 115
Yohn, Frederick C., *158*; pl. 9

Zachrisson, Ruth Conerly, *143*
Zapadores, 76, 90
Zavala, Adina de. *See* De Zavala, Adina
Zavala, Lorenzo de, 8, 24, 43, 125
Zuber, William P., 11, 12, 115, 135, 138, 147

223